Y0-CAN-848

SOCIAL SECURITY
AND INDIVIDUAL EQUITY

SOCIAL SECURITY AND INDIVIDUAL EQUITY

EVOLVING STANDARDS OF EQUITY AND ADEQUACY

Charles W. Meyer
&
Nancy Wolff

STUDIES IN SOCIAL WELFARE POLICIES AND PROGRAMS,
NUMBER 15

Greenwood Press
Westport, Connecticut • London

368.43
M 612

Library of Congress Cataloging-in-Publication Data

Meyer, Charles W.
    Social security and individual equity : evolving standards of
equity and adequacy / Charles W. Meyer and Nancy Wolff.
        p.   cm. — (Studies in social welfare policies and programs,
    ISSN 8755–5360 ; no. 15)
    Includes bibliographical references and index.
    ISBN 0–313–26459–7 (alk. paper)
    1. Social security—United States.   I. Wolff, Nancy.
II. Title.   III. Series.
HD7125.M47   1993
368.4′3′00973—dc20   92–25739

British Library Cataloguing in Publication Data is available.

Copyright © 1993 by Charles W. Meyer and Nancy Wolff

All rights reserved. No portion of this book may be
reproduced, by any process or technique, without the
express written consent of the publisher.

Library of Congress Catalog Card Number: 92–25739
ISBN: 0–313–26459–7
ISSN: 8755–5360

First published in 1993

Greenwood Press, 88 Post Road West, Westport, CT 06881
An imprint of Greenwood Publishing Group, Inc.

Printed in the United States of America

The paper used in this book complies with the
Permanent Paper Standard issued by the National
Information Standards Organization (Z39.48–1984).

10 9 8 7 6 5 4 3 2 1

To N.M.M.

Contents

Figures and Tables

Acknowledgments

Many colleagues, past and present, have contributed to our knowledge and understanding of the social security system. The following deserve special mention. Martin David and W. Lee Hansen commented on earlier drafts of Chapters 3, 4, and 6. B. Dixon Holland, M.D., contributed greatly to our understanding of disability. James C. Hickman provided assistance on actuarial matters. Mark Schlesinger made invaluable and insightful comments on earlier drafts of Chapter 6 and was helpful in the development of the Medicare reform policy. We also acknowledge the helpful comments of members, especially Yu Ping Wen, of the Public Economics Seminar at the University of Wisconsin. The usual disclaimer, however, holds: All biases, shortcomings, interpretations, and conclusions are entirely our responsibility. Donna Otto and Jenny Thomas provided expert assistance in preparation of the manuscript, and Alan McCunn prepared the diagrams.

1

Principles of Social Insurance

Social insurance programs exist throughout the world, and in industrialized market economies, they absorb significant shares of the public budget. Although programs differ in scope and coverage, they share such common features as protection against earnings loss and insurance against part or all of the cost of medical care. Participation is usually compulsory, but in some countries participants may opt out of specified types of coverage. Benefit amounts, benefit eligibility, and means of finance are prescribed by law.

The social security system provides coverage for nearly all of the work force in the United States. Old Age, Survivors, and Disability Insurance (OASDI) pays monthly cash benefits that replace a portion of the earnings lost through retirement, death, or disability. The accompanying Medicare program covers a portion of the medical expenses of the elderly and long-term disabled populations. Social security insures against long-term earnings loss, and unemployment compensation, administered jointly by the federal government and states, insures against short-term earnings loss. These programs are supplemented by a variety of private and public programs, including private pensions and other employer benefits, workers' compensation, and means-tested programs of public assistance. Private programs receive generous tax subsidies.

The term *social security* is sometimes used broadly to describe the entire set of income support programs. This book focuses more narrowly on the federal social security system, encompassing OASDI and Medicare, and attempts to identify and evaluate the competing standards of individual equity and social adequacy embodied within the existing program.

A key issue raised by those calling for reform concerns the extent to which social security should conform to a standard of actuarial fairness. Although the existing system links benefits to prior taxable earnings in covered occupations, the link is tenuous. OASDI cash benefits are tilted toward workers with low earnings; survivors' and auxiliary benefits for dependents favor single-earner married couples at the expense of two-earner couples and single persons. The link between contributions and benefits under the Hospital Insurance component of Medicare is even more remote.

At the heart of the debate over reform are questions about the nature of social insurance. Should primary emphasis be on assuring all beneficiaries an adequate standard of living, or should benefits be more closely related to prior contributions? If we choose the latter, minimal living standards for the elderly and disabled will be guaranteed only through greater reliance on means-tested welfare programs such as the existing Supplementary Security Income (SSI) program. A restructuring of social security to make it conform to actuarial standards would represent a major break from the past. It requires a rethinking of the nature of social insurance and a reevaluation of the basic premises that underlie the current social security system.

PRIVATE INSURANCE, SOCIAL INSURANCE, AND SOCIAL ADEQUACY

Both private insurance and social insurance offer protection against insured risks. In each case, large numbers of individuals contribute to a fund from which benefits are paid to those who suffer losses. Participants limit losses by pooling risks. Seen in this context, social security protects against premature loss of earnings from early death or disability and insures against exceptional longevity by means of old age insurance. (If longevity were predictable, individuals could save for retirement with less fear of outliving their savings.) Medicare provides protection against extraordinary costs of acute medical care for two highly vulnerable groups: the long-term disabled and the elderly. Thus, social insurance, like private insurance, involves sharing of risks. Aside from this common feature, however, the two forms of insurance differ in major respects.

The differences are clearly delineated in a classic article by Reinhard Hohaus (Hohaus 1938). Private insurance markets perform most efficiently when the insured event can be identified and measured without cost and when its probability of occurrence is known for each participant. Premiums must be sufficient to cover expected losses plus the expenses, or load charges, of the insurer. Failure to segregate policyholders according to risk tends to attract those who are poor risks and to discourage those who are good risks. This process of adverse selection encourages insurers in competitive markets to segregate policyholders into homogeneous risk classes and to equate premiums in each class to the expected value of randomly distributed losses. If the conditions for an efficient market are satisfied, an actuarially fair price can be determined for all potential purchasers. If, like Hohaus, one equates individual equity with actuarial fairness, the actuarial standard of individual equity is satisfied in efficient private markets.

Social insurance, according to Hohaus, should insure participating members against income loss that would leave them destitute and cause them to become charges on society. Its first objective is thus to guarantee participants a minimal living standard consistent with accepted norms of social adequacy. Under the social adequacy standard, coverage may be extended to include extraordinary claims against income imposed by high medical expenses. Hohaus considers the social minimum to be "that income which society feels is necessary and economically practicable for the subsistence of individuals comprising it." (Hohaus 1938: 84). He seems to have had in mind something like the federal poverty line that emerged from the antipoverty efforts of the 1960s. Only after achievement of social adequacy should additional benefits be paid in accordance with individual contributions.

Writing in 1938, Hohaus observed that a system linking benefits too closely to prior contributions could not achieve the social adequacy objective during its start-up years. If benefits were restricted to amounts payable out of accumulated prior contributions, even with compounding, it would be years before most annuitants could receive socially adequate benefits from social security alone. Hohaus criticized the benefit formula contained in the original Social Security Act of 1935 for slighting social adequacy in order to achieve greater individual equity. The 1939 Social Security Amendments shifted the balance toward social adequacy by introducing a more progressive benefit structure, adding benefits for wives and widows of insured workers, and commencing the payments of benefits in 1940, only three years after introduction of the social security payroll tax and two years earlier than originally intended. These changes greatly increased intergenerational transfers from working cohorts to the initial beneficiaries. Even so, as of 1949, benefits averaged only $25 per month, and only 16 percent of persons aged 65 and over received them.

The move toward social adequacy continued with the passage of the 1950 amendments. In spite of benefit liberalization, the balance in the trust fund continued to increase throughout the 1940s. In 1950, Congress granted current beneficiaries a 77.5 percent benefit increase, and for the first time since the system's inception raised payroll taxes. From that date until the late 1980s, the system operated on essentially a pay-as-you-go basis with current benefit payments approximately equal to current payroll tax contributions.

Hohaus argued that to be effective and equitable, a system guaranteeing social adequacy had to be both compulsory, to keep the affluent from opting out, and broadly based, to ensure universal sharing of the social burden. During the 1950s, coverage was extended to the self-employed and to some workers in the public sector. By the 1970s, the goal of social adequacy was attained for nearly all workers with extensive work histories. Generous benefits and broad coverage helped to reduce the poverty rate among persons aged 65 and over from 35 percent in 1959 to less than 12 percent in 1989. The existing OASDI system clearly conforms to the model of social insurance envisioned by Hohaus and by the system's founders.

Former Social Security Commissioner Robert M. Ball makes the case for the existing arrangement (Ball 1988). He refers to our four-tiered approach to income security based on a nearly universal and compulsory program of OASDI, supplemented by private pensions, individual private savings, and, as a last resort, the means-tested Supplemental Security Income (SSI) system. Ball argues for a progressive benefit structure, pointing out that keeping minimum-wage workers and their dependents off of SSI while granting all workers the same percentage of earnings replacement would require a substantially larger OASDI program. He concludes that it is better to direct more benefits to less affluent workers, recognizing that those who are better off are more likely to have access to pensions and are better able to save for retirement and emergencies. Ball favors retaining some connection between earnings and benefits in order to attenuate disincentive effects.

CONCEPTS OF SOCIAL INSURANCE

Actuaries such as Hohaus (1938) and Robert J. Myers (1985: 9–17) equate individual equity and actuarial fairness, even as they argue in favor of a social insurance system that combines equity and social adequacy within a single program. Economists such as Michael J. Boskin (1986: 140–171), Alicia H. Munnell (1977: 39), and Nancy Wolff (1987: 137–143) see in the distinction between equity and adequacy a basis for separating the system into two parts: social insurance that relates benefits more closely to earnings or contributions and a separate means-tested welfare program that would provide a guaranteed minimum income for all who are elderly or disabled. Considerations of individual equity would apply only to the earnings-based component. It is clear from the writings of Hohaus and Myers that they regard a program incorporating both equity and adequacy objectives as the very essence of social insurance, but by equating actuarial fairness with individual equity, they may appear to lend support to those who would strip social security of its overtly redistributive elements.

The following chapters examine the case for an earnings-based standard of equity. As we shall see, such a standard is inherent in the current OASDI benefit structure, at least as it applies to worker-only benefits. Issues of equity can be examined with the aid of two competing models of social security, the insurance model and the annuity-transfer model. Each considers the impact of the system on individual workers over the life cycle, explicitly recognizing the connection between benefits and prior taxable earnings, but the two approaches differ in perception of redistribution within the beneficiary population. The basic features of each model have been clearly delineated by Lawrence J. Thompson (1983: 1436–1438).

The insurance model treats social security as a means of insuring against earnings loss resulting from retirement, disability, or death. Since the insured risks are earnings related, a tax on earnings is the appropriate means of finance. The benefit structure balances the conflicting objectives of individual equity and social adequacy. Individual equity is achieved by relating benefits to previous taxable earnings with adjustments for early or delayed retirement. Social adequacy is implemented by a progressive benefit formula that provides a high marginal rate of benefits to earnings in the lowest earnings bracket and successively lower marginal rates of benefits in higher brackets. Benefits to dependents and survivors combine equity and adequacy goals, since like worker benefits, the benefit level is earnings related, but payments go only to families of workers with eligible dependents or survivors.

The progressive benefit formula, coupled with survivors' and dependents' benefits, represents recognition of the fact that low-income workers cannot save enough while working to provide for an adequate standard of living when they are no longer working. More affluent beneficiaries are able to save more and are more likely to receive pension income, so lower marginal benefits (relative to earnings) are justified. Retention of a linkage between prior tax payments and benefits, however, lessens the disincentive effects that would accompany a more purely redistributive program.

The annuity-transfer model recognizes the individual equity and social adequacy components in the current benefit structure but analyzes them separately. As in Hohaus and Myers, individual equity is equated with actuarial fairness as implemented by payment of an actuarially fair benefit annuity stream. Benefits are based on the accumulated value of benefit payments with contributions viewed as a form of compulsory saving. An actuarially fair system insures against uncertainties of life span and incidence of disability. Such a system is regarded as nonredistributive, since any differences in payments to equally situated contributors would be a direct result of random variation in the occurrence of the insured events, either longevity or disability. These differentials are not considered to be redistributive. The model treats benefits not based on actuarial fairness as a form of transfer. Nonactuarial features of the current system, such as the progressive benefit formula and noncontributory auxiliary benefits bring about substantial transfers within generations. As Thompson notes, classification of nonactuarial benefits as transfers raises the issue of how to finance them. He concludes that in the annuity-transfer model redistributive transfers under social security should be treated like any other transfer program. Financing should be analyzed from a current-period rather than life-cycle perspective, implying that transfer benefits should not be treated as a form of insurance against earnings loss. This represents a major departure from the system favored by Hohaus and Myers.

Thompson focuses on issues in the debate over social security reform, and the models that he outlines lie at the heart of the debate. The insurance model represents a reformulation of Hohaus's vision. Hohaus assigned top priority to social adequacy. Once minimal support is ensured for all long-term participants, additional equity-based benefits may be granted to workers with higher earnings. It took nearly three decades for the social security system to reach the goal set by Hohaus. Throughout this period, a series of revised benefit formulas continued to scale benefits to earnings. The goal of social adequacy was never allowed to override completely the goal of individual equity. To reach the adequacy goal without eliminating equity, it was necessary to increase the size of the program well beyond the levels of the 1940s and 1950s. In addition, because of the redistribution built into the system, participation had to be compulsory and, in the interest of equal treatment of the more affluent, coverage had to become essentially universal.

A system based on the annuity-transfer model would look quite different. For example, it might include an actuarial system of old-age and disability insurance, to be supplemented by a means-tested welfare program financed out of general revenues similar to the two-tier system proposed by Munnell (1977: 39–44). As an alternative to a means test for the elderly, all persons over the age of sixty-five or seventy might receive a lump-sum monthly payment, or demogrant, large enough to remove most social security annuitants from the welfare rolls. This plan would spare large numbers of elderly persons the ordeal of means testing, but its high cost makes it politically unattractive.

An annuity-based system of social insurance allows greater flexibility than a redistributive system because it allows participants to opt out of part or all of the program in favor of a private alternative. Its flexibility may be more apparent than real, however, because a continuous flow of tax revenue is needed to cover the unfunded portion of current benefits. Some privatization is possible, especially during the fund accumulation expected over the next three decades, but total privatization cannot be achieved without high and probably unacceptable transition costs and greater willingness to assign beneficiaries to more homogeneous risk classes. The latter change would be necessary to counter adverse selection. It would require benefit formulas specific to gender and perhaps to race and other identifiable personal characteristics and would likely be blocked by constitutional as well as political obstacles.

Thompson identifies a third model, the tax-transfer model, which treats social security in a current-period rather than a life-cycle context. Taxes and benefits are analyzed separately, with taxes evaluated in terms of ability to pay and benefits in terms of efficiency in targeting payments to the pretransfer target population. The tax-transfer model makes no distinction between means-tested categorical welfare programs, universal demogrants to the elderly, and social insurance. Reliance on pure transfers in the form of expanded old age assistance and demogrants like the Townsend Plan was considered and rejected by Congress and the New Deal in 1935. To apply the tax-transfer model to the existing social security system is to ignore its most salient feature, the scaling of benefits to prior contributions. Unlike welfare, a quid pro quo is present so long as an earnings-based individual equity component remains in the benefit formula.

Proponents of the current-period, tax-transfer approach typically express concern over the presumed regressivity of the payroll tax. Such concerns can be easily overlooked when viewing the system in a life-cycle perspective, especially when focusing on the higher returns to contributions for workers with low average earnings.

SOCIAL SECURITY AND INDIVIDUAL EQUITY: AN OVERVIEW

Chapter 2 begins with a summary description of sources of finance, benefit levels, and program trends, followed by an examination of the distributive effects of the cash-benefit programs (OASI and DI). The chapter concludes with a brief review of long-term projections for each of the trust funds.

Chapter 3 describes in detail the equity framework of Dean R. Leimer, Ronald Hoffman, and Alan Freiden (1978). This flexible and insightful framework prescribes a set of procedures for identifying the equity standards embedded in the earnings-based system of Old Age Insurance for retired workers. Workers only benefits are shown to conform to well-defined and internally consistent standards of horizontal and vertical equity.

Chapter 4 extends the analysis to additional program features, including dependents' and survivors' benefits, the earnings test, taxation of benefits, and issues related to benefit notches and transitions. Some of these features weaken the link between benefits and earnings, and each of them raises issues of individual equity.

Chapter 5 examines equity issues associated with Disability Insurance (DI). The DI benefit structure retains basic features of the OASI program, as modified to accommodate the shortened work histories and needs of disabled workers. This aspect of DI may be evaluated within the Leimer et al. framework. On the other hand, DI insures against an event, the occurrence of total and prolonged disability, which is difficult to define and to identify. The fuzziness of the disability concept has serious equity implications. Medical and vocational personnel with responsibility for disability determinations must decide who gets benefits and who does not. This task requires the exercise of complicated professional judgments, often in an atmosphere charged with political strife, public misunderstanding, and threats posed by judicial review.

Chapter 6 explores the individual and social fairness of the Medicare program. Does Medicare treat all elders equally? Are they treated fairly? Should it treat all elders equally if they have unequal medical and financial needs? In examining the program's fairness, we begin by reviewing the basic features of private health insurance—insurance pool, insurable event, benefit coverage, and premium determination and assignment—and then apply them to examine the distributional impact of the Medicare program, a social health insurance program.

Many challenging questions present themselves as we explore issues of fair treatment. What is the appropriate definition of fairness for a social health insurance program? A "community rated" insurance-transfer framework developed by Ronald Vogel (1988) is modified and used to evaluate treatment of equals and unequals within and across retirement cohorts. Our revised framework takes into account differential mortality and expenditure patterns of the rich and the poor to better approximate the ex ante distributional impact of a lifetime social insurance program. How are those in equal (unequal) need defined? Formal conditions are developed for intercohort and intracohort redistribution and companion definitions of horizontal and vertical equity based on principles of individual equity and social adequacy. In reviewing the empirical evidence, we find that the program is neither actuarially nor socially fair.

In the last section of the chapter, we propose and develop an equity-based reform of Medicare. Cost and revenue estimates are provided for a two-tier, age-stratified comprehensive health insurance plan for elders 65 and older that is financed by a combination of income-conditioned premiums and payroll tax contributions. Our plan provides comprehensive hospital, physician, and long-term care benefits to all elders. Fairness is established by requiring elders who are financially able to pay their actuarially fair share; those who are less financially able receive a public subsidy that is adjusted to reflect their relative ability to pay. It is our view that if the Medicare program "is to meet the current and future needs of older Americans, equitably and reliably, reform that focuses on fairness between the poor and nonpoor within an aged cohort is in order."

Chapter 7 briefly summarizes the equity issues developed in the preceding chapters and contrasts the existing equity framework with alternative visions of social insurance. The chapter concludes with a brief discussion of the effect of the pending trust fund buildup on intergenerational equity.

2

Social Security: Scope, Distributional Impact, and Long-Term Financing

From its modest beginnings as a self-financed retirement program for workers in industry and commerce, social security has evolved into a nearly universal system, providing income support for the elderly and for persons with long-term disability. Medicare offers health care coverage for the elderly and long-term disabled populations. The program has grown continuously since its inception, and by 1990 absorbed 6.4 percent of the U.S. gross national product. The economic impact of so large a program can be substantial, and economists have devoted considerable effort to estimating its effect on saving, investment, labor supply, and distribution of income. This chapter describes the means of finance and the variety of benefits that have evolved over the past three decades and sets the stage for subsequent treatment of equity issues by examining the distributional impact of the system's cash benefit programs. The chapter concludes with a brief examination of long-term actuarial prospects.

TAXES AND BENEFITS

Separate trust funds finance each of the system's major programs. Old Age and Survivors Insurance (OASI), Disability Insurance (DI), and Hospital Insurance (HI) are funded by payroll tax contributions earmarked for those purposes. Supplementary Medical Insurance (SMI) is financed jointly by premiums from beneficiaries and appropriations from the federal general fund. Trust fund accumulations are invested in U.S. treasury bonds, but since the funds have operated on close to a pay-as-you-go basis during most of the system's history, interest income has not been an

important source of finance. Anticipated large but temporary fund accumulation in the OASI fund will result in substantial interest income, at
least through the third decade of the twenty-first century. All funds receive
transfers from the federal general fund, but these transfers are minimal
except for the large SMI subsidy.

Tax Rates and Tax Bases

The Social Security Act of 1935 introduced a 2 percent payroll tax,
termed a "contribution" to be applied to the first $3,000 of earnings with
liability shared equally by employee and employer. Maximum liability
was $60 per year. Taxes remained at this level until 1950. Since then,
frequent increases in tax rate and base coupled with the addition of
disability and Medicare coverage have pushed the combined rate to 15.3
percent on a base (as of 1991) of $53,400. As part of the budget agreement
of 1990, the maximum base for the HI component (part A) of Medicare
was increased to $125,000, boosting the maximum payroll tax liability for
1991 to $10,246.60, some 170 times the $60 maximum of the 1940s. Both
the OASDI and HI base maximums are adjusted annually by a wage index
to keep pace with growth in earnings.[1]

Table 2.1 lists the OASI, DI, and HI tax rates applicable to employee
and employer, the combined OASDHI rate, and the corresponding rate
applicable to the self-employed. Rates on self-employment earnings equal
the sum of employee and employer rates. The employer liability and
one-half of the self-employment liability are treated as deductible business
expenses under the income tax. Symmetrical treatment of earnings of
employed and self-employed participants dates only to passage of the
Social Security Amendments of 1983. Prior to that date, self-employment
earnings were taxed at lower rates. The 1983 amendments also introduced
an income tax on a portion of social security cash benefit payments. It
applies only to beneficiaries with substantial income from other sources.
Receipts are earmarked for the trust fund. The tax effectively shifts a
portion of the tax burden from workers to the more affluent beneficiaries.

The earnings base generally includes all money earnings, including
wages, commissions, bonuses, and cash tips if they exceed $20 per month.
Most fringe benefits and payments-in-kind are excluded. Self-employment income creates an additional measurement problem because in many
cases it includes a return to capital as well as to labor. The share attributable
to capital varies widely across occupations, but to achieve simplification,
92.35 percent of net annual self-employment income is counted as earn-

Table 2.1
Old Age and Survivors, Disability, and Hospital Insurance Tax Rates

Years	Employer and Employee				Employer + Employee	Self-Employed			
				(Percent of Taxable Earnings)					
	OASI	DI	HI	OASDHI	OASDHI	OASI	DI	HI	OASDHI
1990-99	5.6	0.6	1.45	7.65	15.3	11.2	1.2	2.9	15.3
2000 and thereafter	5.49	0.71	1.45	7.65	15.3	10.98	1.42	2.9	15.3

Source: Social Security Bulletin, Annual Statistical Supplement, 1990, Table 2.A2, p. 33.

ings for all occupations. Persons with self-employment income of less than $400 are exempt from the payroll tax.

Evolution of Social Security since 1960

By any measure, social security has grown markedly since 1960. In that year, the system included only the cash-benefit OASI and DI programs and paid $10.8 billion in benefits to 14.9 million beneficiaries. By 1990, nearly 40 million beneficiaries received cash benefits of $243.2 billion. Medicare, added in 1965, recorded outlays of $105.5 billion.

Trends in payroll tax receipts appear in Table 2.2. Allocations among trust funds reflect legislated tax rates for each fund. SMI (part B of Medicare), which covers physicians' fees and related medical expenses, is financed by premiums paid by eligible elderly and disabled beneficiaries. Beneficiaries participate by choice and pay monthly premiums, set at $31.80 in 1992 and adjusted annually. Premiums cover only one-quarter of the cost of this heavily subsidized program. As shown by data in Table 2.2, premiums initially accounted for one-half of program costs, but policymakers have chosen to shelter beneficiaries from accelerating medical costs by increasing the share financed from general revenue.

Trust fund expenditures since 1960 appear in Table 2.3. In addition to overall growth, the data reveal shifts in the relative size of program components. The OASI component continues to account for most of the system's expenditures, but its share declined continuously from 95.4 percent in 1960 to 62.8 percent in 1990. Disability Insurance (DI) increased its share from 4.6 percent in 1960, four years after its introduction, to 10 percent in 1980, the end of a decade of rapid growth. By 1990, DI accounted for only 7 percent of system outlays. The Medicare share increased from 18.9 percent of system outlays in 1970 to 30.2 percent in 1990, and this trend is expected to continue despite efforts to cut costs.

The total number of beneficiaries continues to grow, as shown in Table 2.4, but at a reduced rate. Between 1980 and 1990, growth was confined to persons receiving retirement benefits (as workers or dependents), with declines in the number of persons receiving survivor and disability benefits.

Table 2.5 shows trends in average monthly benefits. Average benefits to retired workers, surviving spouses, and disabled workers ranged from $553.00 (surviving spouses) to $602.56 (retired workers) in 1990. Average benefits to workers exceed the official federal poverty line ($552 for a single adult in 1990). Average benefits to surviving spouses, many of whom are elderly widows, remain at poverty level.

Table 2.2
Contributions to Social Security Trust Funds (billions of dollars)

Year	Payroll Tax				Premiums and General Fund		
	OASI	DI	HI	OASDHI	SMI (Premiums)	SMI (Gen. Fund)	Total
1960	$9.8	$1.0	--	$10.8	--	--	
1970	30.0	4.1	4.8	38.9	$0.9	$0.9	$1.8
1980	97.6	16.8	23.2	137.6	2.9	6.9	9.8
1990	264.4	27.4	70.7	362.5	11.1	33.2	44.3

Source: Social Security Bulletin, May 1991, 54(5), Table M-4, p. 35.

Table 2.3
Social Security Benefit Payments: OASDI and Medicare

Year	Cash Benefits			Medicare			Benefit Total	Percentage of Total Cash and Medicare Benefits		
	OASI	DI	OASDI	HI	SMI	HI+SMI		OASI	DI	Medicare
1960	10.3	0.5	10.8	--	--	--	10.8	95.4	4.6	--
1970	26.3	2.8	29.1	4.8	2.0	6.8	35.9	73.2	7.8	18.9
1980	100.6	14.9	115.5	23.8	10.1	33.9	149.4	67.3	10.0	22.7
1990	218.9	24.3	243.2	63.8	41.7	105.5	348.7	62.8	7.0	30.2

Source: Social Security Bulletin, May 1991, 54(5), Tables M-4–M-7, pp. 35–38.

Table 2.4
Number of OASI and DI Beneficiaries (millions)

Year	OASI Retirement	OASI Survivors	OASI Total	DI Workers	DI Dependents	DI Total
1960	10.6	3.6	14.2	0.5	0.2	0.7
1970	17.1	6.5	23.6	1.5	1.2	2.7
1980	23.3	7.6	30.9	2.9	1.8	4.7
1990	28.3	7.2	35.5	3.0	1.3	4.3

Sources: Social Security Bulletin, May 1991, 54(5), Table M-2, p. 33; Social Security Bulletin, Annual Statistical Supplement, 1989, Tables 5.F1 and 5.F4, pp. 194, 196.

Table 2.5
Average Monthly Benefits

| Year | OASI | | | | | DI |
	Retired Workers	Dependent Spouses	Dependent Children	Surviving Spouses	Surviving Children	Disabled Workers
1960	$74.04	$38.72	$28.25	$57.68	$51.37	$89.31
1970	118.10	61.19	44.85	101.71	82.23	131.26
1980	341.41	171.95	140.49	308.12	239.52	370.70
1990	602.56	311.18	259.35	553.07	405.52	587.23

Source: Social Security Bulletin, May 1991, 54(5), Table M-12, p. 43.

Long-term changes in benefit levels can be difficult to interpret without relating them to accompanying rates of inflation and growth in real earnings. Large benefit increases legislated between 1969 and 1972 increased benefit levels of retired workers relative to current wages, as illustrated by the following percentages:

Year	Percentage of National Average Wage
1960	22.2
1970	22.9
1980	32.7
1990	33.3

These percentages should remain relatively stable in the future as a result of indexing procedures included in the Social Security Amendments of 1977.

The trend in social security expenditures (cash benefits and Medicare) as a percentage of gross national product offers another perspective on program expansion. Changes between 1960 and 1990 are as follows:

Year	Percentage of Gross National Product
1960	2.1
1970	3.5
1980	5.5
1990	6.4

Social security has continued to claim an increasing share of the GNP with Medicare accounting for nearly all of the increases since 1980.

DISTRIBUTIONAL EFFECTS OF SOCIAL SECURITY

Social security cash benefits now absorb about 4.5 percent of U.S. gross national product. A program of this magnitude can significantly affect the distribution of income. By combining goals of individual equity and social adequacy, the program achieves primary redistribution, much of which is intentional, within and across cohorts. Secondary redistribution may occur insofar as the program affects savings, labor supply, and factor income.

Studies of Distributional Effects

A number of attempts to measure primary distributional effects have been reported in the literature. These studies employ a variety of methodologies and cover different time periods, but they yield similar qualitative results. As expected, they generally show that the retirement program redistributes income from more to less affluent workers and favors single-earner married couples relative to other participants. In the past, the program transferred large sums from later to earlier cohorts, but this phenomenon should disappear as the system reaches maturity. The focus here will be on two of the many studies, that of Boskin et al. (1987), and that of Pellechio and Goodfellow (1983). These studies are of particular interest because they capture the effects of the post-1983 tax and benefit structure. Each employs a similar methodology. Boskin et al. consider only OASI; Pellechio and Goodfellow estimate the combined effects of OASI and DI.[2]

Boskin, Kotlikoff, Puffert, and Shoven (1987). The authors, hereafter referred to as BKPS, constructed a simulation model to show how households of different ages and configurations fare under OASI. They simulated households representing low, medium, and high earnings levels for six birth cohorts, spaced at fifteen-year intervals between 1915 and 1990. Use of different earnings levels and cohorts enabled them to estimate the effect of the progressive benefit formula across earnings levels and to reveal the impact of increases in payroll taxes, real wages, and life expectancy on different cohorts. Additional computations were made for single males, single females, one-earner married couples, and two-earner couples with equal and unequal earnings. These computations were made only for the 1945 birth cohort.

Workers were assumed to have begun working at age 21 and to have worked continuously until they attained normal retirement age (65 to 67, depending on cohort). Husband and wife were assumed to be of the same age and to have married at age 25. Marriages terminated only by death. Surviving spouses did not remarry, and children's benefits were ignored. Workers were assumed to bear the full burden of payroll taxes including the portion paid by employers.

Low, medium, and high earnings profiles were obtained from historical data and were extended to future years by applying the intermediate earnings projections of social security actuaries.[3] Within each cohort, earnings were assumed to grow at rates above the national average until age 50 and to flatten thereafter so as to resemble more closely the pattern of observed lifetime profiles.

Tax and benefit streams were constructed in 1985 dollars for each representative household by applying statutory tax rates and benefit formulas to earnings profiles. The authors then derived two measures of distributional effects, the internal rate of return and the net present value of expected cash benefits.

The internal rate of return (IRR) was obtained by solving for the discount rate that equated the present value of tax and benefit streams for a representative household. A positive IRR indicates that the dollar sum of benefits exceeds the dollar sum of taxes; a negative IRR indicates the reverse. Table 2.6 lists the simulated IRR for single-earner couples within each of the six birth cohorts and three earnings categories. Reading across each cohort row, the inverse relationship between earnings and IRR becomes apparent. The decline in the IRR at higher earnings becomes more pronounced within the four younger cohorts, revealing the combined effects of changes in tax rates and base, revised benefit computation procedures, and introduction in 1983 of the benefit tax. Reading down the columns, returns within each earnings category decline significantly across successive cohorts before becoming nearly constant for members of the 1960, 1975, and 1990 cohorts. The last three cohorts participate in a fully mature system free of start-up windfalls, and the 1960 cohort is the first that must work until age 67 to qualify for full benefits. The authors speculate that the nearly constant IRR profile for persons in the last three

Table 2.6
Internal Rates of Return from OASI for Single-Earner Married Couples by Birth Cohort and Earnings Levels

Birth Cohort		Earnings Level	
	Low	Median	High
1915	6.34%	5.46%	4.83%
1930	4.37	3.22	2.92
1945	3.50	2.07	1.74
1960	3.08	1.54	1.02
1975	3.02	1.54	1.03
1990	3.10	1.58	1.09

Source: Michael J. Boskin, Laurence J. Kotlikoff, Douglas J. Puffert, and John B. Shoven, "Social Security: A Financial Appraisal across and within Generations," *National Tax Journal*, 40, no. 1 (1987), p. 23. Reprinted with permission of the National Tax Association.

cohorts occurs because increasingly favorable survival probabilities approximately offset the effects of increased taxation of benefits.[4]

BKPS computed the present value of tax and benefit streams for the same grouping of single-earner married households. They used two reference points in computing present values. The first yields present value (PV) as of 1985 for each cohort; the second yields PV for each cohort for the year in which its members attained age 25. All payments were stated in constant 1985 dollars and converted to present value terms by compounding tax and benefit payments prior to the reference year and discounting payments in subsequent years. A 3 percent real rate of interest was used for this purpose.[5]

When a single reference year, 1985, applies to all cohorts, the PV of both taxes and benefits declines continuously from the oldest to the youngest. This result is to be expected because payments prior to 1985 are compounded and those subsequent to 1985 are discounted. The PV of tax payments serves as a standard of individual equity. If the PV of the expected benefit stream exceeds the PV of the expected tax stream, a household enjoys a positive net transfer; if the PV of taxes exceeds the PV of benefits, a household experiences a negative net transfer. From a 1985 perspective, net transfers range from $62,514 for median income members of the 1915 birth cohort to a negative $68,501 for high-earning households in the 1960 birth cohort. All representative households in the 1915 cohort enjoy sizable positive net transfers. Transfers turn negative for high earners in the 1930 and subsequent cohorts and for median earners beginning with the 1945 cohort.

Within cohorts, the PV of taxes increases with earnings, as expected, although among older (1915, 1930, and 1945) cohorts, the difference in taxes among median and high earners is small.

All six cohorts show lower PV of benefits for high-earner than for median-earner cohorts, a surprising result for a program that ties benefits to taxable earnings. This anomaly apparently results from effects of the income tax on benefits, in effect since 1983. High earners are more likely to have adjusted gross incomes above the tax threshold and to fall into higher marginal tax brackets. Because BKPS use the 1985 income tax rate schedule, they overstate somewhat the effect of the tax on net benefits and, therefore, overstate at least minimally the progressivity of the benefit structure.

A change of the reference point to the year in which cohort members attain age 25 offers an ex ante perspective by valuing net transfers early in a cohort's work cycle. One interesting result is the increase in the age 25 PV of both taxes and benefits among successive cohorts. Wage indexing of maximum taxable income and benefit levels ensures this result as long as real earnings continue to grow. Another feature of the age 25 perspective is the very large negative transfer projected for median and high earners in the 1960, 1975, and 1990 cohorts. These estimates range from minus $47,943 (1960 median earners) to minus $105,340 (1990 high earners). In contrast, even from an age 25 perspective, each simulated household in the 1915 cohort receives a positive net transfer of from $12,457 to $16,531.

Two points should be kept in mind when interpreting these results. First, since BKPS used a 3 percent discount rate in all PV calculations, any household with an IRR of less than 3 percent will show a negative net transfer. As indicated by IRR data in Table 2.6, this includes median-earner households in the 1945 and subsequent cohorts and high-earner households in all but the 1915 cohort. The IRR for each of these households is greater than zero, however, indicating that without compounding or discounting, expected benefits exceed expected taxes (in 1985 dollars) for all representative households. Second, the simulations discussed thus far apply only to single-earner married couples. Because these households receive maximum potential access to dependents' and survivors' benefits, they tend to be the most advantageously situated of all program participants.

By simulating rates of return and net transfers for households of the same age but of different composition, BKPS demonstrated the significance of factors other than earnings and cohort designation on returns to OASI contributions. These include eligibility for dependents' and survivors' benefits, which are payable only when eligible family members are present, and the effects of gender-related differences in survival probabilities before and after retirement. The authors selected the 1945 birth cohort for this purpose. Results appear in Table 2.7.

The upper panel in Table 2.7 allows comparison of IRR estimates for single-earner couples, repeated from Table 2.6, with estimates for single males and females. Lower IRR values for single persons stem from ineligibility for dependents' and survivors' benefits. Higher returns for single females than for single males result from differences in survival rates. At retirement age, the life expectancy of females exceeds that of males by nearly five years. Cohort members in each earnings category have identical simulated histories, yet in each case, the IRR estimates for single-earner couples exceed those of single males by close to 2.5 percentage points. Median- and high-income males experience negative returns, indicating that they can expect to get back less in 1985 dollars than they paid in taxes.

Because of peculiarities in benefit computation procedures, returns to two-earner married couples are sensitive to the relative earnings of each

Table 2.7
Internal Rates of Return from OASI across Household Types, 1945 Birth Cohort, by Earnings Level

Household Type	Earnings Level		
	Low	Median	High
Single-earner Couple	3.50%	2.07%	1.74%
Single Male	1.16	-0.44	-0.79
Single Female	2.34	1.00	0.53
Two-earner Couple			
Two-thirds/one-third Split	3.05%	1.46%	0.57%
Equal Split	3.01	1.22	0.44

Source: Michael J. Boskin, Laurence J. Kotlikoff, Douglas J. Puffert, and John B. Shoven, "Social Security: A Financial Appraisal across and within Generations," *National Tax Journal*, 40, no. 1 (1987), p. 28. Reprinted with permission of the National Tax Association.

spouse. The sensitivity results from the dual entitlement provision that applies to spouses who simultaneously are entitled to worker benefits based on their own earnings and spousal benefits (dependent or survivor) based on earnings of their spouse. In such cases, the spouse receives an amount equal to the larger of the two benefits but loses any additional benefits to which he or she may be entitled.

The lower panel in Table 2.7 illustrates the effect of dual entitlement on the IRR when a given amount of earnings is split two-thirds, one-third between husband and wife and when the husband and wife split the same total earnings equally. In each of these cases, two-earner couples experience lower returns to contributions than single-earner couples with identical total earnings. Couples with low and median earnings lose benefits because of dual entitlement. High-earner working couples receive somewhat more than their single-earner counterparts, but their IRR is lower because they pay more in taxes. Couples with equal earnings fare the worst because each spouse receives identical worker benefits, but, because of dual entitlement, neither receives any spousal benefits. These couples fare no better than a single male or single female with the same earnings history.

Pellechio and Goodfellow (1983). The Pellechio and Goodfellow (PG) simulation model resembles the BKPS model methodologically and yields results that are qualitatively very similar. PG incorporated pre- and post-

1983 tax and benefit formulas into their model to allow for analysis of distributional effects of the 1983 amendments. Like BKPS, they differentiated household types by birth cohort, earnings level, marital status, and labor force participation of spouses. Unlike most studies of distributional effects, however, PG measured the combined effects of OASI and DI. They presented results only in PV form.

They estimated the PV (as of 1983) of past and future taxes and benefits and net transfer (gain or loss), all stated in terms of 1983 dollars, for representative households at six annual earnings levels. Earnings range from $10,000 to $35,700 (the 1983 taxable maximum). Household members were assumed to be ages 25, 40, or 55 in 1983, making them members of the 1958, 1943, and 1928 birth cohorts. Household situations included single-earner married couples in which only the husband or wife works, two-earner married couples, unmarried males, and unmarried females. Probabilities of survival and disability were built into the model.

Past tax payments were compounded annually at a rate equal to the yearly average interest rate on new special treasury issues purchased by the social security trust funds. Future tax payments were based on the 1983 intermediate II-B projections of Social Security Administration actuaries. These included projected inflation rates of about 4 percent and real earnings growth that increases from near zero in 1984 to 1.7 percent in 1991 before receding to 1.5 percent in 1993 and thereafter. Future taxes and benefits were discounted at rates contained in the II-B projections. Because projections include an adjustment for inflation, a nominal discount rate was used. The rate declines from 11.4 percent in 1983 to 6.1 percent beginning in 1995. In real terms, the discount rate ranges from 8.3 percent in 1983 to 2.1 percent in 1995 and thereafter.

As expected, households belonging to the 1958 birth cohort experience the least favorable treatment. All households in the top earnings group experience net losses, ranging from minus $3,440 for a single-earner household in which the wife works to minus $80,175 for single males. With one minor exception (middle-income households in which only the husband works), net gain declines consistently as earnings increase. Married households fare better than single households, and unmarried females fare better than unmarried males. Among unmarried households, only low-income females receive positive net benefits (a modest $2,857). Seventeen of the thirty representative households experience net losses.

Although BKPS and PG used similar methodologies, direct comparisons of results are not possible. BKPS presented results for different household types only for the 1945 birth cohort, with 1985 as point of reference. The PG estimates for the 1943 birth cohort, using 1983 as point of reference, provide the best basis for comparison. Results are qualitatively similar, but in all cases, PG showed higher net benefits and more favorable benefit-to-tax ratios. Several factors may contribute to these differences. Cohort effects are likely to be small for cohorts only two years apart. PG included DI taxes and benefits; BKPS did not. One might expect that inclusion of DI would add a progressive tilt to the distribution of net benefits in light of the higher incidence of disability among low earners, but a comparison of benefit-to-tax ratios between the lowest and highest earners reveals greater relative progression in BKPS's results. PG did not tell us whether they differentiated the incidence of disability according to earnings level. If they did not, their results may understate progression. Other factors that could account for the differences include the use of different discount rates and earnings projections and BKPS's use of stylized earnings profiles. Internal rates of return would provide a more direct basis for comparison, but PG present results only in PV form.

To summarize, the PG results seem to indicate that social security offers participants a better deal than was indicated by BKPS. Qualitatively, both studies confirm the progressivity of the benefit structure, and both show that single-earner married couples receive the most favorable treatment while single males fare the poorest. Likewise, both studies show more favorable treatment of earlier rather than later cohorts.

Methodological Issues

Most studies of the distributional effects of social security employ a methodology similar to that of the BKPS and PG models. They compare the tax price of coverage to the expected value of benefits, expressed in terms either of present values or internal rates of return. Results are generated by entering tax and benefit formulas into models that simulate earnings streams. A methodological problem arises because the tax and benefit formulas in the social security statutes are not explicitly connected. Beneficiaries will receive the benefits to which they are entitled only if the trust funds remain solvent. If funding is inadequate, Congress must act to restore solvency, but that requires a tax increase, a benefit cut, or some combination of the two with corresponding changes in simulated tax or benefit streams. At a minimum, the attempt of PG to compare net benefits before and after the 1983 amendments is methodologically suspect. BKPS recognize this and, citing Boskin (1986: 11–13), warn the reader that long-term solvency of the OASI fund is unlikely under current law.[6]

Financial projections of trust fund operations by Social Security Administration actuaries provide Congress and others with information on short-term and long-term prospects for the funds. Each year trustees of the funds publish a set of four 75-year projections, including the most optimistic (alternative I), two intermediate projections (the more optimistic alternative II-A and more pessimistic alternative II-B), and the most pessimistic (alternative III). Each is derived from an underlying set of economic and demographic projections that range from optimistic to pessimistic in terms of their influence on fund balances. Alternative II-B is regarded as most realistic and is most often cited in reference to the program's outlook.

Figures 2.1 and 2.2 show projections for the combined OASI and DI trust funds throughout the projection period. The two funds are treated in combination because of past reliance on interfund transfers in times of stress. Tax and spending formulas in effect since passage of the 1983 amendments will generate tax receipts in excess of expenditures until 2017. This is illustrated in Figure 2.1, which shows cost and income rates as a percentage of taxable payroll. A legislated tax rate of 12.4 percent, supplemented by receipts from the benefit tax and interest on treasury securities held by the funds, will be sufficient to maintain a positive fund

Figure 2.1
OASDI Cost Rates and Income Rates (as a percentage of taxable payroll)

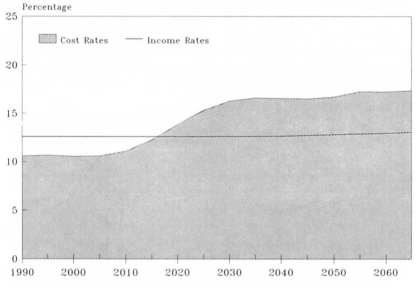

Source: Social Security Bulletin, 1990.

Figure 2.2
OASDI Contingency Fund Ratio (Assets as a Percentage of Annual Expenditures)

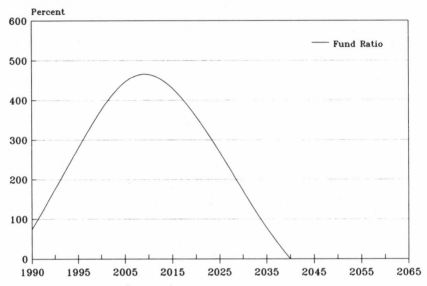

Source: Social Security Bulletin, 1990.

balance until 2043. Figure 2.2 shows the contingency fund ratio that measures assets at the beginning of each year as a percentage of expenditures during the year. This ratio peaks at about 475 percent in about 2014 before declining to zero within the next thirty years. Unlike early retirement cohorts, which enjoyed large transfers from younger workers, the baby-boom cohorts, born between 1946 and 1964, will finance a portion of their own retirement by contributing to a large but temporary fund accumulation.

Turning to the simulations of BKPS, if the alternative II-B projections turn out to be accurate, estimates of returns to the 1975 and 1990 birth cohorts require revision pending corrective action by Congress. These cohorts attain normal retirement age of 67 in 2042 and 2057, respectively, by which time the tax and benefit formulas must be changed unless the "most likely" projection turns out to be too pessimistic.

Nevertheless, the overall impressions one gains from simulations like these may be accurate. The results seem to show that persons born after 1960 will fare less well than their predecessors, but that returns across generations will stabilize if relatively optimistic economic projections and expected improvements in survival rates materialize.

Earlier Studies

Because earlier studies apply pre–1983 tax and benefit formulas, they will not be considered in detail. Most of the earlier studies employ a methodology similar to that of the more recent efforts described above. Simulation techniques are used to compute distributional effects, which are presented in terms of net present value, benefit-cost ratios, or internal rates of return. Aaron (1977) obtained an atypical result when he found that benefit-cost ratios increase with income, indicating that higher survival rates reverse the intended progression of the benefit formula. Hurd and Shoven (1985) found nearly identical return ratios across wealth groups after adjusting for mortality differentials and contributions of deceased husbands of widows receiving survivor's benefits. Other studies employing differential survival probabilities for socioeconomic groups, such as Okonkwo (1976) and Wolff (1987), find that differences in survival rates reduce but do not fully offset progression in benefit awards.

Burkhauser and Warlick (1981) introduced a new technique designed to disentangle the insurance and transfer components in the OASI program for a sample of beneficiaries included in the 1973 Exact Match File.[7] They estimated the annuitized benefit stream that could have been purchased at retirement with each worker's accumulated tax contributions. By comparing the annuity stream with actual benefit payments, they measured the transfer component in each benefit stream. The Burkhauser-Warlick approach conforms to the annuity-transfer model of social security that calls for a clear distinction between actuarially fair insurance benefits and pure transfers. Burkhauser and Warlick measured transfers both as a percentage of benefits and in absolute dollars. They found that transfers were larger in both percentage and absolute terms for the earlier retirement cohorts. Since their sample included only persons retired as of 1972, this finding confirms the belief that earlier cohorts received sizable windfalls during the system's start-up phase. To test for progression, they arrayed households according to income and found that transfers as a percentage of benefits generally diminished as income increased. In absolute dollars, however, transfers tended to be highest among middle-income households.

Wolff (1987) refined and extended the work of Burkhauser and Warlick. For each household, Wolff calculated annuity streams incorporating three survivorship tables: gender merged, sex-race distinct, and socioeconomic. The socioeconomic survivorship tables allow for differentiation for education, income, and marital status. Her findings indicate that married households in the sample cohorts benefited from the system, primarily at the expense of single males. Effects of race on distribution were inconclusive. Tests of the effects of a variety of other variables reveal negative relationships between transfers and years of work in covered occupations, lifetime earnings, early or delayed retirement, and recentness of retirement. Changes in the benefit formula since 1972, especially with respect to computation of the benefit base and adjustment for age at retirement, have no doubt changed these relationships among current and future retirement cohorts. These changes are described in detail in Chapter 3.

NOTES

1. Indexing increased the maximum taxable base to $55,500 for OASDI and $130,200 for HI in 1992. The maximum tax liability increased to $10,715.80 for persons with earnings of $130,200 or more. By placing the HI maximum at more than 2.3 times the OASDI maximum, the budget negotiators shifted more of the cost of financing Medicare to persons with high earnings without increasing their entitlement to future OASDI benefits.

2. Summaries of earlier studies appear in Aaron (1982: 72–81) and Wolff (1987: 15–27).

3. Earnings levels approximate the poverty line, median earnings, and earnings of well-paid professionals. Dollar values vary over time and among cohorts owing to growth in real earnings. For the 1960 birth cohort, they correspond to 1985 earnings of $10,000, $30,000, and $50,000. (Boskin et al. 1987: 22). Maximum taxable earnings in 1985 were $39,600.

4. Boskin, et al. (1987: 25). Benefit taxes become more important over time because the threshold at which they begin to apply is fixed at $25,000 for single taxpayers and $32,000 for married couples filing jointly. Because the thresholds are not indexed, their long-term impact becomes highly sensitive to both inflation and trends in real income.

5. Choice of a 3 percent real discount rate represents a compromise between those who regard it as too high for an essentially riskless investment and those who consider it too low to be consistent with observed behavior. BKPS analyzed the sensitivity of PVs to discount rates of 0 to 4 percent, using 1985 as a reference year. At the extremes, the estimated PV of transfers can vary by more than $200,000 for a given household type, depending on which discount rate is chosen.

6. Aaron (1982) and McBride (1986) also make this point. Aaron raises other interesting methodological points particularly with respect to ex ante–ex post issues and benefit substitution among retired and disabled workers and survivors.

7. The 1973 Exact Match File matches information from census, social security, and Internal Revenue Service for Households in the sample.

3

An Earnings-Based Standard of Individual Equity

The Old Age, Survivors, and Disability Insurance program (OASDI) evolved as a form of earnings replacement for workers who retire or become disabled. Consequently, benefits payments are based on prior earnings. Because the system enables workers to share the risks of earnings loss, a tax on earnings is accepted as the most appropriate means of finance. The OASI and DI benefit formulas relate benefits to earnings but in a complex and indirect way. Benefits depend on the level and timing of earnings, the year of birth of the beneficiary, age at retirement, and the dependency status of members of a worker's family. Benefit formulas accommodate goals of individual equity and social adequacy, in keeping with the philosophy espoused by Hohaus described in Chapter 1.

AN EQUITY FRAMEWORK

The principles that govern the distribution of benefits and taxes constitute an equity framework. In public finance, the most widely accepted principle of equity is the principle of equal treatment of equals. This principle prescribes that economic units in equal positions should be treated equally and, correspondingly, that units in unequal positions should be treated unequally but in a reasonable and consistent manner. Implementation requires an operational definition of the means of positioning or ranking economic units and their consequent treatment. This requires agreement on a standard or index of equality (or inequality). Once such an index has been accepted, equal treatment is achieved by application of a horizontal equity rule; unequal treatment is achieved by application of a vertical equity rule.

Application of rules of horizontal and vertical equity to taxation, particularly to taxation based on ability to pay, is well understood. The principle of horizontal and vertical equity can also be applied to an earnings-based system of social insurance. Past earnings serve as a positioning device or index of equality. An appropriate measure of past earnings then serves as the benefit base. A multibracketed benefit structure, analogous to the graduated rate structure of an income tax, is applied to the benefit base to determine each worker's benefits award. In this manner, the benefit formula implements the horizontal and vertical equity rules.

In the following sections of this chapter, an equity framework will be developed and applied to Old Age Insurance (OAI) for workers. Dependents' benefits, Survivors Insurance (SI), and Disability Insurance (DI) will be analyzed in subsequent chapters. The framework was devised by Dean R. Leimer, Ronald Hoffman, and Alan Freiden (1978). It provides a useful and flexible means of understanding and evaluating the benefit structure.

THE LEIMER-HOFFMAN-FREIDEN EQUITY FRAMEWORK

Leimer et al. (1978) stress the importance of specifying the value judgments embedded within the social security benefit structure. To aid in this task, they provide a step-by-step procedure for analyzing individual equity within and between retirement cohorts. To simplify the exposition, they limit their discussion to OAI, but their framework is easily extended to the other cash benefit components of social security.

Because workers who retire at different times may be treated differently under OAI, criteria must be devised for assigning each worker to a specific cohort. Cohort assignment represents the first step in specifying an index of equality, to be followed by selecting criteria for defining intracohort and intercohort equals and by setting benefits. Cohort assignment will be considered first, followed by an exposition of intracohort and intercohort features of the Leimer et al. benefit framework.

Cohort Assignment and Benefit Eligibility

If social security were a static system that treated each successive retirement cohort identically, cohort assignment would be trivial. To accommodate the phasing in of cohorts during the start-up period and to allow for benefit adjustments as average earnings change, successive cohorts are treated differently. Consequently, assignment takes on substantive importance. The two most obvious criteria for assignment are year of birth or year of retirement. Assignment according to year of birth eliminates worker discretion, but if benefits are adjusted for such factors as age at retirement or presence of a spouse, program parameters will continue to influence retirement decisions. Indeed, the implications of cohort assignment can be understood only with reference to program parameters such as these.

Benefit eligibility may also vary across cohorts. In principle, anyone with prior taxable earnings could be granted benefits, but in practice eligibility may be limited to cohort members whose earnings exceed some threshold level. The intent is to provide earnings replacement only to workers for whom earnings in covered occupations have been a significant source of income. The benefit threshold may reflect both the number of years or quarters with recorded earnings and the amount of earnings. Thresholds may vary over successive cohorts, particularly during the start-up phase of the program when workers with short earnings histories are more likely to be accommodated.

Intracohort Components

Determination of initial benefit awards to members of a cohort begins with specification of the benefit base. Since the benefit base positions each worker within a beneficiary cohort, its specification must be consistent with the intended nature of the program. If the intent is to replace a portion of earnings lost through retirement, some measure of prior earnings would be an appropriate base. The portion of earnings to be replaced may be a function of the magnitude or timing of earnings. For example, the intent may be to replace a lower proportion of lost earnings for high earners than for low earners. This may be achieved by setting an upper limit on the amount of annual earnings to be included in the earnings base or by applying to the base a benefit formula that achieves the desired assignment of benefit awards across the earnings distribution. Earnings profiles over time may be altered by indexing reported earnings. Additional adjustments may alter the benefit award for differences in age at retirement, number of dependents, or other individual characteristics deemed relevant. The Leimer et al. framework allows for separate treatment of each of these program features, thus highlighting the equity or adequacy criteria implicit in each of the various adjustment procedures.

Benefit Base. Once it is agreed that OAI benefits should be related to prior earnings, a decision must be made on how much of the earnings to include in the benefit base. Inclusion of all earnings subject to the payroll tax would seem an obvious choice, since it establishes a link, however tenuous, between tax contributions and benefits, thus reinforcing one of the basic features of social insurance. Administrative simplicity suggests that only money earnings be taxed, even though differences in fringe benefits, working conditions, and locational amenities will cause a ranking based on money earnings to differ from one based on a broader measure of worker compensation.

Some money earnings of covered workers may be excluded from the payroll tax base and, therefore, from the benefit base. For example, earnings in excess of an annual taxable maximum may be excluded on the grounds that OAI should provide only an income floor for retired workers. Replacement of earnings above an annual taxable limit or cap would come entirely from alternative sources, such as private pensions or personal savings. The level at which the cap should be set depends on the perceived role of OAI as a means of support for retired workers. Setting the cap at a level in excess of the annual money earnings of most workers implies reliance on OAI as the primary source of retirement income for most of the insured work force; setting the cap below the annual earnings of most insured workers implies a reduced role for OAI and a correspondingly greater reliance on other sources of retirement income.

If the earnings base of each worker is obtained by summing taxable earnings over a working lifetime, the ranking or position of each worker within a retirement cohort will be sensitive to differences in lifetime earnings profiles. Differences among profiles are particularly significant if the taxable earnings of most workers fall below the taxable limit (or if all earnings are taxed) and if the summed earnings are measured in nominal (current) dollars. Earnings profiles differ across cohort members because of differences in the duration and timing of labor force participation, including the number of years devoted to education. Even moderate rates of inflation cause average earnings to increase several fold over a forty-year working lifetime, and the upward drift receives an additional boost from the tendency of real wages to keep pace with increasing labor productivity. Consequently, a simple summation of annual nominal earnings will be dominated by earnings in later years (assuming that the taxable earnings base grows at a rate commensurate with nominal earnings growth).

The weighting of earnings received in earlier years can be increased by inflating each year's earnings with an appropriate index. As with other components of the benefit structure, the choice of an index depends on the objectives of the program. The two forms of index most often considered for this purpose are a general price index and a wage index.

Price indexing normalizes earnings for inflation by stating all earnings in terms of constant real purchasing power in a benchmark year. Indexing by a price index increases the weight of earnings received early in the work cycle for cohorts experiencing price inflation. This improves the positioning within the cohort of workers with a larger share of earnings concentrated in early years. Typically, the workers most affected would be those who left school to begin working full time at an early age or who retire early. Price indexing does not eliminate the dominance of earnings received in the years just before retirement, however, as long as growth in labor productivity causes real wages to rise.

Wage indexing of annual earnings eliminates the effect of both inflation and productivity growth. Wage indexing converts earnings earlier in the work cycle to a level commensurate with earnings at retirement. Each worker's benefit base therefore reflects growth in real wages plus the effects of inflation during a cohort's work cycle. Wage indexing thus further increases the share of the benefit base assigned to cohort members with a relatively large share of earnings in early years.

Although wage indexing eliminates the effect of inflation and productivity growth on the benefit base, it does not account for the opportunity cost of time. Because market participants, on average, prefer a dollar now to a dollar at some future date, lenders command compensation in the form of interest. In a perfectly functioning capital market, the interest rate provides a measure of time preference. Leimer, et al. offer an example of how treatment of the opportunity cost of time affects the positioning of workers' benefit bases within a cohort (1978: 16–17). To simplify the example, they assume a stable price level, zero growth in general productivity, and perfect capital markets. Suppose that a retirement cohort consists of two workers, A and B. Worker A invests nothing in human capital and begins working at the earliest possible age. Worker B delays entry into the labor force to engage in human capital formation (a college education, for example). Assume that the only cost of acquiring human capital is forgone earnings and that the return to investment in human capital equals the market rate of interest. Worker B has zero earnings in early years but higher earnings than worker A in later years. If earnings are compounded at the market rate of interest, the two workers will have equal benefit bases at retirement. A benefit base of compounded past earnings is neutral with respect to investment in human capital. If earnings are not compounded, worker B will have a larger benefit base and will presumably receive higher retirement benefits.

The example may be extended to the case in which nominal earnings grow in response to inflation and increased labor productivity. Assume that a wage index adjusts earnings in each year for changes in the price level and productivity. This normalization procedure adjusts the earnings of A and B uniformly, maintaining the same relationship between them as in the previous example. (The previous example is a special case in which the wage index does not change). Consequently, only if earnings are compounded by the market interest rate, expressed in real terms, will the present value of the earnings of A and B be equal. Without compounding, the benefit base of worker B will again be higher.[1]

The steps taken in transforming annual nominal earnings into an adjusted benefit base are summarized in equation 3.1.

$$W_i = \sum_{j=1}^{R} E_{ij} \, a_j \tag{3.1}$$

where

W_i = adjusted earnings base of ith worker $\quad i = 1, \ldots, S$
E_{ij} = nominal taxable earnings of ith worker, year j $\quad j = 1, \ldots, R$
R = years of covered employment at retirement
a_j = adjustment factor, year j.

Each worker's share of the intracohort benefit base may then be specified by the ratio b_i:

$$b_i = \frac{W_i}{\sum_{i=1}^{S} W_i} \tag{3.2}$$

These procedures discussed above for indexing or compounding annual earnings can be summarized as follows:

Adjustments of Nominal Earnings to Obtain Benefit Base

1. No adjustments. Benefit base simple sum of recorded nominal earnings.

$$W_i = \sum_{j=1}^{R} E_{ij} \qquad\qquad a_j = 1 \text{ for all } j$$

2. Price indexing

$$W_i = \sum_{j=1}^{R} E_{ij}\, a_j \qquad\qquad a_j = P_R\, /P_j$$

$$P_R = \text{price index, year } R$$

$$P_j = \text{price index, year } j$$

3. Wage indexing

$$W_i = \sum_{j=1}^{R} E_{ij}\, a_j \qquad\qquad a_j = W_R\, /W_j$$

$$W_R = \text{index of average wages, year } R$$

$$W_j = \text{index of average wages, year } j$$

4. Compounding

$$W_i = \sum_{j=1}^{R} E_{ij}\, a_j \qquad\qquad a_j = (1+R)^{\,R-j}$$

$$R = \text{appropriate interest rate}$$

Practical obstacles hinder the application of each of these adjustments to nominal earnings. Available price indices measure changes in the cost of a market basket of goods and services purchased by a "typical" wage earner. The indices ignore the tendency for consumers to respond to changes in relative prices by substituting cheaper for more expensive items. They also deal imperfectly with quality changes, and the market basket (or weights) must be revised periodically to allow for the introduction of new products and the disappearance of old. Inability to adjust for substitution and quality effects introduces an upward bias in measurement of price-level changes, and changes in availability of goods and consumers' spending habits make comparisons of price levels over extended time periods increasingly problematic.

Wage indices measure changes over time in average annual wages. Although average wages are presumed to keep pace with changes in the price level and productivity, at least over long periods of time, various extraneous factors can influence annual wage indices in an unpredictable manner. If the index measures only money wages, changes in the importance of fringe benefits will reduce the accuracy of the index as a measure of changes in compensation. A wage index is also sensitive to changes in human capital formation and labor force composition. A comparison of lifetime earnings profiles indicates that younger workers earn on average less than older workers, women earn on average less than men, and average earnings differ across sectors of the economy. Consequently, variations in age, sex, or sectoral composition of the labor force can cause an index of average wages to fluctuate in ways unrelated to underlying trends in productivity. During the 1970s, the influx into the labor market of young workers born during the peak years of the baby boom depressed average earnings. As these cohorts age and the labor market absorbs the smaller postboom cohorts, the effect on average earnings is expected to be reversed, with a corresponding impact on a wage index. Since wage indices typically are constructed on an annual basis and are more accurately described as annual earnings indices, they are also sensitive to changes in average hours worked.[2]

Finally, data collection problems prevent computation of index series up to the moment of retirement. Only when past price and wage data have been collected can an index series be extended forward. Earnings data are generally more susceptible to collection lag than are price data. Consequently, indexing of earnings must cease a year or two before the year of retirement. Earnings in the final months preceding retirement appear in nominal form.

Practical problems also complicate efforts to adjust an earnings series by compounding. The existence of a perfect capital market enables each individual to borrow or lend at a constant interest rate and to adjust the amount borrowed or lent to equate the interest rate, at the margin, to the individual's marginal rate of time preference. Actual markets are segmented into risk categories. Credit rationing may constrain some borrowers from equating the interest rate to the rate of time preference at the margin. In this environment, the choice of an interest rate to be applied to all beneficiaries becomes of necessity somewhat arbitrary. In subsequent development of the equity framework, it will be assumed that proper price and wage indices and interest rate series are available. Practical problems will be addressed as the framework is applied to the present system.

Adjustment to the Benefit Base. The framework as developed up to this point posits a benefit base encompassing all taxable earnings received over a worker's lifetime. Other factors being equal, this arrangement favors workers with a long and continuous work history over those who entered the labor market late, retired early, or experienced intermittent periods of labor market withdrawal or unemployment. Late entry may follow years of postsecondary education. Intermittent withdrawal and reentry occurs most frequently among women who take time off for childrearing. Early retirement is associated with health problems and is more common among workers in physically demanding occupations and among younger spouses who wish to join older mates in retirement.

Workers with shorter periods of participation in covered occupations gain if the specification of the benefit base allows for the dropping of years of zero or low earnings. If, for example, only the thirty or thirty-five years of highest earnings (indexed or compounded where applicable) are included in the benefit base, cohort members with substantial periods outside the labor force will be awarded larger shares of the benefit base within each cohort. This specification defines intracohort equals as persons who had the same total earnings during a limited number of years of highest adjusted earnings. Emphasis shifts to replacement of earnings during peak years rather than over an entire working lifetime.

Under some circumstances, program goals might require flexibility in specifying the number of years of earnings to be incorporated into the benefit base. This is most easily accomplished by converting total earnings to average annual or monthly earnings. Use of average rather than total earnings as the benefit base simplifies the benefit determination structure by permitting application of a single benefit formula to earnings bases encompassing different numbers of years. As in the previous discussion of dropout years, use of averaging facilitates attempts to define equals in terms other than equal adjusted lifetime earnings. Examples are introduced in the following chapters.

Intracohort equals can be defined in terms of prior earnings, nominal or adjusted, totaled or averaged. Leimer et al. (1978) note that earnings may be subjected to additional adjustments based on characteristics of individual workers before the benefit formula is applied to the base. These adjustments may reflect differences in the number of dependents, income from other sources, or length of service. An adjustment for length of service may be particularly desirable if the earnings base is limited to earnings over only a few years. As in the case of indexing or compounding, any such adjustments must be consistent with the function of positioning of workers within a cohort.

The benefit base specification introduced in equation 3.1 can be restated to allow for averaging and adjustments for individual characteristics, as expressed in equation 3.3.

$$\hat{W}_i = c \sum_{i=1}^{n} E_{ij} a_j k_i$$

(3.3)

where

n =   number of years of highest earnings included in benefit base
c = $1/n$ with averaging
c =   1 without averaging

and

k_i = $k_i(C_i)$ =   individual adjustment factor

where

C_i =   vector of characteristics of ith individual deemed relevant to repositioning

Equation 3.3 incorporates any adjustments of the base that are made after selection of the n years of highest (adjusted) earnings included in the earnings base. Note that $n = R$ if all taxable lifetime earnings are included in the benefit base. If adjustments based on individual characteristics are applied, the earnings base, as defined in equation 3.1, no longer coincides with the benefit base.

Primary Benefit Formula. The primary benefit formula transforms the distribution of benefit bases into a desired distribution of primary benefit awards payable to newly retired workers. The formula takes the form of a rate structure, analogous to the income tax rate schedule. It implements both the horizontal and vertical equity rules within the benefit structure by awarding equal primary benefits to workers with equal benefit bases and unequal awards to workers with unequal bases. Benefit awards are an increasing function of the benefit base, although the benefit structure need not be redistributive. A proportional benefit formula translates the distribution of benefit bases into an identical distribution of initial relative monthly benefit payments. If the vertical equity rule calls for a tilt in favor of workers with lower earnings, this can be achieved by means of rate brackets (called "bend points" in social security jargon) with declining rates in successively higher brackets. If bracket rates decline across higher earnings brackets, benefits as a percentage of the benefit base decline in each successive bracket. This type of benefit formula is referred to as a "progressive" benefit structure.[3]

Primary Benefit Multipliers. The monthly benefit paid to a newly retired worker at the normal retirement age (currently age 65) is termed the "primary benefit award." In social security terminology, it is called the "primary insurance amount," or PIA. The primary benefit award may be adjusted upward or downward according to the circumstances of individual beneficiaries, including early or delayed retirement or presence of eligible dependents.

If adjustments to PIA are proportional in nature, they are made by applying what Leimer et al. term the "primary benefit multiplier" to the benefit base. Because of the proportional nature of the adjustment, the ratio of marginal benefits to base remains constant over the range of benefit bases. The proportionality property retains the vertical equity rule across all beneficiaries with equal primary benefit multipliers and unequal benefit bases.[4]

The Intracohort Benefit Structure: An Algebraic Summary. The framework for computing initial benefits to workers within a cohort is now complete. Following Leimer et al. (1978), the procedure may be restated in equation form.

$$\text{Benefit base} = \hat{W}_i = \hat{W}(W_i, C_i) \quad i = 1, \ldots, S \tag{3.4}$$

$$\text{Primary benefit amount} = B^P_i = B^P(\hat{W}_i) \tag{3.5}$$

$$\text{Primary benefit multiplier} = m_i = m(C_i) \tag{3.6}$$

where

$$C_i = \text{Characteristics of } i\text{th individual incorporated into primary benefit multiplier.}$$

To summarize, the benefit base, $\hat{W}_i$, positions each worker within a retirement cohort. In effect, the base serves as an index of equality. The primary benefit formula, $B^P(\hat{W}_i)$, relates the benefit award to the benefit base. The benefit formula awards equal primary benefits to cohort equals, and implements the vertical equity rule by awarding unequal benefits to unequals. Awards are an increasing function of the benefit base, $\hat{W}_i$.

The primary benefit amount may be augmented or reduced by applying the primary benefit multiplier, $m(C_i)$, to the primary benefit award. The multiplier changes the initial benefit award proportionally across the distribution of PIAs in accordance with individual characteristics such as age at retirement or number of eligible dependents. This step completes the determination of the initial benefit award, B_i^A, as follows:

$$B_i^A = B_i^P \, m \, (C_i) \quad \text{for all } i.$$ (3.7)

Intercohort Components

The framework developed thus far applies only to the determination of initial individual benefit awards within a single retirement cohort. Intertemporal components must be added to specify the relative positions of members of different cohorts and to adjust benefit levels over time. These components provide an operational definition of intercohort equals and prescribe the treatment accorded to equals across cohorts. In the Leimer et al. framework, intercohort equals are defined by the intercohort standard discussed below. Benefit levels awarded to intercohort equals are set by the intercohort benefit adjustment factor.

Intercohort Standard. Benefit bases of successive cohorts can be expected to change over time. The intercohort standard establishes the relative positions of members of successive cohorts by normalizing benefit bases. The standard takes the form of an index series, used to adjust benefit bases of successive cohorts in a manner analogous to the indexing of an annual earnings series for workers within a cohort.[5] Normalization of the earnings base for the ith worker in cohort 1 is illustrated by equation 3.8.

$$W_{i1}^n = \frac{W_{i1}}{S_1}$$ (3.8)

where

W_{i1}^n = normalized benefit base of worker i in cohort 1

W_{i1} = benefit base of worker i in cohort 1

S_1 = index value of intercohort standard for cohort 1

Two workers in different retirement cohorts become intercohort equals if their normalized bases satisfy the following equality:

$$W_{i1}^n = W_{j2}^n$$ (3.9)

where i and j are members of cohorts 1 and 2, respectively. It follows from equations 3.8 and 3.9 that for intercohort equals,

$$W_{j2} = W_{i1} \left(\frac{S_2}{S_1} \right)$$

(3.10)

which states that the percentage difference in benefit bases of intercohort equals is equal to the percentage change in the intercohort standard between their respective retirement years.

Price and wage indices are among the likely choices for an intercohort standard. A price index defines members of different cohorts with benefit bases of equal real purchasing power at time of retirement as intercohort equals. If growth in labor productivity causes average real earnings to increase over time, members of later cohorts will tend to occupy lower relative positions within their cohort distributions than their intercohort equals in earlier cohorts. Selection of a wage index as the intercohort standard implies an intent to specify as equals individuals in different cohorts occupying the same relative position in the distribution of intracohort benefit bases.

Failure to adjust benefit bases of successive cohorts implicitly sets the intercohort standard equal to unity for all cohorts, thereby defining intercohort equals as persons with equal nominal benefit bases at time of retirement. This procedure precludes any systematic relationship between cohorts because of the unpredictable nature of changes in the purchasing power of the dollar.

Intercohort Benefit Adjustment Factor. Once intercohort equals are specified, an operational definition of equal treatment of equals is required. This calls for a procedure that adjusts initial benefit awards over time. Equal nominal benefit awards fail to allow for changes in price level or earnings. If benefit awards are to be adjusted for these or other factors, an additional component, called the *intercohort benefit adjustment factor*, or IBAF, must be added to the benefit structure. The IBAF, like the intercohort standard, takes the form of an index series. It performs the function of normalizing initial benefit awards between cohorts and can be represented algebraically for intercohort equals i and j in cohorts 1 and 2, respectively, as

$$B_{i1}^n = \frac{B_{i1}}{R_1} = \frac{B_{j2}}{R_2} = B_{j2}^n$$

(3.11)

where

B_{il}^n , B_{j2}^n =   normalized initial benefit awards

B_{il} , B_{j2} =   initial benefit awards at retirement

R_1 , R_2 =   value of IBAF for cohorts 1 and 2.

From equation 3.11, it follows that

$$B_{j2} = B_{il}\left(\frac{R_2}{R_1}\right)$$

(3.12)

which states that intercohort equality requires that the initial benefit award to individual i in cohort 1 differ from the initial benefit award to individual j in cohort 2 by the percentage change in the IBAF between the retirement years of the two cohorts.

It follows from the definition of intercohort equals in equations 3.8 and 3.9 that

$$W_{il}^n = \frac{W_{il}}{S_1} = \frac{W_{j2}}{S_2} = W_{j2}^n$$

(3.13)

Combining and rearranging equations 3.12 and 3.13, it can be shown that

$$\frac{B_{j2}}{W_{j2}} = \frac{B_{il}}{W_{il}}\left(\frac{R_2}{R_1}\right)\left(\frac{S_1}{S_2}\right)$$

(3.14)

Equation 3.14 reveals that if, for example, the percentage increase is less for the IBAF (R) than for the intercohort standard (S), the ratio of the initial benefit award to the benefit base (called the "benefit rate") will decline over time. This occurs if the IBAF is a price index series and the intercohort standard is a wage index series, so long as increasing labor productivity causes average earnings to rise faster than the price level. This specification implies an intent to allow the average benefit rate to decline as long as workers' living standards continue to rise. Another reasonable option would be to use a single index series for both the intercohort standard and IBAF. In this case, since S_1/S_2 would be the reciprocal of R_2/R_1, the initial average benefit rate would remain constant over retirement cohorts.

The relationship expressed in equation 3.14 represents one way of defining the replacement rate. A general definition may be expressed as follows:

$$\text{Replacement rate} = \frac{\text{Initial benefit award}}{\text{Replacement base}} \times 100$$

The replacement rate measures the extent to which social security benefits replace lost earnings and provides a measure of the adequacy of benefit levels. Replacement rates must be interpreted with care, however, because of their sensitivity to the specification of the replacement base. If the benefit base serves as the replacement base, the replacement rate and the previously defined benefit rate, B/W, are identical. If, in addition, the same index series serves as intercohort standard and IBAF, the replacement rate for intercohort equals will be constant over time. As previously noted, the benefit base is sensitive to the choice of indexing and averaging procedures used in its computation. To simplify interpretation of the replacement rate, both the benefit award and replacement base are usually stated in annual or monthly terms.[6]

To summarize, a benefit framework must include components that define intercohort equals and specify the level of initial benefits awarded to equals in successive cohorts. In the Leimer et al. framework, these functions are performed by, respectively, the intercohort standard and the intercohort benefit adjustment factor (IBAF). Like other components of the benefit structure, specification of intercohort components makes operational the value judgments underlying the system's benefit structure and establishes the relative importance of the social security program as a source of retirement income across successive generations.

Postentitlement Adjustment. The final component in the equity framework is termed the "postentitlement benefit adjustment factor," or PBAF. It determines the extent, if any, to which initial benefit awards will be adjusted for inflation or changes in living standards. Like the other intertemporal components, the PBAF takes the form of an index series.

A key decision involves the choice between a coupled and a decoupled benefit structure. A coupled benefit structure employs the same series to adjust initial benefit awards and postentitlement benefit increases. If initial benefits and benefits paid after retirement are both adjusted annually by a wage index, persons entering retirement and persons already retired will be granted benefit increases incorporating changes in both prices and productivity. In contrast, benefits to newly entitled workers may be adjusted annually by a wage index, and benefits to those previously retired are adjusted annually by a price index. In such a decoupled system, new retirees receive benefit increases incorporating both price and productivity changes that occurred prior to retirement, whereas benefits paid after retirement are adjusted only for price changes. This arrangement protects the purchasing power of retirees, but they do not participate in changes in average living standards of workers after they retire.

OAI AND INDIVIDUAL EQUITY

The Leimer et al. (1978) individual-equity framework provides a vehicle for examining the Old Age Insurance (OAI) program. Social security has not been static. Although its basic thrust of insuring against earnings loss owing to retirement has not changed since 1935, its tax and benefit structure has been altered by many amendments. Some of the changes significantly affect individual equity. The analysis that follows focuses primarily on the post–1977 structure of OAI, with occasional references to earlier versions to show how individual equity has been affected by program changes. Primary or worker-only benefits will be considered first, since the equity framework for these benefits is the most clear-cut. The following chapter considers the issue of supplemental benefits for dependents and survivors.[7]

Individual Equity under Old Age Insurance

Current statutes specifying OAI benefits contain a number of cohort-specific provisions. These include such key features as benefit eligibility, benefit base computation, and adjustments for age at retirement. Other features of the program, most notably procedures for indexing within and between cohorts, are cohort-invariant, but benefit awards are affected by legislated intercohort adjustments.

Cohort Membership and Benefit Eligibility. The social security system assigns workers to a retirement cohort on the basis of year of birth. Program parameters such as benefit eligibility requirements and adjustment of benefits for age at retirement are specified for each birth cohort.

A worker who has attained fully insured status becomes eligible for retirement benefits under OAI upon reaching age 62. To be fully insured, a worker born in 1929 or later must have a minimum of forty quarters (or ten years) of covered employment. Workers born before 1929 must have one quarter of coverage for each year between 1951 and the year prior to the calendar year in which the worker attained age 62. For example, members of the 1919 birth cohort become fully insured after

30 quarters of coverage, since thirty years elapsed between 1951 and 1980 (the year before they attained age 62). Early cohorts acquired fully insured status under more relaxed rules. Members of the earliest cohorts (persons born before 1893) became fully insured after only six quarters of coverage.[8]

Prior to passage of the 1977 Social Security Amendments, a quarter of coverage was granted for each calendar quarter in which a worker was credited with $50 of wages. The self-employed were awarded four quarters of coverage, but only if net earnings exceeded $400 in a calendar year. Beginning in 1978, a quarter of coverage was awarded for each $250 of taxable wage or self-employment income earned within a calendar year, up to a maximum of four, regardless of the number of quarters in which earnings were actually received. The amount of earnings needed to acquire a quarter of coverage is adjusted annually by an index of average wages and stood at $570 in 1992.

This arrangement for awarding quarters of coverage affects individual equity in two ways. First, it restricts benefit eligibility to those whose employment in covered occupations exceeds a minimum threshold, creating a discontinuity or "notch" in the eligibility formula. Workers who contribute to the program but who fail to attain the minimum level of participation receive no primary benefits. Second, earlier retirement cohorts attained benefit eligibility with less participation in covered employment. Less stringent eligibility requirements for earlier cohorts were adopted to allow broader participation in benefits. Social security came into existence during the working lives of these cohorts and, because many occupations were initially excluded from the program, a number of workers reached retirement age with only a few years of coverage. Results reported in Chapter 2 document the high returns to start-up generations, in part a consequence of relaxed eligibility requirements.

As the program approaches full maturity, intercohort differences in eligibility gradually disappear. Only the earnings minimum for a quarter of coverage will change (owing to wage indexing), but this figure remains so low that all full-time workers, even those earning the minimum wage, receive credit for four quarters of coverage in a calendar year.

The eligibility notch remains, a result of the intention not to provide retirement income to workers with irregular and insubstantial earnings in covered employment. Most workers who fail to qualify for primary benefits on their own earnings record will qualify for supplemental benefits as dependents or survivors, as described in Chapter 4. Others may have worked primarily in uncovered employment in the public sector, thus becoming eligible for federal or state civil service pensions. Vesting provisions impose a similar eligibility notch on many private pensions. Nevertheless, the eligibility threshold creates an arbitrary dividing line between those who are eligible for primary benefits and those who are not.

Extent of Coverage. A truly universal social insurance system would be financed by a tax on all forms of worker compensation received by all workers. Participation would be compulsory. Social security has not yet attained such universality, but as the program has evolved, its coverage has expanded, both in terms of inclusiveness of occupations and in the proportion of earnings taxed.

The original Social Security Act (1935) covered only employees in commerce and industry, about two-thirds of the U.S. labor force. After 1950, coverage was gradually extended. The only major groups not now covered are federal civilian employees who began employment before January 1, 1984, and some employees of state and local governments.

The trend toward nearly universal coverage combined with compulsory participation forces essentially all workers to participate in a single risk pool. Since workers have little opportunity to opt out, it is possible to impose a redistributive benefit structure on program participants. It is also possible to ignore actuarial diversity without fear of adverse selection. If participation is optional, persons who are poor risks find participation more attractive than do those who are good risks. If the good risks withdraw, benefits must be cut or contributions must be raised to maintain financial balance. Compulsory participation accommodates redistribution across risk classes. Some of the consequences were documented in Chapter 2. Equity aspects of risk pooling are addressed in Chapter 7.

Benefit Base. Each worker's record of taxable earnings provides the basic data for computing the benefit base of each cohort member, but, as we have seen, past earnings can be mapped into a benefit base in many ways. Earnings may be indexed to adjust for changes in the price level or average earnings, or they may be compounded to allow for the opportunity cost of time. Benefits may be based on total taxable earnings over a lifetime or on total or average taxable earnings over a more limited time period.

The Social Security Amendments of 1977 introduced wage indexing of annual earnings, commencing with the cohort that reached age 62 in 1979. The wage index used for this purpose is constructed from earnings data reported on W2 forms. It tracks changes in reported average earnings over time. Wage indexing inflates past earnings to a level comparable to that prevailing in the current labor market. As previously noted, the intent is to adjust for the combined effects of inflation and growth in labor productivity, with the assumption that these influences are correctly measured by the index. Consequently, earnings received at any time during a worker's career enter the benefit base on equal terms with earnings recorded as his or her cohort approaches retirement.

Workers may apply for OAI benefits upon reaching age 62, although many delay retirement beyond that date. Differences among cohort members in the timing of retirement complicate indexing and raise equity issues. Under the 1977 amendments, all earnings recorded up to and including the calendar year in which cohort members reach age 60 are adjusted by a wage index. Beyond that point, indexing ceases for all members, regardless of the age at which they retire. Earnings received after the year in which members turn 60 enter the benefit base computation, but only in unindexed or nominal form.

For workers who apply for OAI benefits at the minimum age of 62, lags in the collection of wage data preclude indexing beyond the second year preceding retirement. Framers of the 1977 amendments chose not to reindex earnings for workers who retire later, even though reindexing is administratively feasible, because simultaneous cessation of indexing for all members is consistent with year-of-birth assignment to cohorts. Cessation of indexing after the calendar year in which members reach age 60 stabilizes the distribution of benefit bases accumulated by members of a cohort up to that point. The resulting distribution can be altered by inclusion of additional unindexed earnings recorded in subsequent years, but current indexing procedures make the benefit base less sensitive to age at retirement than would be the case if earnings were reindexed annually for workers who had not yet retired.

Because earnings recorded after a cohort attains the age of 60 enter the benefit base in nominal terms, the base can be sensitive to inflation and other forces that impact money wages. This adds an element of indeterminacy to the computation procedure and, therefore, to the identification of intracohort equals. Most workers now retire by age 65, so the number of unindexed years is generally small. Certainly, the benefit base is much less sensitive to inflation than it was prior to 1979, when all earnings entered the base computation in nominal dollars and the entire base was recomputed annually until a worker retired.

Wage indexing affects the benefit base in another way. Prior to 1975, maximum annual taxable earnings were set by statute. Because only taxable earnings enter into the benefit base calculation, the statutory maximum places a cap on the increment to the benefit base that can be accumulated in a single year. Since benefit awards are an increasing function of the benefit base, the cap imposes an annual limit on rights to benefits accruing to more affluent workers. This feature conforms to the tenet that social security should provide retiring workers with an income foundation, leaving greater scope for supplementation from private sources for those with higher earnings.

The 1972 Social Security Amendments replaced periodic ad hoc adjustments of the taxable maximum with automatic wage indexing. Automatic indexing was suspended for the years 1978 through 1981, as the limit was raised by statute from $17,700 in 1978 to $29,700 in 1981. Wage indexing resumed in 1982. Since then, the taxable limit has been raised annually, rounded to the nearest $300, to keep pace with the rate of increase in the wage index. Increments since 1982 have ranged from $1,200 to $3,300 annually. The limit had reached $55,500 by 1992.

Statutory changes during the 1970s increased the proportion of earnings subject to the payroll tax. (The taxable maximum grew from about 1.3 times average earnings in 1969 to about 2.5 times average earnings in 1989). According to Social Security Administration estimates, about 90 percent of total earnings were subject to the payroll tax in the early 1980s, and about 6 percent of all workers had earnings in excess of the maximum (Thompson 1983: 1426). These percentages will remain constant only if earnings at all levels grow at the same rate as average earnings.

Leimer, et al. (1978) point out that earnings can be adjusted for individual characteristics, such as age at retirement or number of dependents. In this case, intracohort equals would no longer be defined strictly in terms of prior earnings. The OAI benefit structure includes no such adjustments, however, so the earnings and benefit bases coincide, and intracohort equals are defined only in terms of earnings. Benefits may be adjusted to reflect individual characteristics, such as those cited, but the adjustments occur at later stages in the benefit determination process.

The benefit base is not, however, a simple sum of all recorded earnings. Rather, the OAI statutes specify inclusion of a prescribed number of years of highest earnings (wage-indexed through age 60, unindexed thereafter). Earnings in the remaining years, if any, are dropped and do not affect the computation. Earnings for the years to be included are summed and then converted to a monthly average, which serves as the benefit base.

The number of years to be included in the averaging period is cohort specific. It is determined by first counting the number of years that elapse beginning with 1951 or the year after a worker reaches age 21, whichever is later, and ending with the next year in which the worker reaches age 62. Under this formula, in effect since 1975, the number of elapsed years increased by one annually until 1991, when the number reached forty. It remains at forty for all cohorts born in 1929 and thereafter. Next, the number of "benefit computation years," the years to be included in the benefit-base computation, is determined. The law specifies that the number of benefit computation years should equal the number of elapsed years minus five. Thus for persons reaching age 62 in 1991 and following years, the thirty-five years of highest earnings are chosen. The averaging period was shorter for earlier cohorts. For example, the benefit computation period was 25 years for the cohort reaching age 62 in 1981 and 30 years for cohort reaching age 62 in 1986. The final step in determining the benefit base is to sum earnings in the benefit computation years and divide the total by the number of months in these years. Thus, for 1991 and subsequent years, summed earnings are divided by 35×12, or 420, to obtain average indexed monthly earnings, or AIME, which becomes each workers' benefit base. Calculation of AIME completes this stage in the benefit computation process and identifies equals within cohorts.

Gradual lengthening of the averaging period to thirty-five years improves the positioning of workers with sustained participation in covered occupations. Shorter averaging periods during the system's formative years allowed for dropping of a number of years of nonparticipation and helped to accommodate persons who entered the system during later stages of the work cycle. During the 1960s and 1970s, short averaging periods served as a crude substitute for indexing of annual earnings by allowing for the dropping of early years when reported earnings were low. Workers who withdrew from the labor force early did not fare well, but a guaranteed minimum benefit helped to cushion the effect.

Although wage indexing weakens the impact of timing on average earnings, the number of years included in the averaging period can still affect the positioning of workers within cohorts. Assuming that 18 is the earliest age of full-time employment, we have an elapsed interval of 47 years of potential employment for workers retiring at age 65. This allows for twelve drop-out years, enough to accommodate the postsecondary education requirements of even the most demanding professions. The dropping of twelve years also helps to accommodate temporary labor force withdrawal during childbearing years as well as periods of unemployment and early retirement. On balance, the combined effects of wage indexing and lengthening the averaging period increase the share of benefits awarded to workers with long and continuous work histories, but by less than would be the case if the benefit base included all indexed taxable earnings over a lifetime.

A study by Leimer (1978) provides insights into how changes in length of the averaging period affect positioning of workers within cohorts. He assigned beneficiaries from a sample of members of the 1967–70 cohorts to twenty groups (ventiles) ranked according to average indexed monthly earnings (AIME) computed over three different averaging periods. His expectation was that rankings would be more stable over shorter periods because the effect of differences in duration of labor force participation would be largely washed out. Leimer found that when ten- and twenty-year rankings of each of the four cohorts were compared, about three-quarters of the workers shifted at least one ventile in the rankings. Comparisons between ten- and thirty-year rankings show that approximately nine-tenths of the workers shifted at least one ventile and nearly two-thirds shifted positions by at least two ventiles. Clearly, lengthening of the averaging period had a substantial effect on positioning within the cohorts studied.

Computation of Initial Benefit Award. Initial primary benefits payable to a newly retired worker are computed by applying the social security benefit formula to average indexed monthly earnings. The benefit formula assigns to each level of AIME a value called the "primary insurance amount" or PIA. The PIA is the monthly benefit amount paid to a newly retired worker who begins receiving benefit payments upon reaching normal retirement age, currently age 65. The PIA provides a benchmark benefit level that may then be adjusted for early or late retirement or for auxiliary benefits to dependents. These adjustments will be discussed later.

The 1977 social security amendments introduced the current benefit formula, which became effective for workers reaching age 62 in 1979.[9] Bracket rates remain constant over time, but bracket limits are adjusted annually to reflect percentage changes in the wage index. The formula introduced in 1979 took the following form:

PIA = 90 percent of the first $180 of AIME +
32 percent of the next $905 of AIME +
15 percent of AIME over $1,085.

Because of indexing of the bracket limits, by 1992 the formula had become

PIA = 90 percent of the first $387 of AIME +
32 percent of the next $1,946 of AIME +
15 percent of AIME over $2,333.

The progressive nature of benefit awards with respect to the benefit base is apparent. For example, the average benefit rate declines from 90 percent at the upper limit of the lowest bracket to 41.6 percent at the upper limit of the second bracket and 35.8 percent for a worker with the maximum possible AIME (of $2,985 in 1992).

The benefit formula implements the horizontal and vertical equity rules implicit in the social security statutes. It awards equal PIAs to equals within each cohort and unequal awards to unequals, as defined by AIME.

Linking benefits to earnings, rather than to taxes, dilutes the quid pro quo element in the benefit structure. Total taxes paid by each worker over a lifetime are earnings related, but the relationship is by no means proportional. OASI tax rates increased from 2 percent to 11.2 percent (divided equally between employee and employer) between 1950 and 1990. Rates on the self-employed were lower than the combined employer-employee rate until 1984. Allowance for dropout years further erodes the link between taxes and benefits.

Social adequacy is served by the substantial tilt in the benefit formula in favor of workers with low benefit bases. Empirical results reviewed in Chapter 2 illustrate the redistributional effectiveness of the program within retirement cohorts. The role of social security as a primary source of retirement income for less affluent workers has been mentioned. Its redistributional features are consistent with the egalitarian intent of the program's architects, but one feature of the system's revenue structure, the annual maximum on taxable earnings, warrants additional comment. As previously noted, the taxable maximum puts an upper limit on earnings-related benefit payments to the most affluent workers. This feature also imposes on all workers with maximum AIME an identical burden for supporting redistribution within cohorts, even though some persons within this group have earnings at or near the taxable maximum in each of the benefit computation years while others have earnings far in excess of the maximum. In other words, the merely affluent and the "super-rich" bear similar redistributional burdens within the OAI system.

Intercohort Benefit Adjustments. Leimer et al. (1978) identify two distinct intercohort components in the OAI equity framework. The intercohort standard defines intercohort equals; the intercohort benefit adjustment factor (IBAF) establishes the equal treatment to be accorded intercohort equals. These components are incorporated implicitly into the OAI benefit formula.

Bracket limits or bend points are adjusted annually by a wage index. Wage indexing of brackets effectively treats workers in different cohorts whose average indexed monthly earnings (AIME) bear identical ratios to the average indexed earnings of their respective cohorts as equals. Rates within brackets remain constant over time, ensuring equal benefit-to-base (PIA–to–AIME) ratios for intercohort equals. This procedure maintains the same degree of benefit progression over time provided the relative distribution of benefit bases remains constant. Maintenance of constant

PIA–to–AIME ratios for intercohort equals has important long-term implications because it ensures that average benefits will increase at the same rate as average indexed earnings.

The intent of Congress and the Ford and Carter administrations in opting for wage indexing was to maintain constant replacement rates over time for workers occupying comparable positions in the earnings distribution of their respective cohorts. Estimates based on the assumption of smooth earnings trajectories at low, medium, and high earnings anticipate replacement rates (initial annual benefits as a percentage of earnings in the year preceding retirement) of about 56, 43, and 29 percent, respectively, once the new law is phased in (Snee and Ross 1978: 12). This provision ensures that the relative importance of social security as a source of retirement income will be maintained for generations to come.

For reasons of administrative necessity and program consistency, bracket indexing for each cohort is based on the level of the wage index in the second year before cohort members reach minimum retirement age. The lag in collection of data imposes this constraint when computing benefit awards for workers who retire at the minimum age, but since cohorts are defined in terms of year of birth, not year of retirement, the same benefit formula must be used to compute the PIA of all cohort members. PIAs of persons who continue to work after reaching minimum retirement age are adjusted to keep them abreast of the cost-of-living adjustments (COLA) granted to retired cohort members.

Postentitlement Benefit Adjustment. The final step in the specification of the basic OAI benefit structure is selection of a postentitlement benefit adjustment factor (PBAF). The PBAF takes the form of an index series to be used in making periodic adjustments to benefit payments after retirement. As Leimer et al. (1978) make clear, the same index can be used to index initial benefit awards and postentitlement benefit payments. For example, postentitlement benefits could be wage indexed annually, allowing retired workers to experience the changes in living standards enjoyed by working generations, in which case the system would be "coupled." The 1977 amendments decoupled the system, effective in 1979, by adjusting postentitlement benefits according to changes in the consumer price index (CPI).

Use of the CPI to adjust postentitlement benefits maintains the real purchasing power of the initial benefit award. After retirement, beneficiaries receive protection from inflation but do not participate in improved living standards resulting from productivity growth. Other pension plans typically provide incomplete inflation protection or no protection at all. A tax-financed program like social security can guarantee inflation protection throughout retirement, a feature frequently cited in justifying a public program.

The COLA occurs automatically each January. As noted in the previous section, wage indexing ceases when a cohort reaches age 60, but the COLA applies to the PIAs of persons who continue to work after age 62, the age of the initial PIA computation. This feature provides inflation protection for cohort members who continue to work after initial retirement age. Since wage indexing ceases after age 60, OAI benefits keep pace with inflation but do not reflect increases in real income after that age.

The 1983 amendments include a "fund-stabilizer" provision that limits benefit adjustments to the increase in the CPI or the wage index, whichever is smaller. This feature is triggered only if the OASI fund is dangerously low and represents a response to fund crises in 1977 and 1983, which were due in part to the failure of wages and tax receipts to keep up with inflation. The law provides for catch-up benefit increases once the fund rises above crisis levels. Given the large fund accumulation anticipated over the next several decades, the stabilizer is not expected to be operative until at least the middle of the next century unless Congress takes steps to eliminate the buildup.

Although the fund stabilizer is intended to protect against insolvency, a case can be made for implementing its provisions on a regular basis. Ordinarily, wages increase at a faster rate than prices because of increases in labor productivity, but the reverse may occur when the economy experiences supply-side shocks that simultaneously inflate prices and reduce productivity. The two oil shocks of the 1970s are examples. In such cases, social security beneficiaries receive full inflation protection while workers suffer from falling real wages. The full costs of the shock fall on persons of working age, but it might be more equitable for retired persons to share the burden.

Adjustments for Early and Delayed Retirement. Insurance against earnings loss is one of many forms of insurance characterized by "moral hazard," a problem encountered whenever the insured can influence the probability that the insured event will occur. Without proper safeguards, a worker could collect benefits simply by ceasing to work. To counter moral hazard, the OAI system imposes on workers a minimum retirement age of 62, exacts benefit reductions for early retirement, and grants additional benefits for delaying retirement beyond the normal retirement age.

The primary insurance amount (PIA) serves as a benchmark, with a benefit reduction for those who retire before the normal retirement age and a benefit increase for those who retire after. The adjustment may be defended on equity grounds, since monthly benefits will be paid for a longer or shorter period if a person retires before or after the normal retirement age. Because the adjustment also influences the decision to retire, it may be manipulated to discourage early retirement and to encourage delayed retirement. Adjustments are made by multiplying the PIA by an age-related multiplier, an example of what Leimer et al. (1978) call a "primary benefit multiplier." The multiplier need not be a linear function of age, but since its value varies according to age, the pattern of progressivity built into the primary benefit formula applies to all workers in a cohort who retire at the same age.

More than 80 percent of workers begin benefits before age 65, while only about 5 percent delay retirement beyond age 65 (Sherman 1985: 23). Consequently, the multiplier significantly affects average benefit levels and, insofar as the adjustment fails to conform to actuarial standards, program costs as well. The multipliers have frequently been changed, and current law specifies additional changes that, along with a phased-in advancement of the normal retirement age from 65 to 67, will have considerable impact on generations reaching retirement age in the future.

The repeated changes in the adjustments, especially for delayed retirement stem from a lack of consensus on how workers retiring at different ages should be treated, and the earnings-replacement model provides little help in reaching a consensus. One consequence has been asymmetrical treatment between early and delayed retirees. The 1977 amendments retained an earlier provision that reduces the initial benefit award by five-ninths of 1 percent per month for retirement before age 65. This translates into a maximum reduction of 20 percent of PIA for a worker retiring at the minimum retirement age of 62. Reductions for early retirement approximate actuarial equivalence, which means that when averaged over all beneficiaries taking early retirement, the monthly benefit reductions offset the longer time period during which benefits are paid. Early retirement imposes no cost on the trust fund (Myers 1985: 51).

Treatment of workers who delay retirement beyond age 65 has generated more controversy. Prior to the introduction of wage indexing in 1979, the "delayed-retirement credit" granted benefit increases of 1 percent of PIA per year, prorated monthly, up to age 72 for workers who delayed retirement beyond age 65. The 1977 amendments increased the credit to 3 percent per year to offset the effect of wage indexing on benefit recomputation (Myers 1985: 94). In contrast to the benefit reduction for early retirement, the delayed-retirement credit clearly failed to compensate workers for benefits lost by delaying retirement. Its actuarially unfavorable terms no doubt contributed to the decline in labor force participation after age 65 that occurred following World War II.

Concerns about incentives have received more attention than equity issues in recent debates over delayed retirement credits. At the program's inception during the Great Depression, social security offered a means of encouraging workers over age 65 to retire and make room for younger workers. This philosophy is changing, as evidenced by revisions contained in the Social Security Amendments of 1983. These revisions include a gradual increase in the delayed retirement credit from 3 percent to 8 percent per year and an eventual advancement in the normal retirement age from 65 to 67. The first revision increases the award to workers who delay retirement and comes close to satisfying the criterion of actuarial equivalence (Myers 1985: 95). The second encourages people to work longer by requiring beneficiaries to wait an additional two years to qualify for a full benefit or PIA. The changes began with the 1987 cohort (born in 1925) and reach full implementation with the 2022 cohort (born in 1960 and reaching normal retirement age of 2027).

To sort out the effects of changes, we examine their impact on selected cohorts spanning the period 1986 to 2022. The 1986 cohort (born in 1924) is the last to be unaffected by the recent changes. For this cohort, the benefit reduction factor equals five-ninths of 1 percent of PIA per month for retirement before the normal age of 65, yielding a maximum reduction of 20 percent of PIA if entitlement begins at age 62. If retirement is delayed beyond age 65, benefits increase by one-fourth of 1 percent per month (3 percent per year) to a maximum of 115 percent of PIA for retirement at age 70 or later.

The credit for delayed retirement is scheduled to increase by 0.5 percent of PIA every other year beginning with the 1987 cohort and ending with the 2005 cohort, for which it will be 8 percent per year. As with the benefit reduction factor, adjustments are prorated monthly. The delayed retirement credit reaches 6.5 percent of PIA per year for members of the 1999 cohort (born in 1937), the last cohort for which the normal retirement age remains at 65. By delaying retirement, members of this cohort qualify for delayed retirement credits of up to 32.5 percent of PIA, yielding total initial benefits of 132.5 percent of PIA at age 70. Maximum benefit reduction remains at 20 percent of PIA for members who retire at age 62.

Beginning with the cohort reaching age 62 in 2000 (born in 1938), the normal retirement age advances by two months each year until it attains age 66 for the cohort reaching age 62 in 2005 (born in 1943). The delayed retirement credit will be two-thirds of 1 percent of PIA per month, or 8 percent per year, beginning with the 2005 cohort. Workers must now work beyond age 66 to qualify for the credit. A worker retiring at age 70 receives a benefit increase of 32 percent of PIA, yielding a total initial benefit of 132 percent of PIA. This increase is nearly equal to the 32.5 percent increase experienced at age 70 by the 1999 cohort. The increase in the delayed retirement credit almost exactly offsets the advancement in the retirement age. For workers who retire early, however, the monthly benefit reduction increases to twenty-five forty-eighths of 1 percent of PIA, or 25 percent of PIA for workers who retire at age 62. This pattern of benefit adjustments remains in effect for all cohorts reaching age 62 between 2005 and 2016 (born between 1943 and 1954). A comparison of the adjustment patterns shown in Figure 3.1 reveals that, although benefits as a percentage of PIA are nearly identical for members of the 1999 and 2005 cohorts who retire at age 70, the gap widens for workers who retire earlier. Note also that benefits as a percentage of PIA are lower for members of the 2005 cohort than for members of the 1986 cohort who retire before reaching the age of 66 years and 7 months. The 1983 amendments encourage beneficiaries to work longer by accompanying the benefit "carrot," a higher delayed retirement credit, with a benefit "stick," an advancing normal retirement age.

A second advancement in the normal retirement age occurs in annual two-month increments for the cohorts reaching minimum retirement age in 2017 to 2022 (born in 1955 to 1960). The increase for delayed retirement

Figure 3.1
Initial Benefits as a Percentage of PIA by Cohort and Age at Retirement

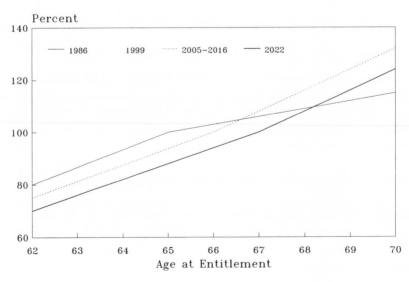

remains at two-thirds of 1 percent per month, but for the 2022 and subsequent cohorts, it applies for a maximum of three years and yields a maximum benefit increase of 24 percent of PIA. Members of these cohorts who retire early receive a benefit reduction of one-half of 1 percent per month for a maximum reduction of 30 percent for workers who retire at age 62. Benefits as a percentage of PIA are lower at all ages for these cohorts than for members of the 2005–2016 cohorts and are lower than benefits for members of the 1986 cohort except for persons retiring after age 68 years 2 months. These relationships are illustrated in Figure 3.1.

Two points should be kept in mind when interpreting these results. First, because of possible benefit-base recalculation and annual COLA adjustments, the PIA typically does not remain static over the age range from 62 to 70. In addition to inflation adjustments, higher earnings late in life can raise the real PIA, but this can occur in all cohorts and need not affect the relative comparisons. Second, if labor productivity continues to rise, increases in average real benefits will cause the average PIA to rise. A smaller percentage of a larger PIA may still produce a higher real benefit.

A final issue concerns the probable effect of an advancing average retirement age on the effective progressivity of benefits. As noted above, the primary benefit multiplier preserves progressivity across benefit bases for workers who retire at the same age. In the future, the penalty for early retirement will increase, and eventually only persons who continue to work until nearly age 70 will gain from the enhanced delayed retirement credit. Since workers in physically demanding occupations on average earn less and retire earlier, effective progressivity across earnings groups may be reduced.

WORKER–ONLY BENEFITS: A SUMMING UP

Alicia Munnell wrote in 1977 that the benefit structure then in effect was "not the product of deliberate policy decisions but rather the result of ad hoc adjustments over the last forty years" (38). Benefits were based on averaged taxable earnings, but earnings were not indexed, making benefit payments sensitive to the timing of labor force participation as well as to changes in maximum taxable earnings and inflation. Short averaging periods discriminated against workers with long periods of covered employment, and a flawed indexing procedure threatened the system with runaway benefit growth and fund insolvency.

The Social Security Amendments of 1977 and 1983 replaced the ad hoc system described by Munnell with a well-defined and internally more consistent tax and benefit structure. A careful examination of the present system makes explicit the value judgments built into the primary or worker-only benefit structure. The new framework retains such basic features of the earlier program as earnings replacement and a progressive earnings-based benefit structure combining goals of individual equity and social adequacy. The following six program features incorporate a more specific set of value judgments built into a revised system.

1. Benefits should be based on prior earnings recorded over an extended period. The maximum benefit computation period of thirty-five years, in effect since 1991, favors workers with long periods of coverage but continues to accommodate a reasonable number of drop-out years for education, childrearing, or prolonged bouts of unemployment.

2. Wage-indexing of recorded earnings up to age 60 adjusts the benefit base for changes in the price level and labor productivity over the course of most or all of a working lifetime. This feature levels the playing field by adjusting earnings to levels comparable to those received in comparable jobs at the time a worker approaches retirement.

3. The progressive benefit formula guarantees a higher replacement rate (benefits as a percentage of average indexed earnings) for workers with low covered earnings. Wage indexing of the brackets in the benefit formula causes replacement rates to remain constant over time for workers occupying comparable *relative* positions in the earnings distribution of successive cohorts. The first provision ensures that OAI will continue as the major source of retirement income for less affluent workers while allowing for greater supplementation from private pensions and savings for the more affluent; the second allows for average real benefits to increase in step with real earnings, thereby allowing OAI to play a more or less constant role as a source of retirement income.

4. A minimum retirement age of 62, a benefit reduction for early retirement, and a benefit credit for postponement of retirement beyond the normal retirement age appear to be motivated by both fairness and incentive considerations. The minimum retirement age denies benefits to workers deemed too young to stop working. The benefit reduction for early retirement, which approximates actuarial equivalence, relieves the program of additional costs owing to early start of benefit payments. Both features serve to counter the moral hazard associated with insurance against earnings loss. Eventual advancement of the normal retirement age from 65 to 67 will help to keep the program in actuarial balance by forcing workers to remain in the work force longer to qualify for full benefits. This change brings the retirement system more closely into line with the lengthening of life expectancy. A phased-in increase in the delayed retirement credit provides a greater incentive for workers to remain in the labor force until age 70. Benefit adjustments for early

or delayed retirement differ for each month in which age at entitlement falls short of or exceeds normal retirement age. Adjustments apply proportionally across the distribution of PIAs, thereby retaining the pattern of progressivity in the benefit formula for all cohort members who retire at the same age.

5. Annual COLAs keep postentitlement benefit levels abreast of changes in the consumer price index. Recent experience indicates that prices are likely to more than double during the expected life span of a worker retiring at age 65, and for most retired workers only OAI provides full lifetime inflation protection.

6. Because coverage is compulsory and nearly universal, a substantial amount of redistribution can be imposed on participants in the social security risk pool. In addition to the progressive benefit formula, which tilts benefits toward workers with lower lifetime earnings, the benefit structure includes a single award structure for all cohort members. Aside from adjustments for differences in age at benefit entitlement, no allowance is made for differences in life expectancy, even though the OAI risk pool is quite heterogeneous. Any redistribution attributable to differences in survival rates among racial, gender, or socioeconomic groups is regarded as a normal outcome of risk sharing within a nearly universal social insurance system. In contrast, a system that adjusted for differences in survival rates would equalize the present value of expected postretirement benefit payments at time of retirement, but such a system would appear to be inconsistent with generally accepted principles of social insurance.

NOTES

1. See Leimer et al. (1978: 17–22).

2. For more on the shortcomings of price and wage indices, see Kaplan (1977). Leimer (1978) offers a detailed critique of wage indexing.

3. Some writers refer to a benefit formula tilted toward lower earnings as regressive. An example is Shoup (1969: 34). The more common convention applies the word "progressive" to formulas favoring the less affluent.

4. See Leimer et al. (1978: 29–30) for an elaboration.

5. If the earnings base is not adjusted for individual characteristics, the earnings base and benefit base coincide. In this case, $\hat{W}_i = W_i$ for all i. To simplify the exposition of intercohort adjustments, we assume that the earnings and benefit bases coincide. This assumption is reflected in the notation.

6. Other frequently used specifications of the replacement base include earnings in the year preceding retirement or earnings averaged over several years preceding retirement. These specifications capture the more immediate change in income that accompanies the transition from work to retirement.

7. Analysis of individual equity requires description of the social security benefit structure. An attempt has been made to avoid unnecessary entanglement in the technical details of a very complex and evolving system. More complete descriptions of the system appear in U.S. Department of Health and Human Services (1988) and Myers (1985).

8. Quarters of coverage may be earned at any age, not just during designated elapsed years. The number of quarters required for benefit eligibility is reduced for workers experiencing periods of disability. This so-called disability freeze is described in Chapter 5.

9. To limit the sudden drop in benefit awards between adjacent cohorts, the 1977 amendments included transitional provisions for cohorts reaching age 62 between 1979 and 1983. These provisions awarded benefits based on a modified version of the old benefit formula if they exceeded awards based on the new formula. The transition, which generated great controversy over the so-called notch cohorts, is discussed in Chapter 4.

4

Extending Social Adequacy

The earnings-related benefit structure of Old Age Insurance (OAI) provides benefits to retired workers according to clearly delineated rules of horizontal and vertical equity. Equal initial benefit awards to equals within cohorts conform to the principle of equal treatment of equals. A progressive benefit formula achieves vertical equity and promotes social adequacy. Prior taxable earnings serve as the equity standard in defining equals within and across cohorts.

Other features of social security designed to promote social adequacy depart to varying degrees from an earnings-based standard. For example, auxiliary benefits to dependents and survivors' benefits to survivors of deceased workers, although earnings related, are paid only if eligible beneficiaries are present. An earnings test reduces benefits payable to beneficiaries whose earnings exceed an annual exempt amount. The Social Security Amendments of 1983 introduced partial taxation of benefits received by high-income recipients. By channeling revenue from the tax on benefits back into the OASI trust fund, some of the burden of financing the system has been shifted from workers to affluent beneficiaries. Legislative changes to the benefit structure alter benefit levels across generations in other ways. These changes may create discontinuities or "notches" in benefit awards to adjacent retirement cohorts unless they are accompanied by transitional provisions. The remainder of this chapter examines the effects of these program features on individual equity.

AUXILIARY AND SURVIVORS' BENEFITS

Auxiliary and survivors' benefits, like primary benefits for workers, are derived from a worker's primary insurance amount (PIA). A spouse or dependent child may qualify for auxiliary benefits if a worker retires or for survivors' benefits if a worker dies. Eligibility criteria and benefit levels will be discussed first, followed by an examination of the alleged inequities that such benefits create among subgroups of beneficiaries.

Auxiliary Benefits

Old Age and Survivors Insurance (OASI) provides auxiliary benefits to qualify spouses and dependent children of retired workers. Among retired workers, spousal benefits are the more important. The spouse or divorced former spouse of a retired worker qualifies for a spousal benefit of 50 percent of the worker's PIA if payment begins when the spouse is age 65 or over. An additional benefit equal to 50 percent of PIA is payable for each unmarried child up to age 18 (or up to age 19 if the child is enrolled full-time in elementary or high school). These benefits may be constrained by the family maximum or reduced by the earnings test, as described below.

Spousal and children's benefits cannot begin until a worker retires and becomes entitled to benefits. Benefits payable to a divorced former spouse are determined in the same manner as spousal benefits, but a divorced spouse need not wait until the primary worker retires to begin receiving benefits. To be eligible, a divorced spouse must have been married to the worker for at least ten years and, to discourage abuse of the nonretirement provision, must have been divorced for at least two years prior to filing for benefits.

Spousal benefits, like primary benefits, may begin once a spouse attains age 62, subject to a reduction for early entitlement. Maximum benefit reduction at age 62 is currently 25 percent. The minimum age for entitlement will remain at 62 when the normal retirement age advances, but the reduction at age 62 will increase to 30 percent when the normal retirement age advances to age 66 and 35 percent when it advances to age 67. Even though the percentage reductions for early retirement exceed those of workers, the spousal reduction falls short of the percentage required for actuarial equivalence. This occurs because spousal benefits are payable only during the joint lifetime of both spouses, a shorter period than the expected lifetime of an individual beneficiary. As a consequence, early entitlement by spouses adds to the cost of the program (Myers 1985: 58).

Spousal benefits initially were payable only to wives, but current law treats the sexes symmetrically. At retirement, many married and divorced workers become dually entitled to primary benefits based on their own earnings record and auxiliary benefits based on the earnings record of a current or former spouse. If a workers' primary benefit exceeds the auxiliary benefit payable on a spouse's earnings record, the worker receives only the primary benefit. If the auxiliary benefit is greater, the difference is added to the primary benefit award. This arrangement effectively limits the total benefit payment to the larger of the two awards and frequently deprives two-earner couples of most or all of the spousal benefits that they otherwise would receive.

Survivors' Benefits

OASI pays survivors' benefits to two categories of survivors, elderly spouses of insured workers and households that include surviving dependent children of deceased insured workers. Surviving divorced spouses are eligible if the marriage lasted ten years or longer. Benefits derive from the PIA of the insured worker as calculated at time of death or retirement.

The PIA on which survivors' benefits are based is computed in the same manner as that of retired workers. If a worker dies before attaining age 62, the benefit computation period is shortened by one year for each year that elapses between age at death and age 62. For example, the computation period for a worker who attained age 21 in 1961 and died in 1990 at age 50 includes the twenty-three years of highest indexed earnings. The minimum computation period is two years. For workers who die before age 62, a special deferred benefit provision allows for recomputation of the benefit base and PIA if the beneficiary is not yet eligible for SI benefits. Recomputation adjusts benefits to widows or widowers for increases in real earnings occurring between year of death and the year the worker would have attained age 60 (Myers 1985: 84–85). In all other cases, the PIA adjusted only for changes in cost of living.

Widowed spouses and divorced spouses of deceased workers become eligible for benefits at age 60 (age 50 if the survivor is totally disabled). Benefits equal the decreased worker's PIA, subject to cost of living adjustment and recomputation when applicable. If the deceased worker received primary retirement benefits prior to death, the benefit award to the survivor also includes any early retirement reduction or delayed retirement credit experienced by the worker. If the survivor becomes entitled to benefits prior to attaining normal retirement age, an additional benefit reduction is assessed up to a maximum of 28.5 percent of the deceased worker's PIA at age 60.[1]

Unmarried children of deceased workers qualify for benefits up to age 18 (or age 19 if enrolled full-time in primary or secondary school). A widow, widower, or divorced spouse is eligible for a widowed mother's or father's benefits if a child or a deceased worker is in the parent's care. These benefits cease when the child reaches age 16. Child and widowed mother's or father's benefits equal 75 percent of the deceased worker's PIA (indexed when applicable). The mother's or father's benefit enables the surviving parent to remain out of the labor force to care for children under age 16. A surviving parent who works full-time usually loses this benefit because of the earnings test, as described below.

Survivors' Insurance (SI) benefits are awarded only to survivors of workers who have attained currently or fully insured status. To attain currently insured status, a worker must have accumulated at least six quarters of coverage during the thirteen-quarter period ending with the quarter of death. Special allowance is made for workers who were totally disabled prior to death. As previously noted, workers acquire fully insured status by accumulating a specified minimum number of quarters of coverage over a lifetime. For workers born in 1929 and thereafter, the minimum is forty quarters. Insured-status restrictions function as a benefit threshold by ensuring that benefits go only to survivors of workers deemed to have had recent or substantial labor force attachment.

As with auxiliary benefits, a beneficiary eligible for both primary worker and SI benefits receives a monthly payment equal to the larger of the two. Again, two-earner couples frequently receive little benefit from this form of insurance, especially if the deceased spouse and the survivor have similar earnings records. SI benefits are also subject to the family maximum and earnings test.

Maximum Family Benefit

Auxiliary and survivors' benefits are determined by applying a benefit multiplier to a worker's PIA. After allowing for adjustments for early or delayed retirement, benefit-formula progressivity is preserved across the distribution of benefit bases within each subset of cohort members having an identical configuration of dependents or survivors. Preservation of benefit progression within each of these subsets is constrained, however, by a formula setting maximum benefits payable to each family.

The maximum family benefit is determined by applying a bracketed, wage-indexed formula to the PIA. The family maximum ranges from 150 percent of PIA for workers with low earnings to a maximum of 187.5 percent in midrange, decreasing to 175 percent of PIA for workers with maximum earnings. Its effect is to reduce progressivity of benefits within subsets of cohort members affected by the constraint. The family maximum overrides the vertical equity rule inherent in the benefit formula in an apparent violation of the social adequacy goal. Its justification rests on two considerations. First, it limits transfers within the system by capping benefits to individual families. Second, it reduces the likelihood that benefits after entitlement will exceed earnings before retirement or death. For workers approaching retirement, benefits in excess of earnings exert an overwhelming disincentive effect, but extension of the provision to SI benefits seems to reflect a desire to keep initial benefit awards below prior earnings for nearly all new beneficiaries.

Because the family maximum applies only to awards in excess of 150 percent of PIA, it is binding only on families with more than two beneficiaries. Benefit awards may exceed the family maximum if the worker qualifies for a delayed retirement credit since the credit is excluded from the maximum benefit amount.

Auxiliary and Survivors' Benefits and Individual Equity

The original Social Security Act of 1935 prescribed benefits for retired workers only. In 1939, Congress added wife's benefits equal to one-half of the worker's benefit and widow's benefits equal to three-fourths of the worker's benefit. At the same time, the benefit formula was made more progressive. The motivation for these changes was both programmatic and political. Benefits payable to retired workers were low, and they were seen as particularly inadequate when a retired worker had to support both a wife and himself. An across-the-board benefit increase would be too costly, but the addition of benefits for wives and widows offered an attractive opportunity to channel benefits where they were most needed.[2]

The political motivation for the 1939 amendments came from the architects of social security who desired to establish its dominance over a means-tested welfare program for the elderly. During the political struggle that preceded passage of the 1935 act, many in Congress and elsewhere expressed a preference for a federally subsidized welfare program over compulsory social insurance. As part of a compromise package, the 1935 act introduced Old-Age Assistance (OAA), a precursor to Supplemental Security Income (SSI), to be administered by the states with a federal subsidy. OAA benefit levels varied among states but frequently approximated old-age benefits payable under the original social security benefit formula. By adding auxiliary benefits and making the benefit formula more progressive, social security provided elderly beneficiaries with more generous benefits than did OAA. Political support for social security increased among both the elderly and budget-conscious state officials, and support for a means-tested alternative weakened.

Introduction of auxiliary and survivors' benefits created an anomaly that remains today. The contributing unit is the individual, but the benefit unit is the family. Workers with dependents receive additional coverage for which they make no additional contributions. Critics see this arrangement as a source of horizontal inequity, discriminating against two-earner married couples and, even more so, against single persons who are not a part of a larger, legally recognized family unit.

The strongest criticism is directed against dual entitlement, which is condemned for discriminating against married women who work. More precisely, the present system treats couples differently depending on the division of preretirement earnings between spouses (Holden 1982: 63; Campbell 1977: 101–103). Several examples illustrate how this can happen.

Example 1. The husband works full-time in a covered occupation, whereas the wife works full-time as a homemaker with no earnings in a covered occupation. Assuming that benefits commence when both spouses reach normal retirement age, monthly benefits will equal $1.5 \times \text{PIA}$. Benefit payments exceed by 50 percent the payments to a single worker with the same benefit base. Spousal benefits to the wife are totally noncontributory.

Example 2. Same as example 1 except that the wife works briefly in a covered occupation but not long enough to qualify for primary benefits on her own account. Benefit payments are not affected, but the wife gets no return on her contributions.

Example 3. The husband and wife work full-time in covered occupations. Each has a benefit base equal to one-half the benefit base of the husband in example 1. Under dual entitlement, neither member receives spousal benefits. Note that the aggregate earnings base of the couple in this example equals the earnings base of the husband in example 1. Progression in the benefit formula will generate PIAs in excess of one-half of the PIA of the husband in example 1. Frequently, however, the total monthly benefit payable to the one-earner couple will be greater than the sum of worker-only benefits paid to the two-earner couple with equal total earnings. A more formal statement of the relationship appears in the appendix to this chapter.

Example 4. Now suppose that the husbands in examples 1 and 3 die, leaving their wives as survivors. The surviving wife of example 3 draws no survivor's benefits, since her PIA (adjusted for inflation) equals her husband's. The surviving wife in example 1 receives a monthly payment equal to her husband's PIA (adjusted for inflation). Thus, the noncontributing wife receives more as a survivor than the contributing wife receives as a retired worker, even though the two households had identical aggregate benefit bases at retirement.

The criticisms implicit in these examples elicited a response from Robert J. Myers, chief actuary of social security from 1947 to 1970 and a participant in the design of the system for half a century (Myers 1985: 440–442). Myers begins his response by contending that the critics of auxiliary and survivors' benefits consider only individual equity while ignoring social adequacy. By contrast, most long-time students of the program believe that the best results come from a blending of the two elements. Under social adequacy, benefits meet presumptive need regardless of prior contributions. He concedes, however, that political support for the program may wane if the link between contributions and benefits becomes too weak.

Commenting specifically on examples of the type given above, Myers notes that they are based on the simplistic assumption that both spouses begin drawing benefits at age 65 and ignore the fact that spouses qualifying for primary benefits can retire at different times, whereas spouses in a single-earner household cannot. Two-earner households qualify for child-survivor benefits upon the death of either spouse, and each spouse is covered by disability insurance. Critics who consider only retirement benefits overlook these important benefits to two-earner households (Myers 1985: 441).

The particular circumstances illustrated in the examples given above may not hold in all cases, but the examples demonstrate that when auxiliary benefits are considered, the clearly defined relationship between benefit base and benefit awards no longer holds. The relationship breaks down because of the sensitivity of benefit payments to the family circumstances of beneficiaries. Because of this sensitivity, OASI no longer conforms to the standards of horizontal and vertical equity built into worker-only benefit structure.

Horizontal Equity. Horizontal equity may be viewed from an individual or family perspective. The individual perspective will be considered first. In keeping with the principle of equal treatment of equals, we compare initial benefit awards to individual workers having equal benefit bases and retiring at the same time and age. Workers within this category who qualify only for primary benefits receive equal benefit awards. Those with eligible dependents draw additional auxiliary benefits. Among the latter group, auxiliary benefits will vary in accordance with the number of dependents and will be reduced dollar for dollar if a spouse qualifies for primary benefits. Additional benefits may be paid to one or more divorced former spouses. From an individualistic perspective, this arrangement clearly violates horizontal equity.

Seen from a family perspective, households are defined as horizontal equals if their respective aggregate benefit bases are equal. To avoid for the moment the difficulty of defining equals when spouses belong to different cohorts, consider the case of married couples, all of the same age, all retiring at the same time with benefit bases equal in the aggregate but divided unequally between spouses. Division of the base between spouses affects the benefit award to the family unit because the progressive benefit formula applies separately to the benefit base of each spouse. In the absence of auxiliary benefits, family units with equally divided benefit bases would receive the highest benefit awards. As example 3 demonstrates, however, family units in which spouses have equal or nearly equal benefit bases will be denied auxiliary benefits. Inclusive of auxiliary benefits, the benefit structure typically favors couples with highly unequal division of the aggregate benefit base and favors single-earner couples most of all.

Survivors' benefits confound the principle of equal treatment of equals in a similar manner. Seen from an earnings-based individualistic perspective, SI provides additional coverage to workers with dependent children. As noted by Myers, SI provides two-earner couples with protection in case of the death of either parent. This feature redresses somewhat the discrimination against two-earner couples that exists elsewhere in the benefit structure, but it creates horizontal inequities between households with and without children.

In contrast to primary and auxiliary benefits, survivor's benefits provide a means of beneficiary substitution when an insured worker dies. This feature seems most defensible in cases of workers who die before becoming entitled to retirement benefits. Survivor's benefits redress the redistribution inherent in an age-contingent program of old-age insurance, but only if eligible survivors are present. From a family perspective, limits on benefits under dual entitlement deprive many two-earner couples of some or all of the potential SI benefits payable to elderly surviving spouses. Potential benefits to couples with equal aggregate benefit bases remain highly sensitive to the division of bases between spouses and frequently result in higher awards to surviving spouses with no recorded earnings than to those who worked full-time (as illustrated in example 4).

Evaluation of horizontal equity from a family perspective becomes more complex if marriage partners belong to different retirement cohorts. Since benefit computation formulas are cohort-specific, the specification of interfamily equals must include a procedure for normalizing intercohort benefit bases.

Vertical Equity. From an individualistic perspective, the vertical equity rule inherent in the benefit formula carries over to auxiliary benefits, since the latter are determined by applying a primary benefit multiplier to a worker's PIA. The award may be altered by application of an additional benefit multiplier if entitlement occurs at other than the normal retirement age. Strictly speaking, therefore, the precise progressivity pattern implicit in the primary benefit formula is repeated only across subsets of cohort members with an identical set of primary benefit multipliers, and even within these subsets, the pattern holds only for beneficiaries not affected by the maximum family benefit constraint or reductions associated with dual entitlement. Thus, the impact of the vertical equity rule on the distribution of benefits becomes clouded when allowance is made for age at entitlement, maximum family benefits, and dual entitlement.

Vertical equity becomes even more problematical when viewed from a family perspective. This is to be expected, since the benefit formula is applied separately to the earnings record of each spouse, not jointly to their combined earnings record. Implementation of a vertical equity rule from a family perspective would require a redesign of the OASI system.

THE EARNINGS TEST

The earnings test reduces benefit payments to beneficiaries whose earnings exceed the annual exempt amount. A more stringent test applies to recipients under age 65 than to recipients age 65 to 69. The test does not apply after age 70. As of 1992, the annual exempt amount for persons under age 65 was $7,440, or less than one earns working full-time at the minimum wage. The annual exempt amount for persons age 65 to 69 was $10,200, which for full-time workers translates into wages of about $5.10 an hour. To keep pace with rising wage levels, the exempt amounts are adjusted annually to the nearest multiple of $120 by a wage index. For recipients under age 65, benefits are reduced by $1 for each $2 of earnings in excess of the annual exempt amount. For those age 65 to 69, the reduction is $1 for each $3 in excess of the exempt amount.[3] Reductions apply to earnings by recipients by auxiliary and survivors' benefits as well as to earnings of primary beneficiaries. An alternative test based on monthly earnings may apply in a year in which benefit payments begin or in which survivors become ineligible for children's or surviving parent's benefits.

A worker who becomes entitled to benefits before attaining normal retirement age experiences an early retirement benefit reduction. Individual equity requires restoration of the benefit reduction for each month in which a worker loses benefits because of the earnings test. The law prescribes restoration of the early retirement reduction for each such month, but the restoration is not implemented until the worker attains normal retirement age.

The case for the earnings test rests in part on the premise that social security insures against earnings loss and that one must cease or curtail working to qualify for benefits. Thus, the earnings test is sometimes referred to as a retirement test and, at least among elderly beneficiaries, it serves this function. The other category of potential beneficiaries most affected by the earnings test is surviving spouses who are eligible for SI parent's benefits for having in their care dependent children of deceased workers. In many cases, surviving spouses find it necessary to work full-time and must forgo mother's or father's benefits for which they are eligible. Again, this denial of benefits must be defended on social adequacy grounds. Widowed parents who work full-time are deemed not to be in need of additional income. Thus, the earnings test implies that a full-time worker has no need for benefits and a worker who has withdrawn partially from the labor force has only a partial need.

Concern about vertical equity lies at the heart of much of the support for retention of the test. Workers with substantial earnings rank among the most affluent within their cohorts, and they would appear to benefit the most from elimination of the test (Pattison et al. (1990). The consequences of elimination of the test, both in terms of program costs and distributional effects, depend on the relationship between age at entitlement and adjustments for early and delayed retirement. As noted in Chapter 3, the benefit adjustment for early retirement approximates actuarial fairness, whereas the adjustment for delayed retirement is actuarially unfair. Once the delayed retirement credit is fully adjusted to 8 percent per year, beginning in 2009, it is anticipated that corrections for both early and delayed retirement will approximate actuarial fairness. If this should be achieved, horizontal equity would be served by eliminating the earnings test and treating the retirement benefit as a form of annuity rather than as a need-based earnings replacement, provided an actuarial standard is accepted as an equitable adjustment mechanism for this purpose. It does not necessarily follow that the earnings test should be eliminated for auxiliary and survivors' benefits, since social adequacy justifies the latter.

Congress has repeatedly liberalized the earnings test, which prior to 1954 denied all benefits for any month in which a beneficiary recorded more than minimal earnings. Critics of the test argue that it discourages older persons from working, although evidence indicates that its disincentive effects may be small.[4] The argument that the test discriminates against persons with earnings implies that OASI is a form of annuity, not a means of earnings replacement, and waiver of the test for persons age 70 and over indicates congressional ambivalence on this point.

The earnings test, like the benefit tax, reduces benefit payments to the more affluent elderly and, in an indirect way, shifts some of the burden of financing OASI from younger workers to persons of retirement age. It distorts the pattern of progression embedded in the benefit formula and dilutes implementation of the vertical equity rule, but it does so in the name of social adequacy, itself a rather vague concept. If the test should be further eroded or eliminated, the move would reflect a shift in emphasis away from adequacy toward greater concern for work incentives, labor market efficiency, and individual equity.

TAXATION OF BENEFITS

Social security benefits traditionally have been exempt from the individual income tax, while employees have been denied deductibility of contributions. Employer contributions are deductible as a form of business expense. Prior to 1984, contributions of the self-employed were fully taxable, but the 1983 amendments raised self-employment tax rates to the level of combined employer-employee rates. To complete the task of making tax treatment of employees and self-employed symmetrical, the self-employed are now allowed to deduct one-half of their contribution from taxable income. This arrangement became effective in 1990, following a phase-in period that granted tax credits in lieu of deductions.

The following formula shows how benefits are taxed:

Benefit tax   =   (Adjusted gross income + Nontaxable interest income +
                  1/2 of social security benefits – Base amount) × Marginal
                  income tax rate

subject to the constraint that benefit tax liability cannot exceed the tax due on one-half of social security benefits. The base amount is $25,000 for single taxpayers and $32,000 for couples filing jointly. Taxes collected on benefits are earmarked for the social security trust funds and were introduced to help close the projected fund deficit. The benefit tax shifts some of the burden of supporting each retirement generation to its own more prosperous members, reducing the need to rely on intergenerational transfers.

The benefit tax has been described as a benefit reduction, akin to reductions under the earnings test, and it clearly has the effect of increasing the progressivity of net benefits within each retirement cohort. Representative William Archer, a dissenting member of the National Commission on Social Security Reform, described the tax as a means test for full benefits and criticized it for taxing those who save for retirement while rewarding those who do not (National Commission on Social Security Reform 1983: 2–3). The tax represents yet another departure from the earnings-based principle inherent in the worker-only benefit formula. Its introduction marks another concession to social adequacy, but in time, the progressivity of the benefit tax will erode. Congress chose not to index the base amounts, so a tax that initially affected only a small fraction of beneficiaries will gradually become more inclusive unless the law is changed.[5]

NOTCHES AND TRANSITIONS

Since its inception, the social security system has been marked by many abrupt and unforeseen changes. Indeed, its creation provided the first generation of retirees with windfall benefits denied to their predecessors. Most of the subsequent changes increased benefits and liberalized eligibility, so those receiving benefits did not complain. Such was not the case when the 1977 amendments introduced benefit reductions of 5 to 10 percent or more for cohorts born after 1916.

Congress recognized that an abrupt transition to the new benefit formula would have imposed an unacceptably large drop or "notch" in benefits. To ease the transition, the 1977 amendments allowed for a special alternative benefit computation for members of the 1917–1921 birth cohorts. The transitional procedure allowed for benefit computation under both the old formula, based on unindexed average monthly earnings (AME), and the new formula, based on average indexed monthly earnings (AIME). Workers received the higher of the two benefit awards, but the transition rule prescribed that earnings in years after a worker reached age 61 could not be included in the transitional AME computation. Since earnings in the most recent years frequently weigh heavily in the AME computation, the transition rule significantly affected the PIA of members of the notch cohorts who continued to work full-time after age 62. Even though the PIA was adjusted annually for increases in the CPI, benefits were lower than they would have been under the old formula. Members of the transitional cohorts who retired at age 62 were little affected, however, because their benefit awards were not subject to recomputation.

To illustrate the effect of the 1977 and 1983 amendments on successive cohorts, Kollmann and Koitz (1988) prepared hypothetical benefit computations for workers who always received average earnings and who retired at age 65 between 1960 and 2000 (the 1895 to 1935 birth cohorts). Computations are based on actual earnings through 1988 and projected earnings thereafter. All benefit levels are stated in 1988 dollars. Benefit awards increased from $494 for a worker retiring in 1960 to $586 for a worker retiring in 1973. Awards then increased from $599 in 1974 (1909 birth cohort) to $740 in 1981 (1916 birth cohort), a 23 percent increase in real benefits during a seven-year period that saw average real wages decline by more than 7 percent. The benefit award declined to $670 for a worker retiring in 1982 (the first transitional cohort) and bottomed out at $596 for a worker retiring in 1985 (1920 birth cohort). Awards increase slowly in real terms and are projected to reach $719 by the year 2000, still $21 less in constant dollars than the award received by the 1916 birth cohort.

Experience with the notch cohorts of 1917–1921 illustrates the potential difficulties that occur when major changes are made in the benefit structure. The flaw in the previous benefit formula had to be corrected. Otherwise, retirement benefits eventually would have exceeded earnings received during the recipient's work life. Politicians who promise to remove the notch by paying higher benefits to affected cohorts conveniently overlook this point and fail to acknowledge that the notch cohorts receive higher benefits than they would have received had the new AIME–based benefit formula been in effect since 1972. It would have been more equitable to have dealt with the notch by rescinding the windfall benefits to pre–1917 birth cohorts, but that would have required a politically sensitive benefit cut. As a less contentious compromise, beneficiaries of the windfall could have been denied cost-of-living adjustments until the windfall disappeared. Congress chose the notch, which turned out to be larger than expected because of the effects of high inflation rates of the 1970s on nominal earnings.

If major changes in the benefit structure are contemplated, political acceptance is likely to be contingent on the inclusion of an acceptable transitional procedure. In particular, the adjustment in benefit awards to intercohort equals must be gradual so as not to violate perceived standards of horizontal equity. Public acceptance of change seems also to depend on the remoteness of the impact. Benefit reductions introduced in 1977 and 1983 elicited barely a whimper from the generations most affected. Perhaps this reflects in part a perception that lower lifetime benefits will in some way be accompanied by lower future taxes.

EROSION OF THE EARNINGS-BASED EQUITY FRAMEWORK

Auxiliary and survivor's benefits erode the earnings-based framework of OASI by granting noncontributory benefits to dependents and survivors of some workers. The benefit structure is particularly generous in its treatment of single earner married couples. To be politically acceptable, elimination of noncontributory benefits would require a lengthy and potentially costly transition period. A possible compromise solution would phase out auxiliary and survivor's benefits and implement earnings sharing, under which the combined earnings bases of spouses would be split equally between them during each year of marriage, regardless of how they shared actual earnings. Benefits would then be based on individual earnings bases, not on family circumstances. This option, which treats marriage as an equal economic partnership, has attracted limited political support because of transition costs and, perhaps, because of fear of offending conservative proponents of traditional family values.[6]

The earnings test, a permanent feature of OASI, and the benefit tax, added in 1983, also erode the connection between earnings and benefits. Horizontal equity would be served if elimination of the earnings test were accompanied by actuarially fair adjustments for early or delayed retirement.[7] Both the earnings test and the benefit tax reduce net benefits to more affluent households, thus adding distributional considerations to concerns over program costs. The earnings test remains under pressure, as evidenced by its gradual liberalization. With the social security payroll tax already under fire from ability-to-pay advocates, the benefit tax seems more likely to remain.

APPENDIX

The following example shows how the initial benefit award to families with equal total benefit bases is affected by the distribution of benefit bases between spouses.

Let $B_H = B_H' + B_W' =$ benefit bases of two household units.

$F(B) =$ progressive benefit formula

$\alpha =$ auxiliary benefit multiplier

$PE =$ progressivity effect

Then,

$$B_H' \, f(B_H') + B_W' \, f(B_W') \quad \underset{<}{\overset{>}{=}} \quad B_H f(B_H) \, (1+\alpha)$$

so that

$$\frac{B_H' \, f(B_H') + B_W' \, f(B_W')}{B_H f(B_H)} \quad \underset{<}{\overset{>}{=}} \quad 1+\alpha$$

Relative benefit awards then depend on the relative magnitude of the progressivity effect (PE) versus the multiplier effect, $1 + \alpha$, where

$$PE + \frac{B_H' \, f(B_H') + B_W' \, f(B_W')}{B_H f(B_H)} \quad \underset{<}{\overset{>}{=}} \quad 1+\alpha$$

In the special case described in example 3, the following relationship holds:

$$B_H' = B_W' = 1/2 B_H$$

By substitution

$$\frac{1/2 B_H \, f(B_H') + 1/2 B_H \, f(B_W')}{B_H f(B_H)} = \frac{[f(B_H') + f(B_W')]}{B_H f(B_H)}$$

so that

$$\frac{1/2 \, [f(B_H') + f(B_W')]}{B_H f(B_H)} \quad \underset{<}{\overset{>}{=}} \quad 1+\alpha$$

The direction of inequality depends on which dominates, the progressivity effect or the multiplier effect.

NOTES

1. When the normal retirement age advances, the early entitlement reduction for SI benefits will become operative at corresponding later ages. The reduction at age 60 will remain at 28.5 percent, however, resulting in a decline in the prorated monthly reduction between ages 60 and 66 or 67. See Myers (1985: 60–61) for an elaboration on this point and a discussion of complications that occur when benefit reductions are inherited from a deceased worker.

2. Holden (1982: 42–43) summarizes the historical evidence.

3. When the normal retirement age advances, corresponding changes will be made in earnings-test age variables.

4. Packard (1990) found the removal of 70- and 71-year-olds from the earnings test had little effect on labor supply. As Packard notes, the effect may be greater among workers age 62 to 69.

5. Interaction between the earnings test and the benefit tax adds an interesting twist. Insofar as the earnings test reduces social security benefits, it reduces the benefit tax liability of beneficiaries with earnings in excess of the annual exempt amount. The benefit tax also adds complexity to the tax treatment of affected individuals, especially those subject at the margin to federal and state income taxes, payroll taxes, earnings-test benefit reductions, and the benefit tax.

6. See U.S. Congress, House Committee on Ways and Means (1985) for an evaluation of the cost and benefit redistribution effects of earning sharing.

7. Myers (1985: 470) suggests automatic adjustment of the normal retirement age be tied to life expectancy at age 65. This arrangement would parallel other automatic indexing features in the tax and benefit structures.

5

Disability Insurance and Individual Equity

Social Security Disability Insurance (DI) extends protection against earnings loss to insured workers found to be unable to work because of severe physical or mental impairments. Auxiliary benefits are provided for eligible dependent children and spouses of disabled workers. A worker's disability must be long term in nature, expected to last for at least one year (or until death). Applicants must wait a minimum of five months after onset before becoming entitled to benefits.

DI benefits, like other social security benefits, are contingent on prior work in covered occupations. To be eligible, a worker must be both fully insured and disability insured at time of disablement. Requirements for both types of insured status vary with age. To be fully insured, persons age 31 and over must have accumulated one quarter of coverage for each year beginning with the year after attainment of age 21 and ending with the year of onset (or attainment of age 61, whichever comes first). Persons age 24 to 30 must have accumulated coverage for at least one-half of the quarters that elapsed beginning with the quarter after they attained age 21 and ending with the quarter of onset. Persons under age 24 must have accumulated a minimum of six quarters of coverage during the twelve-quarter period ending with the quarter of onset. To be disability insured, workers age 31 and older must have earned at least twenty quarters of coverage in the forty quarters immediately preceding onset. The latter requirement ensures recency of labor force attachment, thereby establishing a claim for earnings replacement. This requirement is waived in the case of blindness. Workers under age 31 simultaneously satisfy fully insured and disability insured requirements.

The DI program pays monthly benefits to more than 3 million disabled workers and auxiliary benefits to more than 1.2 million dependents. Benefit awards are comparable to those received by beneficiaries of Old Age and Survivors Insurance (OASI). Differences in benefit computation procedures are discussed later in this chapter.

Although DI and OASI share similar benefit structures, the very nature of disability raises issues of individual equity not present in a retirement program. Retirement benefits are payable only to workers who have attained a minimum retirement age. Disabled workers may begin receiving benefits at any age, as long as they meet requirements for insured status and satisfy disability criteria. Because DI benefits are intended only for workers whose disabilities are total and of long duration, program designers seek to establish disability criteria that enable claim examiners to separate those who are capable of significant gainful activity from those who are not. The task of determining which claimants are truly disabled has been assigned to state agencies operating under the regulation of the Social Security Administration (SSA). This joint state-federal operation handles more than one million new claims each year. Numerous appeals, reviews of previous benefit awards, and challenges in federal courts add to the administrative burden. The disability determination process continues to create controversy as policymakers struggle to balance issues of equity, cost containment, and compassion for the afflicted.

DISABILITY IN THE UNITED STATES

Because disability is an ill-defined concept, no accurate count of disabled working-age adults exists. Haveman and Wolfe (1987) classify as disabled persons of working age who report work limitations that prevent them from working full-time, full-year, or who receive benefits from one or more major public disability programs. Using data from the Current Population Survey, they calculated the percentage of working-age adults (age 18 to 64) classified as disabled during the period 1962 to 1984. The percentage ranged from 7 percent (1962) to 11 percent (1973). It exceeded 10 percent between 1968 and 1980 but declined to 9.5 percent by 1984. This measure is sensitive to changes in the number of program participants, as Haveman and Wolfe note, but the count of disabled persons far exceeds the number receiving benefits from public disability programs. For example, Haveman and Wolfe report that in 1984 about 5.4 percent of the working-age population received a disability-related transfer. Only 1.8 percent received Social Security DI benefits. These figures indicate that roughly one-half of disabled working-age adults received cash benefits for the disabled but that less than one in five received DI benefits.

Several explanations exist for the differences between incidence of disability and program participation. Many persons with work limitations may not have impairments of sufficient severity to qualify for benefits. Others may prefer to continue working in spite of severe disablement, thereby earning enough to make them ineligible for benefits. Disability is not just a medical phenomenon. It is, as noted by Berkowitz and Hill (1986: 6), a socioeconomic phenomenon, affected by individual motivation and job opportunities for workers with impairments as well as by availability of public programs for the disabled.

Viewed from this perspective, the application rate among potential claimants is responsive to DI benefit levels, the stringency and predictability of the disability determination process, and the availability of Medicare and other contingent benefits. All of these are policy variables subject to manipulation by Congress and program administrators. Not surprisingly, econometric evidence indicates that the labor supply of workers with disabilities declines in response to increases in benefits, although the various studies differ in their estimates of the magnitude of the response. Leonard (1986) summarizes results through 1985.[1]

Designing a DI System

Market economies rely on two distributive regimes, one based on factor earnings, the other based on need. Public policy superimposes a need-based system (which is secondary) upon an earnings-based system (which is primary). Labor accounts for about 75 percent of factor earnings and 80 percent of money income. Thus, it becomes clear that labor earnings provide the primary means of support for most households. Able-bodied working-aged adults are expected to be self-supporting, and social policy seeks to deny them access to the need-based system. A social consensus seems to support this denial, as evidenced by persistent attempts to force or induce adults on public assistance to find jobs.

Although a social consensus supports benefits for the truly disabled, the imprecise nature of the disability concept complicates program design. Policymakers face the task of defining disability in a manner that facilitates the separation of claimants into two categories: those who are capable of substantial gainful activity (SGA) and those who are not. Implementation requires teamwork between medical and vocational experts, and criteria must be sufficiently precise to enable examiners to make a determination based on evidence in a claimant's medical file. Unfortunately, efforts to achieve such precision have not been very successful.

Owing to individual differences in motivation, sensitivity to pain, vocational background, and education, a given medical impairment may or may not render an individual incapable of SGA. This difficulty was recognized before the introduction of DI and helps to explain the cautious manner in which social security administrators approached the issue (Stone 1984: 70–71; Derthick 1979: 279). Nevertheless, Congress added DI to the system in 1956. Since its inception, the program has experienced alternate periods of expansion and retrenchment as Congress and successive administrations have grappled with conflicting goals of need and fiscal constraint. Federal courts, operating within a legal framework of rights and entitlements, have at times undermined congressional intent and restrained administrative practices.

Intractable problems of administration along with the usual disagreements over the role of social insurance have kept the disability program in a state of flux. Its benefit structure and award procedures can be better understood by first examining the program's evolution.[2]

The Era of Expansion. Initially, the DI program paid benefits only to insured workers age 50 to 64. Auxiliary benefits to dependents were added in 1958, and in 1960 benefits were extended to workers under age 50. In 1965, the definition of disability was liberalized from "permanent and total" to include nonpermanent disabilities expected to last for at least one year. Each change enlarged the pool of potential beneficiaries. This broadening of the definition of disability was accompanied by an increased willingness to consider age and vocational factors in making awards, increasing the number of awards to older workers, especially those with limited education and a work history in physically demanding occupations.

A series of ad hoc benefit increases enacted by Congress between 1969 and 1973 added to work disincentives. These increases, which became effective between January 1970 and June 1974, increased nominal benefits by 78 percent. In contrast, average earnings in covered occupations increased by only 36 percent. Prices, as measured by the consumer price index, increased by 38 percent between 1969 and 1974. The net result was a nearly 30 percent increase in real benefit levels.

An indexing error introduced in the 1972 Social Security Amendments increased real benefits even more beginning in 1975, especially for disabled workers with short earnings histories. This effect is apparent in initial benefit awards for 1978, which averaged $300 per month for disabled workers compared to $262 for newly retired workers. Estimates by Myers (1985: 107) show that replacement rates (benefits as a percentage of predisability earnings) for workers disabled at age 29 in 1978 were 78.5 percent for those with low earnings, 60.3 percent for those with average earnings, and 45.3 percent for those with maximum earnings. When a revised, wage-indexed formula replaced the flawed formula in 1979, the corresponding replacement rates declined to 53.4 percent, 42.7 percent, and 34.1 percent, respectively. In the long run, the ratios are expected to stabilize at 56.4 percent, 43.3 percent, and 29.1 percent, less than three percentage points above the rates for newly retired workers. These rates do not reflect the added disincentive effects of auxiliary benefits, Medicare, or other disability-related transfers.

Increases in DI benefit levels during the 1970s appear to be unintentional spillovers from congressional and administration efforts to increase retirement and survivor benefits. One study (Lando et al. 1979) found that in 1973, a quarter of all newly entitled DI beneficiaries received more in benefits than they had received from working during the previous year. Program growth exceeded projections as the number of primary beneficiaries climbed from 1.3 million in 1968 to 2.7 million in 1976. Working-age DI beneficiaries increased from 1.2 percent to 2.1 percent of the adult working-age population (Haveman and Wolfe 1987: 7). Growth in the number of beneficiaries slowed by 1979 and the number peaked in 1980, but not before policymakers became alarmed over a program that many thought was out of control (Lando et al. 1982).

The Era of Retrenchment. Throughout DI's history, a tension has existed between a benevolent desire to extend support to the disabled and attempts to restrain growth in program costs. Efforts at restraint began to dominate after 1976 in the form of stricter standards of eligibility and reductions in benefits. The Social Security Amendments of 1977 reduced benefit awards to all new beneficiaries, retired and disabled, beginning 1979. The Social Security Disability Amendments of 1980 focused directly on the disability issue by amending the benefit formula, restricting auxiliary benefits, and adding incentives for beneficiaries to return to work. This legislation also directed SSA to exercise stricter control over new awards and to schedule periodic review of eligibility of previous awardees.

When an allegedly overzealous review of the continuing eligibility of current beneficiaries by the Reagan administration led to the termination of benefits for 316,910 disabled workers, a political and legal backlash erupted.[3] Federal courts reversed many terminations, and Congress reacted by placing new limits on SSA termination procedures. Benefit limits and return-to-work features enacted in 1980 remain in effect, and the DI benefit structure seems to have stabilized. Attempts to apply uniform standards of disability to all current and new beneficiaries failed, however, a victim of judicial resistance and a turnaround in Congressional senti-ment. Growth resumed after 1984, and by 1990, the number of worker beneficiaries for the first time passed the 3 million mark. The era of retrenchment is over.

BENEFIT STRUCTURE

The DI benefit structure generally parallels the OASI structure de-scribed in Chapters 3 and 4. Notable differences include a shortening of the averaging period to accommodate shorter work histories of disabled workers and stricter limits on the maximum family benefit. The latter provision stems from concern over the work-disincentive effects of gen-erous auxiliary benefits.[4]

Benefit Computation: Worker-Only Benefits

For retiring workers reaching age 62 in 1991 or later, benefits are based on average indexed monthly earnings (AIME) averaged over thirty-five years of highest indexed earnings. The DI computation procedure shortens the averaging period for workers who become disabled prior to age 62. The number of benefit computation years is obtained by first counting the number of elapsed years beginning with the year after a worker attains age 21 and ending with the year of disablement, but with a minimum of two years. Next, a variable number of dropout years is subtracted from the elapsed years to determine the number of benefit computation years. The number of dropout years varies with age at entitlement, starting at zero for workers under age 27 and increasing by one for each five years of age between 27 and 47 up to a maximum of five. Table 5.1 illustrates how this provision affects the number of benefit computation years.

Variation in the number of dropout years equalizes the proportion of total working years included in the benefit computation period. Prior to 1980, the law allowed for five dropout years for DI beneficiaries of all ages (subject to a minimum of two benefit computation years), frequently resulting in abnormally high benefit awards to younger workers whose benefits were based on a very few years of highest earnings. The change introduced in 1980 reduces this inequity.

Wage indexing of prior earnings of disabled workers extends through the second year preceding initial entitlement. The prescribed number of years of highest earnings constitutes the benefit base for computation of AIME. The benefit formula in effect in the year of entitlement is applied to a disabled worker's AIME to determine the primary insurance amount

Table 5.1
Benefit Computation Period for Workers Becoming Disabled at Different Ages

Age at Entitlement	Elapsed Years	Dropout Years	Benefit Computation Years (BCY)	BCY as Percentage of Elapsed Years
22	0	0	2	--
23	1	0	2	200%
27	5	1	4	80
32	10	2	8	80
37	15	3	12	80
42	20	4	16	80
47	25	5	20	80
62	40	5	35	87.5

(PIA). Thus, each new DI beneficiary receives treatment equivalent to that of a member of the current age 62 retirement cohort with the same earnings base or AIME.[5]

A newly entitled disabled worker typically receives an initial benefit award equal to the PIA. DI and OASI benefit awards are granted identical postentitlement treatment. Each receives annual cost-of-living adjustments and each becomes subject to the benefit tax if adjusted gross income exceeds $25,000 for a single taxpayer or $32,000 for a married couple filing jointly. DI beneficiaries switch automatically from DI to OASI upon reaching normal retirement age.

Benefit Offset

Benefit payments may be reduced to DI recipients who receive monthly Worker's Compensation benefits for work-related disabilities. In most cases, the offset constrains total disability benefits to 80 percent of monthly earnings as averaged over the year of disablement and the five preceding years.[6] Like the cap on family benefits, the offset is designed to weaken work disincentives by limiting total benefit payments to affected workers. Benefits under the offset cannot be less than benefits under DI alone.

Disability Freeze

Periods of disability of five months or longer are exluded in determination of a worker's insured status and in computation of AIME. The freeze serves to maintain a worker's insured status and keeps benefits from being depressed by inclusion of periods of low or zero earnings in the computation of the benefit base. Myers likens the freeze to waiver-of-premium clauses in life insurance policies. (1985: 64)

Pooling the Risk of Disability

Shortening the benefit computation period for disabled workers has the effect of granting equal benefit awards to newly entitled workers with identical AIME averaged over different time intervals. All such newly entitled workers, retired or disabled, are treated as intracohort equals. Benefits to disabled workers conform to social adequacy standards intended for newly retired workers, and any resulting redistribution is regarded as the intended outcome of social insurance arrangements. Given the generally higher mortality rates experienced by disabled workers, disability benefits may also be viewed as a substitute for the retirement benefits that such workers earn but frequently fail to receive.

The Work Test: Substantial Gainful Activity

The OASI earnings test allows beneficiaries to replace a portion of lost earnings with social security benefits while they continue to work, often on a part-time basis. A more stringent limit on earnings applies to DI beneficiaries. The function of DI is to replace earnings of beneficiaries who are totally disabled, not to supplement earnings loss for persons with partial disability. Thus, benefits are denied to beneficiaries whose labor market activities are deemed to be both gainful and substantial. SSA establishes the earnings level indicative of substantial gainful activity. After remaining at $300 per month throughout the 1980s, the SGA amount increased to $500 per month beginning in 1990. The latter figure is less than one would earn working full-time at minimum wage. Disability-related expenses may be deducted in determining whether earnings exceed the SGA amount. In contrast to the various legislated or indexed amounts so common in the social security tax and benefit structure, the SGA amount is changed at the discretion of SSA.

AUXILIARY BENEFITS

Eligibility requirements for auxiliary benefits to dependents of disabled workers are identical to those under OASI. A dependent spouse qualifies for spousal benefits beginning at age 62, subject to an early retirement reduction if entitlement begins prior to normal retirement age. Dependent children qualify for children's benefits until age 18 (age 19 if enrolled full-time in primary or secondary school). Mother's or father's benefits are payable to a dependent spouse if the household includes dependent children under age 16. Auxiliary benefits are set at 50 percent of a worker's PIA subject to the early retirement reduction for elderly spouses and to the earnings test for all dependents with earnings.

Disabled Child's, Widow's, and Widower's Benefits

A disabled child of an insured worker may also qualify for benefits. To be eligible for disabled child's benefits, the recipient must be age 18 or over, must have become disabled before age 22, and must be the dependent child of a retired, deceased, or disabled worker. Criteria for disability are the same as for disabled workers. The monthly benefit rate equals one-half of the parent's PIA if the parent is disabled or retired, three-fourths if the parent is deceased. Benefits may be reduced if the family maximum applies or if the child receives benefits on his or her own account.

A disabled widow or widower may qualify for disability benefits based on the earnings record of a deceased spouse. Eligibility is limited to persons age 50 to 59. The initial benefit award equals 71.5 percent of PIA (the rate applicable to widows and widowers at age 60). At age 60, beneficiaries transfer to OASI. To qualify for disability benefits, a widow or widower must meet the same standards of disability as a disabled worker.

Maximum Family Benefit for DI Beneficiaries

A special maximum family benefit cap applies to families of disabled beneficiaries. It imposes a benefit maximum equal to the smaller of 85 percent of AIME or 150 percent of PIA, but not less than 100 percent of PIA. The special maximum places a lower cap on family benefits for DI than for OASI in order to reduce the number of cases in which benefits exceed a worker's previous earnings. Since the cap affects only auxiliary benefits, its primary impact is on families of disabled workers with dependent children. The lower cap was added by the 1980 amendment to counter work-disincentive effects.

Medicare Eligibility

After twenty-four consecutive months on DI, a beneficiary becomes eligible for Medicare, including Hospital Insurance (HI) and optional

Supplementary Medical Insurance (SMI). If a DI beneficiary recovers, Medicare coverage ends with the last month of cash benefits, but the two-year waiting period for Medicare is waived if a former beneficiary returns to the DI rolls. Loss of Medicare coverage deters beneficiaries from returning to work, and waiver of the waiting period for former recipients represents a modest attempt to weaken this disincentive.

Returning the Disabled to Work

Policymakers have long expressed a hope that disabled workers might be able to return to work. Efforts to return workers to the labor market include requirements that beneficiaries accept rehabilitation services and availability of temporary support during trial work periods. These efforts have met with limited success.

Vocational Rehabilitation and Medical Recovery. The law requires that DI applicants be referred to state vocational rehabilitation agencies for possible rehabilitation services. Benefits may be withheld from beneficiaries who refuse to cooperate. Rehabilitation services must be performed in accordance with federal regulations, and state agencies receive a cost reimbursement only in cases in which services result in return of a worker to SGA for a minimum of nine consecutive months. The law also requires beneficiaries to inform SSA of medical improvements that might make them ineligible for benefits.

Trial Work Period. Beneficiaries who have not experienced medical recovery are allowed to test their ability to work during a nine-month trial work period. During this period, earnings may exceed the SGA amount without suspension of benefits. The nine trial months may occur at any time within a sixty-month period. Earnings must exceed $75 per month to count as a trial month. Upon completion of the trial work period, benefits continue for an additional three months, followed by a thirty-three-month reentitlement period during which benefits will be restored if earnings cease. In addition, Medicare benefits continue for forty-eight months after the beginning of the trial work period. A worker is allowed only one trial work period per period of disability. These provisions do not apply to workers who experience medical recovery.

DISABILITY DETERMINATION

The social security statute (United States Statutes at Large 1968: 868) defines disability as follows:

The inability to engage in any substantial gainful activity by reason of any medically determinable physical or mental impairment which can be expected to result in death or which has lasted or can be expected to last for a continuous period of not less than 12 months. [A person must be] not only unable to do his previous work but cannot, considering his age, education, and work experience, engage in any other kind of substantial gainful work which exists in the national economy, regardless of whether such work exists in the immediate area in which he lives, or whether a specific job vacancy exists for him, or whether he would be hired if he applied for work.

The statute requires examiners to determine whether a claimant's impairment is of sufficient severity and duration to meet the statutory definition of disability. In addition to medical findings, examiners are instructed to consider a worker's age, education, and vocational history. To deny entitlement, the government must show that job opportunities for an impaired worker exist somewhere in the national economy, but it is not necessary to show that such work exists in a worker's immediate area or that a specific job is available. The reference to work opportunities conveys Congressional intent to prevent the DI program from becoming a form of unemployment insurance.[7]

Steps in the Determination Process

A worker begins the process by filing a claim at a local SSA office. At this point, it is determined whether the claimant has acquired insured status. If the claimant is employed, earnings must remain below the monthly amount that establishes SGA, currently $500 per month. For claims that satisfy insured status and limits on earnings, the local office assembles required information including names of physicians and hospitals that can provide medical evidence. Completed applications are then forwarded to the state disability determination agency in the claimant's state of residence.

Initial Determination. Once a claim reaches the state agency, it proceeds through a sequential evaluation process. Each claim is assigned to a two-person evaluation team consisting of a physician and a disability examiner. The examiner is responsible for acquiring and organizing the information needed to process the application. SSA regulations contained in the Disability Insurance State Manual (DISM) set out in detail the procedures to be followed. Examiners are instructed to acquire relevant medical evidence from treating physicians and other personnel who may have examined a claimant, and they may ask a claimant to provide additional information. Treating physicians are instructed to fill out forms designed to elicit information descriptive of the claimant's condition and, when relevant, to provide test and other clinical data such as electrocardiograms, Xrays, or chemical profiles. Respondents may also be asked to evaluate the effect of impairments on functional capacity, but they are not asked to judge whether the patient is or is not able to work.

If information obtained from treating physicians and other sources is judged to be insufficient, the examiner may request a consultative examination (CE), to be performed at government expense by a physician under contract with the state agency. Because of cost and time delays, regulations discourage routine reliance on CEs, but the DISM instructs examiners to acquire additional information if it is needed to develop a claim. The burden of proof rests not on the claimant but on the examiner, who is instructed to give first priority to the interests of the claimant. Thus, the purpose of CEs is to ensure fairness in adjudication, not to exercise quality control over evidence obtained from treating physicians.

To guide determination teams and to promote uniformity of standards, SSA publishes a set of medical and vocational guidelines. Medical guidelines take the form of a listing of more than 100 medical conditions presumed to be so incapacitating as to render a person incapable of engaging in SGA on an ongoing basis. The listings specify diagnostic signs, symptoms, and clinical findings that establish the requisite severity and duration. If medical evidence indicates the presence of one or more conditions included in the listings, the claim is allowed automatically.

Allowances are granted automatically to claimants with impairments not listed but judged to be equivalent in severity and duration to listed conditions. Allowances are also granted if a combination of multiple impairments is judged to be equivalent in severity and duration to listed conditions, even if none of the impairments considered individually is deemed to be severe. Equivalency judgments must be made by the physician member of the determination team.

To be considered severe, a set of impairments must significantly limit a person's physical or mental capacity to perform one or more work activities required in most occupations. Basic physical activities include walking, standing, reaching, sitting, lifting, pushing, pulling, carrying, and handling. Also included are the capabilities of sight, hearing, and speech. Mental capacities include the ability to understand, to follow simple instructions, to remember, and to exercise judgment, and behavioral factors such as the ability to respond appropriately to supervision or the actions of co-workers and to handle unusual work situations (Mashaw 1983: 114–117).

If a claimant's medical condition fails to meet the standard of disability implied by the listings but meets the twelve-month duration rule, regulations require the examiner to consider other factors. If it is determined that the claimant can meet requirements of his or her former occupation, the claim will be denied. If the claimant cannot meet these requirements, a determination must be made as to whether, considering age, education, and vocational experience, the individual can engage in any other kind of SGA that exists in the national economy.

To assist agency personnel in making this determination, SSA created a grid that relates worker characteristics (age, education, work experience) to the residual functional capacity (RFC) to perform work-related physical and mental activities. RFC categories range across a spectrum that includes sedentary, light, medium, heavy, and very heavy work capabilities. Examiners determine RFC from the evidence in a worker's file and refer to the grid to ascertain whether, given age, education, and work experience, a worker retains the capacity to engage in SGA. If evidence in the claimant's file is deemed to be inadequate for this purpose, an examiner may request an examination and evaluation by vocational experts. At this point, the examination team makes an initial determination to allow or deny the claim.

The law authorizes SSA to review and reverse any state agency determination and requires federal review of 50 percent of all allowances and a sufficient number of denials to ensure accuracy. Reviewers target cases deemed most likely to contain errors.

Reconsideration. Upon completion of state agency determination and SSA review, if any, the claimant receives notification of the result. The number and percentage of initial allowances varies from year to year, but the rate has consistently remained below 50 percent. In fiscal year 1990, initial allowances were granted to 39 percent of the nearly 1.1 million applicants. Claimants who are denied benefits may request reconsideration by state agencies within sixty days of notification, and approximately 30 percent of the unsuccessful applicants did so in 1990. Reconsiderations are handled by a different team but follow the same rules as initial determinations. In fiscal year 1990, 17 percent of the initial denials were allowed after reconsideration.

Appeal. A claimant denied benefits upon reconsideration may request a hearing before an SSA administrative law judge (ALJ) within sixty days of notification. At this stage, the claimant may add new evidence, appear in person, and be represented by counsel. The ALJ may request additional evidence. This is the first stage at which a claimant is allowed a face-to-face hearing. ALJs operate under less rigid guidelines than state agency personnel. In particular, ALJs are less likely to base decisions on objective medical data and are more likely to consider the more subjective circumstances surrounding individual cases. Although these hearings are non-adversarial, they tend to be quasi-judicial in nature, and ALJs are more likely than state agency personnel to show deference to rulings of federal courts. The ALJ is seen by some as a guarantor of individual rights and by others (including some SSA administrators) as a weak link in the determination chain. In fiscal 1990, ALJs received 272,141 appeals from more than half of all the claimants denied upon reconsideration and reversed denials in 63 percent of the cases. Such high rates of reversal are typical at this stage of appeal. Among appeals not reversed, 24 percent were denied and 12 percent were dismissed.[8]

The Appeals Council, a fifteen-member board in the SSA's office of Hearings and Appeals, provides the final stage of administrative appeal. A claimant may request a hearing before the council within sixty days of notification of denial by an ALJ. Among 22,904 appellants, the Appeals Council in fiscal year 1990 allowed claims in 8 percent of the cases, denied or dismissed claims in 86 percent, and remanded the remaining 6 percent to ALJs for further consideration.

Claimants whose denial is upheld by the Appeals Council may commence civil action in a U.S. district court within sixty days of notification. In fiscal year 1990, 4,668 cases reached this stage. Once an appeal reaches federal court, the case becomes subject to legal rules of evidence, proof, and constitutionality. In fiscal year 1990, federal courts allowed 29 percent of appeals, denied 63 percent, and dismissed 7 percent. As a result of the reconsideration and appeals process, 27 percent of initial denials were reversed, increasing the eventual allowance rate from 39 percent to 55 percent.

Continuing Disability Reviews

Following the legal, political, and administrative disruption that accompanied the massive review and termination effort of 1981–84, SSA implemented a much less ambitious program of review. During the early Reagan years, SSA attempted to apply the same standards of disability to the review of persons currently on the rolls as to initial determinations of new applicants. Such a procedure would seemingly improve equity by subjecting all current and potential beneficiaries to equal treatment, but it was not so perceived by many of the hundreds of thousands removed from the rolls or by members of Congress besieged by angry constituents. Two factors generated resistance to the administration's efforts. First, SSA implemented the grid system of classifying claimants according to medical condition and personal characteristics in 1979. The new procedures, at least as they were applied, appear to have been stricter than procedures in effect during the early 1970s. Second, during the 1970s, an increasing number of beneficiaries were admitted to the rolls after appeal to ALJs, and given the differences in standards applied by state agencies and ALJs, it is not surprising that a disproportionate number of those admitted on appeal were later terminated (Derthick 1990: 43n). Thus, many beneficiaries whose medical condition had not improved were shocked to receive a totally unexpected termination notice.

The effort to apply a uniform standard to the entire beneficiary population was halted by a series of adverse court decisions imposing some form of medical improvement standard on SSA (Derthick 1990: 140–143). Congress responded with passage of the Disability Reform Act of 1984. This act established a medical improvement standard under which benefits may be terminated only (1) if there is substantial medical evidence of improvement in a person's work-related impairment, (2) if advances in medical or vocational therapy now enable a person to perform SGA, (3) if evidence based on new or improved diagnostic techniques indicates that a person's condition is less disabling than originally thought and that it is now possible to perform SGA, or (4) if there is substantial evidence indicating that the prior determination was in error or was fraudulently obtained. The act also specifies that the combined effect of multiple impairments be considered in cases in which any one impairment would not be severe enough to qualify a claimant for benefits. This feature applies to both new determinations and reviews (Koitz 1984).

Because many recipients of termination notices were caught by surprise during the 1981–84 review, the act requires SSA to notify all beneficiaries of pending review, to inform them of the right to submit new medical evidence, and to warn them that review could result in termination of benefits. Recipients of termination notices have the same rights of reconsideration and appeal as persons experiencing initial denial, and they may continue to receive benefit payments (subject to repayment) during the appeal process.

SSA halted reviews in 1984 while under duress from courts, Congress, and a number of governors who resisted and, in some cases, suspended reviews by state agencies. Although the law allows SSA to assume responsibility for determination and review in states that refuse to comply with federal regulations, no such action was taken. Reviews did not resume until 1986, and then at a much reduced rate. During the first year, SSA reviewed 317,000 cases. By 1991, this number had dropped to 183,000, or about 6 percent of disabled workers in beneficiary status. Under the new statutory guidelines, initial termination rates among those reviewed dropped to about 11 percent, and reversals at subsequent stages in the reconsideration and appeal processes reduced the effective rate to less than 10 percent. The review process is no longer controversial, nor does it purport to apply equivalent standards to reviews and initial determinations. Rather, it perpetuates inequities that come about as standards change over time.

The Social Security Disability Amendments of 1980 were to have improved equity by requiring systematic review of disabled beneficiaries in accordance with current disability standards. The effort failed, not only because of the recalcitrance of ALJs and the courts, but also because of the ambiguities inherent in the disability concept and because of disagreement over what it really means to be disabled. The following section examines each of these obstacles to achieving equity within the DI program.

Obstacles to Equity in the Determination Process

The law requires disability adjudicators to determine which applicants for DI benefits are capable of SGA and which are not. Only the latter become entitled to benefits. Whether an applicant is truly disabled must be inferred from available medical information plus such personal characteristics as age, education, and vocational background. When Congress introduced the disability freeze (1954) and DI benefits (1956), thereby recognizing disability as a social insurance category, legislators emphasized the importance of basing determinations on objective medical evidence. The Social Security Amendments of 1967 reiterated the key role of clinical and laboratory findings in disability determinations.

When gathering medical evidence, state agency examiners are instructed to look for signs—objectively verifiable evidence of impairments—in preference to symptoms—the subjective testimony of claimants. For example, reports of the presence of pain should be substantiated by evidence of underlying physiological causes.

If medical evidence indicates the presence of a physical or mental condition that severely impairs a person's ability to perform work-related functions, a judgment must be rendered as to whether the individual retains sufficient residual functional capacity to gainfully perform any job that might be available in significant numbers in the local or national economy. This requirement reflects a belief that diagnostic techniques of modern medicine, including clinical and laboratory data and tests of strength, motion, and endurance, can distinguish genuine from feigned disability (Stone 1984: 130). Congress persisted in this belief despite warnings from physicians that more might be expected of the medical profession than it could deliver. Medical experts appearing before Congressional committees prior to introduction of the freeze and benefit payments explained that disability is an elusive concept, frequently requiring subjective judgments that undermine efforts to achieve objectivity, accuracy, and consistency. Honest disagreements are unavoidable. Physicians also expressed concern over the therapeutic impact of a program that rewards individuals for being disabled and encourages malingering (Stone 1984: 80–81).

In spite of this cautionary testimony, Congress introduced and subsequently expanded the DI program with the expectation that most awards would be based on medical criteria alone. Upon implementing the freeze in 1954, Congress directed state agency disability examiners to acquire information from treating physicians and other private practitioners selected by the claimant. This practice allayed fears of creation of a new federal bureaucracy and forestalled opposition from the American Medical Association, but it forced physicians to assume conflicting roles as agents of both the patient and the government. Concerns over such conflicts were conveyed to Congressional committees in testimony of physicians prior to Congressional action, and the issue has never been resolved (Stone 1984: 81).

As previously noted, examiners may request CEs if they conclude that evidence from treating physicians is incomplete, but such examinations are not to be used as routine checks on information from sources selected by the claimant. Results from one study indicate that information provided by CEs may actually increase the probability of a favorable determination, as might be expected in light of SSA instructions that examiners place primary emphasis on protecting the claimant's interest (Mashaw 1983: 128–131).

Use of the listings and the grid represents an attempt to implement what Mashaw (1983: 25–26) calls "bureaucratic rationality" at the state agency level. Claimants with medical conditions included in the listings, or their equivalent, are presumed to be so impaired as to be incapable of SGA for at least one year. Persons with impairments judged to be severe but potentially less disabling than those in the listings are evaluated in accordance with the grid, a decision matrix that bases determination on age, education, and vocational data combined with measures of functional capacity (generally inferred from medical data). The grid allows for a trade-off between human capital and functional capacity in determining work potential. Disability standards within the grid are most lenient for

older workers (age 55 and over), progressively stricter for younger workers, and strictest for workers age 18 to 44. Use of the age factor seems to
imply that, other things equal, capacity to work declines with age, but it
may also represent implicit recognition of the increasingly bleak employment opportunities facing older workers, especially those with impairments.

The listings and the grid represent a consensus of medical opinion
regarding the relationship between impairment, functional capacity, and
ability to work (Stone 1984: 128–129). Although not billed as such, this
approach creates an "average person" standard for determining which
impairments are truly disabling (Stone 1984: 159). It implies the existence
of a disability continuum ranging from the most severely impaired (those
with medical conditions included in the listings or their equivalent) to
persons with severe impairments that may be totally disabling for some
individuals but not for others (the grid), to those with work-limiting but
nonsevere impairments (not disabled) and, finally, to those with no work-
limiting physical or mental impairments whatsoever.

An approach of this nature is probably necessary in a program that
processes more than 1 million initial determinations and nearly half a
million reconsiderations and reviews each year. It seems to be the only
way that SSA and the state agencies can handle so large a case load at an
acceptable cost and without undue delay.

As Weaver (1986: 50–51) notes, any particular impairment will be
associated with different degrees of disability among different people or
for the same person at different times. Consequently, an average-person
approach almost certainly results in erroneous determinations for claimants who may be atypical. Errors are of two types: false positives in which
allowances are granted to claimants who are not disabled, and false
negatives in which allowances are denied to claimants who are disabled.
Improved diagnostic techniques and evaluation procedures can reduce
both types of error. Otherwise, efforts to reduce one type of error by
tightening or relaxing standards generally increase the likelihood of the
other. Whether standards should be strict or relaxed is, of course, a
normative question. In a social insurance program, the choice becomes
political and depends, ultimately, on the willingness of a society to provide
earnings replacement to people with varying degrees of impairment. Since
the introduction of DI in 1956, the standard has shifted over time in an
ongoing political and judicial tug-of-war between those concerned with
fiscal constraint and those emphasizing compassion and the presumed
rights of beneficiaries. Although standards have been flexible, the statutory
definitions of disability and employability have not changed since 1967.

Sources of error in disability determination are not limited to matters of ease or stringency in standards. Stone (1984: 129–133) raises serious questions about the quality of medical evidence available to adjudicators. She cites evidence of unreliability of clinical results, including frequent errors in laboratory tests and differing interpretations of Xrays and electrocardiograms. She also notes difficulties in evaluating some of the more subjective tests, specifically citing tests used to diagnose pulmonary diseases, and concludes that it is not surprising that "substantial inconsistencies" are found in decisions that rely on clinical evaluations. Thus, at least some of the errors in determination arise because of insufficient or inaccurate medical information.

Quality assurance (QA) programs operate at three levels within the determination hierarchy to promote accuracy and timeliness. Within state agencies, QA analysts review a sample of claims to check on the quality of case development and on compliance with regulations. The SSA central office implements a similar postdetermination review of state agency decisions, and cases in this sample are subjected to a third-level review that, in effect, monitors the performance of the monitors. Information obtained from QA analysts is used by administrators to discern and correct weaknesses in the decision-making process.[9] Nevertheless, consistency may continue to suffer owing to the irreducible role of individual judgment in the diagnosis of impairments (Stone 1984: 133).

Inconsistency resulting from what could be termed "measurement error" may be unavoidable, but it might be reduced by changing the way in which the system operates. Mashaw (1983: 204–205) suggests that claimants could be examined by an evaluation team of three physicians, employed by state agencies for that purpose, to replace treating physicians as sources of medical evidence. Claimants would experience personal contact with agency personnel prior to initial determination, and the team would prepare a clinical evaluation for agency examiners. A less radical restructuring would introduce physician teams only at the reconsideration stage. Use of specialized physician teams would eliminate the conflicting roles now assigned to treating physicians, and early personal contact could help to legitimize a determination process that now seems remote and impersonal.

A more ambitious proposal calls for multidisciplinary evaluation teams. Mashaw (1983: 206–209) finds a prototype in a study by Nagi (1969). Clinical teams consisting of a social worker, physician, psychologist, occupational therapist, and vocational counselor evaluated a sample of 2,454 DI applicants. The purpose of the study was to discover how better information would affect determinations by state agency examiners. In each case, examination teams in three state agencies first made determinations using information from the usual sources. Examiners in the same agencies (not necessarily the same teams) made redeterminations based on information from the five-person evaluation teams. Upon redetermination, 8.2 percent of allowances and 20.8 percent of denials were reversed (Nagi 1969: 60).

Nagi's study predates by a decade the introduction of the grid. Insofar as it truly represents the effect of more information on determinations, Nagi's results indicate that the use of multidisciplinary evaluation teams would increase somewhat the rate of allowance. There is a presumption that more information would improve accuracy and consistency, but given the elusiveness of the concept of disability, the degree of improvement is difficult to predict. Not surprisingly, reversal rates in the Nagi study were lowest for impairments found in the listings, somewhat higher for equivalent impairments, and much higher when decisions hinged on vocational factors (Nagi 1969: 62). Nagi's findings indicate that if SSA were to incur the greater expense of team examinations, the payoff would be in the form of greater consistency in granting allowances within the claimant population. The number of awards at the initial determination stage might increase, but this could, in turn, reduce subsequent appeals and reversals.

The complicated state-federal adjudicatory hierarchy has long been questioned by critics who argue that federalization of the initial determination function would bring greater uniformity to decision making. Besides, states have a conflict of interest because persons who are denied DI benefits and eventual Medicare coverage frequently become clients of state welfare and Medicaid programs. It is not certain, however, that federalization would improve upon the existing state-federal QA program under which states with low performance ratings are subject to corrective action by SSA. Mashaw (1983: 166–168) reports that, upon visiting offices in different states, he finds similarities in routine and structure and, while differences remain in what he calls "decisional culture," he senses an incremental convergence among state agencies. Reliance on state agencies prevents lateral transfers of personnel across geographical regions, however, thus limiting the opportunity for agency personnel to experience the homogenizing effects of different work environments.

Administrative Appeal. Of greater concern is the apparent inconsistency between state agencies and ALJs in granting allowances. The two groups employ a quite different approach to case development and adjudication. Whereas state agencies operate within the confines of the listings and the grid and rely totally on written evidence, ALJs operate under much more lenient guidelines. They may request additional medical evidence. Claimants may appear in person at ALJ hearings, may be represented by counsel and may present expert testimony and additional clinical evidence. These procedures allow for more consideration of individual circumstances and permit decision makers to make more subjective assessments of an applicant's potential for gainful activity.

Appeals are handled de novo, meaning that each case is developed anew, frequently with new medical evidence. ALJs typically do not monitor state agencies for compliance with SSA instructions, nor do they provide them with corrective feedback. Rather, the ALJs operate in accordance with their own less restrictive procedural rules and make what amounts to new determinations. Since the statutory intent is to grant allowances on the basis of disability, not on the basis of medical and vocational status per se, ALJs could, by placing more emphasis on individual circumstances, add a desirable flexibility to the more rigid standards imposed upon initial determinations. The hearings process itself could help to legitimize the determination process simply by granting the most dissatisfied applicants an opportunity for personal contact with a decision-making representative of SSA (Mashaw 1983: 143).

On closer examination, however, it appears that ALJs contribute to inconsistency by applying less stringent standards than state agencies. Only denials are appealed to ALJs, so that only false negatives may be corrected at this stage. False positives are not corrected once they slip by internal review samplings, and under the medical improvement standard now in effect, subsequent correction via continuing disability review has become more difficult. Cases appealed to ALJs are likely to involve relatively less severe impairments, since the severest cases are generally granted allowances at the initial determination stage. Yet the reversal rate of ALJs has always been high, ranging from 40 to 50 percent in the early to mid-1970s and reaching or exceeding 60 percent in more recent years (Derthick 1990: 40; U.S. Congress, House, Committee on Ways and Means 1991: 59).

The final stage of administrative appeal, the Appeals Council, handles much smaller case loads and has much lower reversal rates. In contrast to ALJs, the Appeals Council has authority to conduct "own motion" reviews of ALJ decisions, but its role in the adjudication process attracts little comment or controversy.

Judicial Appeal. Until the controversy over continuing disability review, federal courts played only a limited role in the evolution of disability policy. A notable exception was *Kerner v. Flemming* (283 F.2d 916 (2d Cir. 1960)), in which the court placed upon the secretary (of Health, Education and Welfare) the burden of proving that, if a claimant could no longer perform in his or her previous occupation, jobs that the claimant could perform were currently available. Congress responded in 1967 with an amendment introducing the national economy test.

During the 1980s, the judicial climate changed, as a series of circuit court rulings forced upon SSA an improvement standard for benefit termination.[10] Initially, the agency adopted a policy of nonacquiescence, accepting the verdict in the case in question but refusing to apply the same principles to other termination cases. Nonacquiescence has precedent elsewhere in administrative-judicial relations and was further justified because of inconsistencies in rulings across the twelve circuits. In the absence of a Supreme Court resolution, acquiescence would have threatened the SSA policy of maintaining a single, nationwide DI program.

Ultimately, SSA was forced to back down, both by Congress and because of lack of support by the Department of Justice (Derthick 1990: 144). Mashaw, in a post mortem on the experiences of 1981–84, refers to the "juridification" of the DI debate and concludes that, once entitlements have been granted, the courts will evaluate them to the status of a legal right that cannot be rescinded (1988: 174–175). He sees the episode as marking the end of the vacillation between relaxation and stringency that marked the period from the late 1950s to the 1980s, to be followed by an era of long-term expansion.

The Determination Process: A Summary

State agency determination teams are expected to conform to the bureaucratic mode of decision making as prescribed in SSA regulations (specifically, in the DISM). To achieve consistency, team members must understand the appropriate definition of disability and must collect sufficient information about each claimant's medical condition to enable them to reach a proper decision. Teams must attempt to predict how a claimant's medical condition will affect the ability to perform various jobs existing in the economy even though, in many cases, the individual has never performed such jobs. Criteria laid out in the listings and the grid provide guidance, but they emphasize objectively determinable medical conditions and factors such as age, education, and job experience. This procedure allows only limited scope for evaluation of more subjective individual characteristics like motivation or the capacity to endure pain and discomfort. Criteria included in the listings and the grid represent a distillation of views of medical specialists as to the work capabilities of the average person with a given set of medical-age-vocational characteristics.

The statutory definition implies that each decision should be made after considering the personal circumstances of each applicant, a view that has been reinforced by the courts. Unfortunately, the bureaucratic procedures required of state agencies make such individualized treatment almost impossible, particularly in light of pressures to limit the use of CEs and to expedite the processing of claims.[11] Add to this the apparently unavoidable errors and judgment calls that appear in the information base of many claims, and it becomes clear that the potential for error is inherent in the decision process. Even with procedural changes, such as those suggested by Mashaw, an irreducible potential for decision error will remain.

Although the statutory definition of disability has been unchanged since 1967, its implementation has changed substantially. Some of the changes stem from advances in medical treatment and diagnosis. These advances allow practitioners to diagnose and correct a variety of medical conditions that once may have been totally disabling. The existence of jobs available to severely impaired persons may change over time as a result of economic development and legislation, such as the Rehabilitation Act of 1973 and the Americans with Disabilities Act of 1990. Yet the employability provision in the statute remains amorphous. The Kerner doctrine (*Kerner v. Flemming*) made benefit denials contingent on the ability of the secretary to show that job opportunities existed within an applicant's state or region. In 1967, Congress amended the statute to relieve the secretary of the obligation to show that specific vacancies existed or that the claimant would be hired if he or she applied for a job, but courts continued to render liberal interpretations of the employability provision (Stone 1984: 153–154).

Mashaw (1983: 58) refers to the "pervasive instability of the DI value matrix," as evidenced by cycles in the share of awards based on factors not included in the listings. For example, the percentage of initial allowances based on the listings (the most rigorous standard) increased from 29 percent in 1976 to 74 percent in 1983 but then declined to 59 percent by 1990. In contrast the percentage of allowances based on the medical-vocational grid (the most liberal standard) declined from 26.7 percent in 1975 to 17.7 percent in 1983 before increasing (but not continuously) to 29.2 percent in 1990. The remaining awards were based on medical conditions judged to be equivalent to conditions included in the listings. This category, considered to fall between the listings and the grid in terms of stringency, allows substantial scope for medical judgment. It served as the basis for about 45 percent of awards during the mid-1970s, but it dropped markedly later in the decade, especially after introduction of the grid in 1979, accounting for only 8.3 percent of awards in 1983 and 11.8 percent of awards in 1990. The determination mechanism appears to adjust quite rapidly to changes in signals from its political overseers.

DISABILITY INSURANCE AND INDIVIDUAL EQUITY

Equity standards inherent in the DI program may be inferred in general terms from the statutory definition of disability and from the benefit structure. The statutory definition of disability specifies that worker benefits be awarded only to insured workers who, on the basis of objective medical evidence, are judged to be incapable of substantial gainful activity for a period of at least one year (or until death), but the particular set of medical and personal characteristics that qualify a claimant for benefits have varied over time. Some of the changes result from improved diagnostic techniques and treatment; others represent accommodations to judicial pressure and the shifting political climate. Differences in standards, or at least in points of emphasis, between the initial determination stage and subsequent stages of appeal (most notably ALJs and federal courts) add to the inconsistency. As a result, for the relatively less impaired members of the entitlement population, success in obtaining a benefit award may depend on when one applies and on how vigorously one presses the appeal of an initial rejection. Implementation of the medical improvement standard for benefit termination, forced upon SSA by the courts and codified in the 1984 amendments, will block any serious effort to correct for past inconsistencies through reconsideration of prior awards.

Even if a stable consensus could be reached as to where on the disability continuum to draw the line between those eligible for benefits and those to be denied, imperfections in the evaluation process would preclude the achievement of total consistency. Errors in measurement and interpretation of results and the subjective nature of evaluations, especially when unobservable symptoms such as pain or anxiety may be present, impose upon the system an irreducible margin of error. The task of selecting a boundary is made more difficult by the dichotomous nature of the determination. Either you are disabled or you are not. No allowance is made for partial disability, and no earnings replacement is provided for lost earnings potential of workers with severe but nondisabling (in statutory terms) impairments. For workers close to the boundary between "disabled" and "nondisabled," small differences in medical condition can result in large differences in public support and economic well-being. There is little doubt that applicants who receive allowances are generally more severely impaired than those who are rejected, but the fact that one-third or more of the rejected applicants never return to the work force indicates that many of the rejectees may differ little from many of the marginal awardees.[12]

The fact that many rejected applicants do not return to work or work only intermittently does not prove, of course, that they are incapable of SGA. It may mean that some of them fail to find jobs, perhaps because they refuse to relocate or because the labor market cannot absorb all who want to work. DI was never intended to provide unemployment insurance. On the other hand, relaxed eligibility requirements for older workers, especially those age 55 to 64, indicate that the program enables older workers with severe impairments to take early retirement, especially if they have long work histories in physically demanding occupations. This feature makes it easier to impose age limits on retirement benefits, a consideration that will become increasingly significant when the normal retirement age advances to 67, with corresponding benefit reductions for early retirement. Relaxed eligibility standards for older workers can be defended on allocational grounds as well, since the payoff to investments in rehabilitation and job training is lower for older persons who would work for only a few years under any circumstances.

Turning to the benefit structure, it incorporates the progressive benefit formula of OASI, which provides higher replacement rates for workers with lower average earnings (AIME). Auxiliary benefits to workers with eligible dependents resemble those under OASI, but they are subject to lower maximum family benefits because of greater concern over work disincentives. Workers with low earnings account for a larger share of beneficiaries under DI than under OASI, both because of the higher incidence of disability among lower-income groups and because of vocational factors in the grid that favor persons with less education and lower skill levels. This "triple tilt" is not unexpected in a social insurance program, and it serves to offset to some degree the benefits of longevity that accrue to the more affluent under both OASI and Medicare.

NOTES

1. Leonard (1986: 92) concludes that inability to observe the potential wages of persons not working or disability-related benefits forgone by persons who are working complicates estimation and explains most of the differences in results. Bound (1989) criticizes the econometric studies on methodological grounds and argues that the disincentive effects of DI are much weaker than econometric results would imply.

2. The standard reference for developments through 1977 is Derthick (1979: 295–315). Weaver (1986) describes and analyzes developments through

1984. Her discussion is enhanced by an application of basic insurance principles to disability. Derthick (1990) brings the story up to date with an analysis of the impact of the disability review controversy of 1981–84 on the DI program and the Social Security Administration.

3. Estimates at the time placed the number of terminations as high as 495,000. Derthick (1990: 211n) attributes the lower figure to the General Accounting Office and blames the inflated estimate on duplicate counting and inclusion of cases not part of the review process.

4. U.S. Department of Health and Human Services (1988: 75–87, 102–103) contains a detailed description of the DI benefit structure. For a succinct but thorough description of the entire program, see U.S. Congress, House of Representatives, Committee on Ways and Means (1991: 48–73).

5. The parallel nature of each year's disability and retirement cohorts holds with one exception. Since the benefit formula applies to a retirement cohort at age 62, newly entitled retired workers must wait until normal retirement age (currently 65) to receive the full PIA. Newly entitled disabled workers receive the PIA immediately, since they are not subject to the early retirement benefit reduction.

6. See Myers (1985: 108–110) for a description of various means of arriving at average earnings to be used in the offset.

7. The current language was introduced in a 1967 amendment intended to soften the effect of a 1960 court decision, *Kerner v. Flemming*, which required the government to prove by substantial evidence the availability of jobs the claimant is capable of performing. Current language requires only that such jobs exist in the national economy. Mashaw (1983, 188–189) casts doubt on the effectiveness of the amendment in altering the burden of proof.

8. Data on determinations and appeals appear annually in the *Green Book*. Information presented here appears in the 1991 edition (U.S. Congress, House, Committee on Ways and Means 1991: 59). Appeals data include both Title II (DI) and Title XVI (SSI) applications. Disability standards for the two programs are identical, but appeal and reversal rates may differ. Some applicants apply simultaneously for each program. Data for federal courts include appeals of both initial determinations and disability reviews, but the number of reviews appears to be small enough to have little effect on the current case load.

9. Mashaw (1983: 153–155) describes efforts to improve QA after issuance of General Accounting Office recommendations in 1978. In 1980, Congress mandated SSA review of 65 percent of all state awards, but Mashaw notes that legislators in that era saw QA more as a means of containing costs than as a means of quality control.

10. Some of the key cases applied to Supplemental Security Income (SSI), but since the statutory definition under DI and SSI is identical, the court rulings threatened terminations under both programs. Derthick (1990: 138–152) provides a detailed account of the termination debacle.

11. The DI manual (DISM) sets out time guidelines. Most initial determinations are processed within two or three months, and delays of four months elicit

inquiries from the SSA central office. SSA expedites the processing of claims that are the subject of Congressional inquiry, even though this practice disrupts the processing of other claims (Mashaw 1983: 129, 135–136).

12. Bound (1989: 486) summarizes results of the 1972 and 1978 Surveys of the Disabled, which found that between 40 and 45 percent of rejected applicants had worked in the previous years and less than one-third were employed when interviewed. More recent data on applicants rejected in 1984 show that 58 percent were not working in 1987 (U.S. Congress, House, Committee on Ways and Means 1991: 66). These studies also show that rejectees who are working earn substantially less than they had earned prior to applying for DI. The multidisciplinary teams in the 1969 Nagi study found that 67 percent of applicants were granted initial allowances and 36 percent of those receiving denials were "not fit for work" (Nagi 1969: 94).

6

Individual and Social Fairness of the Medicare Program

INTRODUCTION

Medicare, appended to the Social Security Act of 1935 in 1965, is a two-part social health insurance program for persons 65 and older and the long-term disabled. The two parts are commonly referred to as Part A, the Hospital Insurance (HI) program, and Part B, the Supplementary Medical Insurance (SMI) program. Each part covers a different dimension of acute medical care services; each is separately administered and uniquely structured and financed. Part A covers a variety of medical care services provided by hospitals, skilled nursing facilities, and home health agencies. This insurance coverage is automatically extended to all persons age 65 and older who are eligible for monthly OASI benefits and to persons younger than 65 who have been disabled for a minimum of twenty-four months or who have end-stage renal disease. HI expenditures are financed mainly by a flat-rate payroll tax assessed on a portion of earnings during working years. Persons who are age 65 and who do not qualify for monthly OASI benefits can voluntarily enroll in Part A by paying a monthly HI premium. In 1990, Medicare expenditures for inpatient services for roughly 33 million enrollees equaled $63.8 billion. Medicare Part B covers physician services, outpatient hospital services, and such ancillary services as diagnostic tests, medical supplies, and some prescription drugs. Unlike HI, SMI is financed partly by monthly premiums paid upon enrollment and partly by matching general revenue funds. All HI enrollees are eligible to purchase SMI coverage; those persons age 65 and older who are not eligible for HI but who choose to buy into HI are also required to buy SMI coverage. Medicare spending for SMI services equaled $41.2 billion for the 32 million enrollees in 1990.

Like the OASDI portions of Social Security, the intent of Medicare insurance is to protect the elderly and the long-term disabled populations from financial loss resulting from a defined event. In the case of Medicare, the defined event is temporary or acute loss of health when retired or disabled. The financial loss is potentially large medical care expenses associated with this loss of health. Experiencing impaired health may lead to an unexpected need for extensive, as well as expensive, medical care services. These unanticipated expenses may impose large financial consequences on persons suffering a health loss, especially the retired and disabled on fixed incomes. In the absence of Medicare, the earnings replacement intention of OASDI would be compromised by elders' large medical care expenses. Such expenses may leave little or no additional income to defray the costs associated with other basic necessities, such as food and housing.

Medicare insurance, however, does more than just protect financial independence. It also ensures access to the medical care system in times of impaired health. Health insurance, in general, effectively reduces the price of a defined package of medical services to encourage their use in times of medical need. An insurance-induced price reduction has two separate, though mutually reinforcing, effects. First, it dampens the ill person's sensitivity to price and encourages use of medically necessary, but expensive, medical services. It may also encourage insurance abuse, whereby the insured person overuses medical services because the effective price is less than the true market price. Safeguards, such as deductibles and coinsurance payments, are necessary to moderate "moral hazard." Second, limiting the financial liability associated with using medical care services through price reductions minimizes the variation in income and wealth over periods of changing health status. Medicare, like other health insurance plans, is best viewed as encouraging access while protecting income and wealth.

MEDICARE: SOCIAL HEALTH INSURANCE

Unlike other health insurance plans, Medicare is social health insurance; it blends principles of individual equity and social adequacy. Private health insurance is based on principles of individual equity or actuarial equivalence. Individuals can buy private insurance against the financial impact of illness at a price equal to an actuarially fair premium plus administrative overhead. An equitable assignment of premiums requires that each insured be assigned a premium that closely approximates his or her risk exposure level or average expected medical expenditures. Persons who are unable to pay the assigned premium rate are precluded from private coverage, requiring instead that they self-insure. Social insurance would not necessarily adhere to actuarial principles in the calculation or assignment of premiums or coverage. Adherence to social adequacy principles may require using funds other than premiums to defray medical claims costs for the group; it may also require assigning premiums on the basis of ability to pay, as opposed to risk exposure levels. Allocating premiums on an ability to pay principle allows for coverage to be extended to persons who are unable to pay actuarially fair premiums.

The social adequacy features of Medicare insurance can be summarized as follows: (1) *Universal coverage.* All persons 65 and older who receive OASI and persons younger than 65 who are sufficiently disabled are deemed equally financially and medically needy and as such are guaranteed equal financial access to the medical care system. No formalized need or means test is required. (2) *Uniform benefits.* All insured persons are provided access to a uniform and identical package of medical care benefits independent of income or contribution levels. (3) *Unequal contribution/premium levels.* Contributions for Hospital Insurance are differentiated among members of a retirement cohort in accordance with taxable earnings up to a ceiling, a weak measure of ability to pay. Workers with more ability to save (as indicated by higher taxable earnings) are required to pay more of the true cost of the uniform benefit package. Supplementary Medical Insurance premiums are equal for all elders, except for poor elders whose premiums are paid for by Medicaid.

Rationale for Universal and Equal Coverage

Providing universal and equal access to a social health insurance program has been explained in several ways. The first explanation focuses on the intrinsic nature of medical care services. Because medical care services have health palliative, restorative, and lifesaving qualities, they are not viewed as standard market commodities to be rationed strictly by market prices and impersonal market forces. Rather, medical care is seen as a set of services that should be extended as a basic human right to all people with a potential medical need independent of their ability to pay the market determined price. Commenting on this view, Senator Edward M. Kennedy (1972: 17) stated:

I believe good health care should be a right for all Americans. Health is so basic to man's ability to bring to fruition his opportunities as an American that each of us should guarantee the best possible health care to every American at a cost he can afford. Health care is not a luxury or an optional service we do without.

In this context, Medicare insurance guarantees access to a basic human right for a special target population who may be in peril of losing this right by virtue of retirement or disability.

Whether all persons within this target population are equally vulnerable to this loss leads to the second explanation. Implicit in the provision of equal access to Medicare is the assumption that all elderly and disabled persons have equal medical and financial need. This two-pronged assumption was reasonably defensible prior to the enactment of Medicare. In the 1950s, elders had the highest rate of illness and lowest income relative to the rest of the nation. Age and poor health are known correlates, which makes the elderly as a group a poor insurance risk. In 1960, 75 percent of the 16 million persons age 65 and over were reported to have one or more chronic illness. Elderly persons were also found to be more frequent users of short-term hospitals and nursing homes than their younger counterparts (Cohen 1963: 98–99).

Poor and deteriorating health in advancing years in combination with greater use of the health care system results in above-average health care costs for elders. Higher expected medical care costs translate into higher health insurance premiums. Paying these premiums, however, was a major problem for most elders. Prior to the introduction of Medicare, the elderly as a group were in poorer economic standing than the nation as a whole. The poverty rate of the elderly was considerably higher than for working-age Americans. For example, in 1959, the percentage of elders living in poverty was 35 percent, compared with 22 percent of the nation as a whole (Gornick et al. 1985: 31). Obtaining and maintaining meaningful medical care insurance at affordable premiums was a serious problem for poor and nonpoor elderly alike (Feder 1977: 11; Long and Settle 1984: 610–19). According to Cohen (1963: 100),

There are some 76 Blue Cross plans in the United States; 73 have offered nongroup insurance to the aged. Of the 73, 32 have premiums of over $100 a year (exclusive of physicians' coverage) per person and 15 that offer only Blue Cross-Blue Shield combination plans have premiums of over $125 per person a year. Even the $100 per person premiums amount to 10 percent or more of the median income of the nonmarried aged and almost 10 percent of median income for couples, without covering physicians' services or drugs outside of hospitals, or many other medical costs.

This financial reality may in part explain why only a minority of the elderly had meaningful hospital insurance prior to Medicare (Corning 1969: 72–73, 101–103; Harris 1969: 62). In 1962, less than 40 percent of nonworking elders had any health insurance (Marmor 1970: 19). It is important to note, however, that there were no market failures that prevented the private sector from offering comparable Medicare-like coverage at an actuarially fair premium to elders.[1] Access to this coverage was limited by the individual's ability to pay the premiums and to meet medical requirements (due to the presence of preexisting medical conditions).[2]

Contemporary Appropriateness of Universal and Equal Coverage

Although this equal presumption of need was defensible in 1965, it is becoming less so over time. Undeniably, the elderly, as a group, have an above average incidence of illness and impairment, but over time there are a higher number of elders who are generally healthy and living longer. This leads many to question whether age is a reliable indicator of medical or financial need. This questioning really raises two different issues. First, is age per se a reliable predictor of need? And, second, is age 65, in particular, the appropriate age for indicating onset of need?

Focusing on age as a predictor of medical need is based on the observed correlation between age and poor health status (Rice 1986; Rice and LaPlante 1988; Verbrugge 1984). On average, the elderly are more physically impaired than their nonaged counterparts. Being over 64, however, does not necessarily imply poor health. According to data from the 1980 National Medical Care Utilization and Expenditure Survey, roughly 60 percent of elders (1) rated their health as "excellent or good," and (2) reported having no major activity limitations (Kasper 1985). Other factors in combination with age are more likely to predict relative medical need of persons within and across age cohorts. In particular, health status has been found to vary systematically with income (Davis and Schoen 1978; Gottschalk and Wolfe 1991). People with lower incomes tend to encounter more health-related problems and have greater medical need. For example, in 1984, 44 percent of poor elders reported that they were not in good health as compared with 22 percent of elders with moderate or high incomes (Kasper 1988: 50). Functional abilities were also found to vary by income; 41 percent of elders with multiple activity in daily living limitations had annual incomes less than 150 percent of poverty in 1984, in contrast to 31 percent of all elders (Rowland 1989: 45). Focusing on ages 65 and older as an indicator of medical need tends to overlook important subgroups within the aged population who are similarly aged but dissimilarly impaired.

Today's elderly compose a heterogenous group with unequal medical needs and financial abilities. In terms of health status, this age group is more accurately conceptualized as having its own life cycle—young-old, old, old-old, frail, with needs and abilities changing with advancing age categories (Neugarten 1974). Table 6.1 shows the persistent increase in impairment with advancing age. For example, in 1982, people older than 84 were more than three times as likely to have one or more selected activities in daily living (ADL) limitations than people age 65 to 69 (6.6 percent versus 7.7 percent). The proportion of elders needing assistance from another person was also found to vary over the aged life cycle; 44 percent of persons 85 and older required assistance, compared to 7 percent of persons 65 to 74 (Rabin 1985: 36). Nearly one-fifth of people over age 84 are institutionalized, compared to only 1 percent of people age 65 to 69 (column 4, Table 6.1). The breakdown by age categories shows that different age groups have different levels of impairment (i.e., ability to care for oneself) and dependency, with differences being greatest between the age categories at either extreme of the aged life cycle.

It is even more challenging to justify universal and equal coverage beginning at age 65 on the basis of financial need. The absolute and relative economic status of the elderly has risen dramatically over the past twenty years, largely as a result of generous increases in social security benefits and pension benefits over this period (Gornick et al. 1985: 30–33; Hurd 1989: 659–661; Schultz 1988: 44–61). Between 1970 and 1987, the average income (expressed in 1983 dollars) of households headed by an elder increased by 28 percent, from $13,907 in 1970 to $17,827 in 1987. Their relative economic standing also improved over this 17-year period; the average household income for elders in 1987 was 63 percent of the average income of all households, up from 54 percent in 1970 (Hurd 1989: 659). Caution is warranted, however, in comparing income across the elderly and nonelderly groups since these summary measures are sensitive to the definition of income and household adjustment factors.[3] Adjusting for differences in household size, Hurd (1989: 660) reached the conclusion that "by 1984 the elderly were at a minimum as well off as the nonelderly, and possibly substantially better off."

Looking at poverty statistics, by 1984, 12 percent of the 27 million elders were poor as compared to 14 percent of the nation as a whole (Gornick et al. 1985: 31). This represented a 40 percent decline in poverty since 1959. It is important to note, however, that while the percentage of elders in poverty has fallen over time, there were still 3.3 million elders

Table 6.1
Estimated Percentage of Aged Persons with Functional Limitations by Age

Age	Number of Medicare aged enrollees in thousands July 1982 (1)	Percent of Medicare enrollees with ADL limitations and living in the community 1982[a] (2)	Percent of Medicare enrollees with ADL or IADL limitations and living in the community 1982[a] (3)	Percent of aged persons institution- alized 1980[b] (4)
Total	26,539.6	12.6	19.1	4.6
AGE				
65-69 years	8,652.1	7.7	12.8	1.1
70-74 years	7,021.6	9.7	15.8	2.1
75-79 years	5,063.9	13.7	21.1	4.3
80-84 years	3,284.9	19.1	27.8	9.0
85 years or over	2,617.4	26.6	34.5	18.7

a Activities of daily living (ADL) include bathing, getting in and out of bed, and so on. Instrumental activities of daily living (IADL) include shopping for groceries, housework, and so on.

b Aged persons in homes for the aged, including nursing and convalescent homes.

Source: Adapted from Marian Gornick, Jay N. Greenberg, Paul W. Eggers, and A. Dobson, "Twenty Years of Medicare and Medicaid: Covered Populations, Use of Benefits, and Program Expenditures," *Health Care Financing Review*. 1985 Annual Supplement, HCFA Pub. No. 03217, Office of Research and Demonstrations, Health Care Financing Administration (Washington, DC: U.S. Government Printing Office, 1985), Table 3, p. 22.

who were poor. These income and poverty statistics cast doubt on the stereotypical belief that all elders, measured either in relative or absolute terms, are financially vulnerable, but they are supportive evidence that some elders are financially vulnerable.

As with health status, income changes systematically across the aged life cycle. In 1984, the average real incomes of elders (adjusted to 1982 dollars and by household size), as a group was $14,160, with the averages for the 65 to 69, 70 to 74, 75 to 79, 80 to 84, and 85 plus groups equaling $16,496, $14,401, $12,617, $11,496, and $11,825, respectively (Radner 1987: 14). Note that the income of the oldest group is 28 percent less than that for the youngest. Also, as shown in Table 6.2, their poverty rates differ. In 1983, elders age 85 and older were twice as likely as elders 65 to 74 to be poor (21.3 percent versus 11.9 percent). An additional 22.4 percent of elders age 85 and older had money incomes between 100 and 149 percent

Table 6.2
Percentage of Older Persons by Ratio of Income to Poverty Level by Age Group, 1983

Ratio of income to poverty	Age of Person		
	65-74	75-84	85+
< 100%	11.9%	16.7%	21.3%
100-124%	6.7	10.6	12.7
125-149%	6.7	9.6	9.7
Total < 150%	25.3	36.9	43.7

Source: G. Lawrence Atkins, "The Economic Status of the Oldest Old," *Milbank Memorial Fund Quarterly* 63, no. 2 (1985), p. 399. Reprinted with permission of the author and the *Milbank Quarterly*.

of the poverty level as compared to an additional 13.4 percent of elders age 65 to 74 (Atkins 1985: 399). Economic vulnerability appears to increase with advancing age, with the old-old being at greatest risk of financial need. Hurd (1989: 660) notes that "one would expect the oldest to have the highest poverty rates because they have lived beyond their life expectancies; thus, they have had to spread their lifetime economic resources over more years."

Uniform Benefits and Unequal Contributions

Despite the health and economic advancements made by elders over the past twenty years, and thus their changing age-based needs, the basic design of Medicare has remained largely unchanged. The benefit structure, target population definition, and financing mechanism reflect the normative belief that access to medicare care services is a basic human right; they also reflect the positive assumption that elderly and disabled persons are equally vulnerable to losing this basic right due to their shared financial and health vulnerabilities. To this end, social adequacy principles have been uniformly and persistently substituted for traditional actuarial principles of insurance. For the most part, the benefit provisions under Medicare are similar to those offered by private insurance (Feder 1977: 2–3). For example, Aetna Insurance Company's health insurance plan for federal employees was used in designing SMI (Marmor 1970: 67). Not until the methods used to finance medical care liabilities and to assign premiums are examined does the fundamental difference between social and private insurance become apparent.

An actuarially fair, private health insurance plan would spread the total expected medical care costs plus administrative load charges across the members composing the insurance pool (in the case of Medicare, a retirement cohort). Premiums would be assigned to each subgroup of the insurance group in accordance with the subgroup's expected average medical expenditures. Uniform premiums would be assigned only if all members of the insurance pool had equal expected average expenses. In cases in which subgroups have different risk exposures, premiums would differ across subgroups and would reflect each subgroup's risk exposure level. For example, groups of high expense users in the pool would be charged higher than average premiums, and the opposite would hold for groups with low expenses.

Medicare insurance is based on a different financing and premium assignment structure. First, the ex ante expected medical care expenditures for a given retirement cohort are not fully funded by the premium payments made by the members of a retirement cohort. Medicare relies on pay-as-you-go financing. This transfers resources from the current working population to cover the medical care expenses incurred (but not fully financed) by nonworking elderly and disabled populations. In fact, the phase-in retirement cohort (1966) did not pay any HI contributions prior to enrollment in HI. All the Medicare-covered medical expenses over the life of this retirement cohort were externally financed by the current working population. Second, for that portion of benefits internally financed by members of a retirement cohort, contributions for HI and premiums for SMI are unrelated to the risk exposure experience of those members. Taxable earnings levels, number of elapsed years, and HI tax rate determine mandatory payroll contributions paid for HI benefits. No additional contributions are assessed in persons who receive derivative HI benefits as dependent spouses and survivors. A uniform ("one-price-for-all") SMI premium is assessed on persons enrolled in SMI. SMI premiums are set to cover one quarter of the expected expenditures of persons age 65 or older. No further adjustment is made to account for systematic differences in expected claims payments or ability to pay.

INSURANCE FRAMEWORK

Individual principles require that each person in a retirement cohort be charged a premium that closely reflects his or her likelihood of loss—expected medical care claims payments arising from illness. In the remainder of this chapter, principles of individual equity will be developed and used to evaluate the performance of Medicare insurance in terms of individual equity and social adequacy. Because HI and SMI are not earnings-based programs, the Leimer et al. (1978) earnings-based equity framework developed in Chapter 3 cannot be used. Instead, an alternative "community rating" insurance-transfer framework developed by Vogel (1988) will be modified and used to evaluate treatment of equals and unequals within and across retirement cohorts. This framework will also permit an examination of intra- and intercohort redistribution within Medicare.

Health insurance protects an individual against large medical care costs. How much to charge an individual for this protection depends on several factors, including the size and characteristics of the insurance pool, the nature of the insurable event, and the amount and nature of benefit provisions. These factors are discussed in advance of the discussion of the determination and assignment of actuarially fair premiums for health insurance.

Insurance Pool. Through insurance pools, unrelated persons consolidate resources to share the costs related to a defined, but uncertain and potentially costly, event. Health insurance pools allow a large number of people to spread illness risks so that they can reduce expected costs associated with illness to an amount equal to the premium plus any cost sharing. Insurance pools need to be sufficiently large and representative. The larger the pool, the better the actuarial prediction of total medical care cost for the members of the pool. Large numbers ensure the functioning of the law of averages. It is also necessary to have a pool that is representative of reasonable expected medical care costs. Voluntary enrollment into an insurance pool allows for the possibility of adverse selection—too many high-risk persons buying insurance and driving up costs. To avoid adverse selection in voluntary insurance plans, all members of the group may be subjected to a preliminary physical examination. Alternatively, the group may be experience rated so that adverse selection leads to higher subsequent premiums.

Insurable Event. An ideal insurable event can be described as follows: The event occurs at a predictable rate in the aggregate, but at a relatively low and random rate for any one person (the probability of occurrence is close to zero) in the pool. It is associated with high monetary costs. The best examples of such events are fire, theft, and natural disasters. Medical care costs associated with impaired health are not ideal insurable events for several reasons. First, use of medical care services is not an unlikely event; in fact, such an event, on average, is very likely to happen *multiple* times to an individual over the course of a year. For example, in 1989, persons age 65 and older contacted a physician an average of 8.9 times and visited a physician roughly 5 times (National Center for Health Statistics 1991: 137). These types of events are "assured" to occur. In the British system, assurance is distinguished from insurance, where the former pertains to events that will occur and the latter pertains to events that are not likely to ever occur (*Encyclopedia Britannica* 1970: 337).

Compounding this is the nonrandomness of the probabilities of occurrence for an individual. Although illness is a random event, the use of medical care services does not occur at a random rate. Individuals and their medical care agents can and do influence the rate or probability of medical care use during the course of the year. Current and future medical care expenditures are likely to be related to personal, clinical, and economic factors that influence the demand for care, such as age, gender, race, diagnosis, prior use and health status, help-seeking attitudes and preferences, income, and prices. Also, the level of demand for medical care services will be influenced by the structure of health insurance—the service coverage definition and cost-sharing provisions. Nonrandom variation in medical care utilization introduces the need for risk classification and experience rating of premiums to reflect the systematic differences in medical care utilization patterns within the insurance pool. It also provides a rationale for the imposition of cost sharing and peer review safeguards to constrain the individual's (and his or her agent's) control over the probability of the event occurring.

Policies designed to control moral hazard (i.e, use of a larger amount of medical care services as a result of having insurance and, hence, not having to pay fully for individual services) discourage the use of costly services by constructing a financial barrier (higher prices) to health care. The effect of cost sharing on the demand for health care services has been studied extensively over the past twenty years (Acton 1976; Keeler et al. 1988a, 1988b; Manning et al. 1987; Newhouse 1981; Phelps and Newhouse 1974). Empirical evidence shows that use of health care is price responsive; that is, an increase in the price of services (say, an increase in the coinsurance amount) paid by the consumer will decrease the use of health care services. According to the Rand Health Insurance Experiment, increasing cost sharing from 0 to 25 percent reduced the use of services by roughly 20 percent (for an under-65 population) (Manning et al. 1987: 267–269).

Most insurable events are associated with high unexpected costs. In the absence of insurance, these costs would impose large financial losses on the majority of unlucky persons experiencing the peril. Whether medical care costs associated with a health loss meet this condition depends on how broadly or narrowly medical care services are defined, since medical care services vary in their relative costliness. Health losses requiring medical care provided in an institutional setting would most likely qualify as a high-cost event. An inpatient day in a community hospital cost, on average, $586.33 in 1988, varying between $360 per day in South Dakota and $961 in Alaska (Health Insurance Association of America 1990: 51). The average length of stay in 1988 for persons 65 and older was 8.9 days (National Center for Health Statistics 1991: 142). In contrast, physician and ancillary services are relatively low-cost services but are used frequently; hence, the total cost of such services is likely to be high. It is unlikely that most users of these services would be financially devastated if they were required to pay the full market price associated for some of these types of services. However, the total costs for these kinds of medical services are unpredictable, and few households have sufficient savings to finance all such costs. On average, with Medicare and supplement insurance policies, the elderly spent 18.2 percent of their income on health care and health insurance premiums in 1988 (U.S. Congress, House Select Committee on Aging 1990: 24).

Benefit Coverage. Insurers limit their financial liability by prespecifying the losses they are willing to cover if the event occurs. Total financial liability depends on the multiplicative relationship between the quantity of services covered and the prices charged for the services for a time period, such as a year. In the case of health insurance, insurers limit financial liability by confining coverage to certain types of medical care services and restricting the average and total payment amount for these services. For example, preventive, experimental, custodial, and/or cosmetic medical services may be excluded from coverage. Average prices paid for services rendered may reflect provider costs, charges, or some other reimbursement method. Because chronic or severe illnesses may require medical services over an extended period of time, insurers may try to close the back end of coverage by stipulating maximum limits. Maximum coverage may be specified in dollars or days covered.

Determination and Assignment of Premiums. Insurers set premiums such that the sum of premiums assigned to all members of the insurance pool will cover total expected medical care expenditures for the pool plus administrative load charges. Notationally, the total costs for the insurer (which, by definition, also equals the total value of health insurance received by the insureds) are

$$TV = \sum_{j=1}^{m} \sum_{i=1}^{n_j} \sum_{g=1}^{X} P_{gij} \, Q_{gij} + A$$

$$(6.1)$$

where the price and quantity of $g, \ldots, x$ medical care services received by individuals $i, \ldots, n$ in $j, \ldots, m$ experience-rated subgroups in the insurance pool are represented by P_{gij} and Q_{gij}, respectively, and A is the administrative load charge (plus profit for for-profit insurers). At the time of purchase, the actuarial value of the expected medical benefits to any member in an experience group is TV_j/n_j. Each insured is assigned a premium equal to the average medical care costs for those comprising the experience group. Actuarially fair insurance does not redistribute income ex ante; it does, however, redistribute income ex post. Over a defined time period, income is transferred from those insureds who did not experience a health loss to those who did.

Clearly, the total value of the health insurance is positively related to the comprehensiveness of the benefits covered and prices paid by the insurer and the utilization and illness patterns of individuals within the insurance pool. Insurers can influence total expenditures by carefully screening persons accepted into the pool and by stipulating to providers what services will be covered and at what rate. But once the insurance pool and benefit structure are defined, insurer expenditures are insured and provider driven. That is, insurers can provide guidelines on covered services and specify reimbursement arrangements, but ultimately expenditures depend on the incidence of illness, the help-seeking practices of insureds, and clinical practice patterns of providers.

Definition of Horizontal and Vertical Equals

Central to the evaluation of the distribution impact of the Medicare program is defining what is meant by equal and unequal treatment of individuals and establishing principles of equity. Within the context of health insurance, equals and unequals are defined by risk exposure levels. Unequals are those persons who have different expected average medical expenditures. Persons with unequal risk exposures are assigned unequal but actuarially fair premiums. Individuals who have the same expected average medical care expenditures, reflecting the combined effect of their illness distributions and help-seeking practices, are risk exposure equals and as such would be assigned equal insurance premiums. The principles of equity used herein are horizontal and vertical equity. Horizontal equity pertains to the equal treatment of equals, whereas vertical equity focuses on the unequal treatment of unequals.

Uniform premiums are charged within an insurance pool only if the variation in medical care expenditures is purely random. Community rating is appropriate when all individuals in an insurance pool have identical ex ante expectations and likelihoods of experiencing the expected loss. In this case, a set of benefits is offered at a uniform rate to all individuals.

When the variation in expected medical expenditures is nonrandom, charging different premiums to individuals in an insurance pool is fully consistent with principles of insurance and individual equity. Nonrandom variation may be a result of systematic differences in illness patterns, use of medical care services, and/or expenditures. Insurers use experience rating to rank and then subset individuals according to expected average medical care expenditures. The success of experience rating for tailoring premiums to risk exposures depends on the quality of actuarial prediction. The challenge with experience rating is to find meaningful correlates for predicting future medical expenditures. Future medical expenditures may be related to age, gender, race, diagnosis, prior spending history, income, and occupation, as well as other identifiable characteristics. Some of these correlates may not be politically or legally permissible discriminators. Moreover, consumer preferences may play an important role in determining the utilization of medical care. Identifying the appropriate and reasonable correlates for subjective preferences is even more challenging and speculative.

MEDICARE PAYMENT AND BENEFIT STRUCTURE

Each part of Medicare insurance will be described using the four features of insurance discussed above: insurance pool, insurable event, benefit coverage, and determination of premiums and assignment of premiums. Following the descriptive discussion of HI and SMI, a stylistic model of each program based on the framework developed by Vogel (1988) will be presented. Issues of equity and adequacy will be examined within an insurance-transfer framework in the following section. Empirical evidence is presented at the end of this section.

Hospital Insurance (HI)

Insurance Pool. Three distinct groups are targeted for inclusion in the HI insurance pool: persons age 65 and older, persons under 65 who are disabled, and persons under 65 with end-stage renal disease. Each person within a targeted group must satisfy entitlement criteria to be eligible for inclusion. In contrast to private insurance, Medicare does not require a physical examination, nor does it exclude persons with preexisting conditions.

The largest target group is persons age 65 and older. Any person 65 or older who is entitled to monthly OASI benefits is automatically enrolled in the HI insurance pool. This would include persons collecting worker, dependent spouse, and survivors' benefits. Persons 65 or older who are ineligible for monthly OASI benefits because their earnings credits were insufficient to qualify them are eligible for HI under transitional provisions. Two groups are excluded from coverage under the transitional provisions: retired federal employees and aliens with less than five consecutive years of permanent residence. With the 1972 amendments, ineligible persons age 65 or older (except aliens) can voluntarily enroll in HI provided they pay a monthly premium, equal to $177 in 1991, and enroll in SMI. In 1990, 30 million persons 65 or older, equaling roughly 95 percent of all persons 65 and older, were covered by HI. Approximately 90 percent of Medicare enrollees are age 65 or older. Because of the nearly universal coverage of persons 65 or older, adverse selection problems that plague private health insurers do not exist for Medicare.

The 1972 amendments extended HI coverage to the two other target groups whose members are disabled and younger than age 65. The second target group includes the long-term disabled. To qualify as having a long-term disability, a person must have received disability payments from the social security or railroad retirement program for a total of 24 months. Derivative HI coverage is not extended to a disabled person's spouse or children. The third target group includes persons diagnosed with end-stage renal disease. Persons with end-stage renal disease who have sufficient quarters of coverage to meet insured status, or who are entitled to monthly OASDI or railroad benefits, or who are the spouse or child of an insured worker or beneficiary are eligible for HI coverage. Approximately 3 million persons with disabilities were enrolled in HI in 1990.

Insurable Event. Hospital insurance protects against a health loss requiring the use of expensive hospital, nursing home, or home health care services. This defined event is insurable; it is a high-cost event with a relatively low, but predictable, probability of occurrence. It is not an ideal insurable event, however, since the rate of occurrence is not purely random. Use of institutional services can be influenced by the joint preferences of the insured and his or her agent, the physician. Physician behavior and incentives, in particular, are likely to influence the rate of the insured event since physicians admit patients into hospitals and nursing homes (Wennberg et al. 1982; Chassin et al. 1986).

Nonrandom, physician-induced variation in the rate of loss can be controlled by monitoring the admission and treatment decisions of physicians. Medicare has introduced two methods for monitoring physician decision making. The first method is to pay for a second doctor's opinion in cases of surgery. Due both to the cost and risk of unnecessary surgery, Medicare has agreed to cover (under SMI) the additional cost of a second doctor's opinion. Because there is for many diagnoses considerable latitude in identifying preferred treatment, second opinions may eliminate some unnecessary and expensive treatments. Medicare Second Opinion Referral Center is available to provide information to beneficiaries on local doctors who provide second opinions.

The second method involves peer review after medical care has been delivered. Medicare will pay only for care that is considered reasonable and necessary according to standards accepted by the medical profession and provided in the most appropriate care setting. Created in 1982, Peer Review Organizations (PROs), composed of practicing physicians and other health care professionals, are impaneled at the state level but at the federal government's expense. They review the hospital care received by Medicare patients. PROs, upon review of a case, can deny Medicare payment for services rendered if the care provided was deemed not medically necessary, not delivered in the most appropriate setting, or not meeting approved standards of quality. Most of this review is retrospective. But PROs are increasingly incorporating review procedures that operate before care is provided. These are often referred to as "prior authorization" requirements.

Benefit Coverage. Medicare covers the standard set of services provided by inpatient institutions, including semiprivate room with meals, operating room, regular nursing and rehabilitative services, laboratory and X-ray tests, medication, medical supplies, and use of medical appliances. According to the most recent legislation, Medicare covers 90 days of inpatient hospitalization for each benefit period (i.e., hospital stay or illness episode). Additional hospital days thereafter are subtracted from the individual's "lifetime reserve" of 60 additional hospital days. The first 60 days of hospitalization are fully paid by Medicare after the individual has paid the hospital deductible per benefit period, equal to $628 in 1991. A daily coinsurance amount equal to 25 percent of the benefit period deductible, or $157 in 1991, is assessed on each of the next 30 days of care. Each additional hospital day after 90 days is subtracted from the person's 60-day lifetime reserve, with a coinsurance amount of 50 percent of the benefit period deductible, or $314. Medicare coverage ceases for hospital stays in excess of 90 days plus the lifetime reserve balance—full financial responsibility for hospital care shifts back to the elder. In addition to inpatient treatment in "participating" hospitals, HI coverage extends to inpatient tuberculosis care, inpatient psychiatric hospitalization (190-day lifetime limit, although no limit applies to mental health treatment received in general hospitals), and emergency inpatient care in a nonparticipating hospital.

The HI program also partially covers inpatient care provided in skilled nursing homes.[4] Skilled nursing care coverage is designed for hospital patients who no longer need the full complement of hospital services but who still need constant skilled nursing or rehabilitative services. Medicare covers 100 days of skilled nursing care per benefit period for persons who have at least 3 consecutive days of "medically necessary" hospital care. Services delivered must be prescribed by a physician and deemed appropriate for the treatment of the patient's medical condition. The first twenty days of nursing home care are fully paid by Medicare; cost sharing begins on the twenty-first day of care, when the coinsurance amount becomes one-eighth of the hospital deductible for each of the next eighty days, equaling $78.50 in 1991. Skilled nursing homes are reimbursed on a reasonable-cost basis.

Medicare coverage was expanded to include extended-care home health and hospice care services in the early 1980s. Beginning July 1, 1980, Medicare paid for health care visits provided by Medicare-approved home health agencies to beneficiaries who meet three conditions: (1) they are homebound due to medical problems, (2) they require part-time or recurrent skilled nursing care as physical or speech therapy, and (3) they are under a physician's care and prescribed plan. Services covered include medical social services; physical, occupational, and speech therapy; intermittent services of nurses and home health aides; medical supplies; and durable medical equipment. Current legislation provides coverage for unlimited "intermittent" home health visits with no coinsurance or deductibles. Patients must pay 20 percent of the reasonable cost of durable medical equipment.

The Tax Equity and Fiscal Responsibility Act (TEFRA) enacted in 1982 established Medicare certification and coverage of hospice care. Medicare covers a lifetime maximum of 210 days of comprehensive hospice care (in lieu of other hospital services) for terminally ill beneficiaries (with life expectancies less than six months) who could receive all necessary medical and support services outside of a hospital setting. Care can be extended past the 210 day limit if the patient is certified as terminally ill by a physician or hospital director. Only care provided in Medicare-certified hospice programs is reimbursed by Medicare. Hospice care is not subject to deductibles or coinsurance, although a 5 percent cost sharing for inpatient respite care and a $5 maximum fee on outpatient pain medication are imposed.

Services not covered by HI include custodial care, homemaker services, long-term care, personal convenience services (e.g., telephones or televisions in rooms), private duty nurses, private rooms, and services that are not reasonable and necessary under Medicare program standards.

Medicare uses several methods for controlling the costs associated with covering the above package of benefits. One the demand side, deductibles, coinsurance, and premiums can be raised to increase the elderly's share of health care cost burden in an effort to encourage more judicious use of covered medical services. For example, the Omnibus Budget Reconciliation Act enacted in 1981 included a 12 percent increase in the Part A deductible. Moral hazard (i.e., the overuse of covered services resulting from generous insurance coverage) is moderated by the use of coinsurance and deductibles.

Congress also attempted to control escalating health care costs in the 1980s through a series of cost-saving legislation targeted at reimbursement charges for hospitals. Until October 1983, Medicare reimbursed hospitals on a retrospective "reasonable" cost basis. Under cost-based reimbursement, hospitals were reimbursed according to the actual costs incurred in providing covered services to Medicare patients. This method of reimbursement provides an incentive for the hospital to hospitalize patients longer and to provide more covered services and tests since days and services were paid for separately.

Major reimbursement changes designed to control Medicare expenditures for inpatient hospital services were mandated with the enactment of the TEFRA of 1982. Effective October 1983, Medicare replaced cost-based reimbursement by a prospective payment system (PPS). Under PPS, hospitals are paid a preestablished fixed amount for hospitalized acute care patients in 468 diagnosis-related groups, or DRGs. These fixed prices reflect average hospital costs with adjustments for wages, teaching intensity, proportion of indigent care, and rural versus urban location. Hospitals have the financial incentive under PPS to (1) reduce the patient's length of stay, (2) alter the mix and intensity of services used to treat the patient, (3) increase the number of new admissions, and (4) expand hospital services to include those services not covered by the new system (e.g., psychiatric care, home health, and alcoholism treatment). Hospitals, under the new system, profit by shortening the length of stay for Medicare patients and omitting or reducing the services received during a hospital stay. If the patient's treatment costs less than the preset rate for his or her particular diagnosis, the hospital retains the savings; if the patient's treatment costs more than the preset rate, the hospital absorbs the loss.

Fears of deteriorating hospital care for elders under the new payment incentive system led to the introduction of PROs.

The prospective payment system has affected hospital behavior and costs. The average length of stay for a Medicare patient decreased 9 percent per year between 1983 (pre-PPS) and 1984 (post-PPS), from 10.0 days in 1983 to 9.1 days in 1984, roughly one full day of care in the course of one year (Guterman and Dobson 1986: 103). This trend continued until 1985, but has stabilized since then (Latta and Keene 1990: 91); the average length of stay for a Medicare patient decreased from 9.1 days in fiscal year 1984 to 8.4 days in fiscal year 1985, about an 8 percent decline (Moon 1988: 382). Although the sharp decline in length of stay for elderly patients is consistent with the PPS incentive structure, not all of the observed decline can be attributed to PPS. Historically, hospital stays have become shorter, although not at the rate observed since the introduction of PPS (Russell 1989: 24–35). Admission rates were also expected to increase under PPS; however, the reverse has been observed. Aged admissions per 1,000 increased by approximately 2 percent from 1982 to 1984, but declined by at least 2 percent in each of the next three years (Guterman and Dobson 1986: 103). This has been attributed to a shift in services from hospital to outpatient settings (Russell (1989: 83–84). Both the decline in the length of stay and in the admission rate contributed to slowing the growth in Medicare expenditures on hospital care. Real costs for hospital care under Medicare in 1984 grew at half the 1983 rate and at one-third the rate between 1975 and 1982 (Guterman and Dobson 1986: 111–12).

The prospective payment system has slowed the growth of inpatient payments to hospitals, in part by shifting care (and hence costs) to outpatient treatment covered largely by SMI (Russell 1989: 72–74) and to families (Moon 1988). The PPS encourages earlier discharge from the hospital, but not earlier recovery from an ailment. Accordingly, patients are sent home with a new problem: finding needed health and support care outside the hospital setting. Medicare does cover posthospital care provided by nursing homes and home health care agencies, but often these services are not available or are inadequate. Patients, as a consequence, are sent into the "no-care zone," relying on privately financed formal care or informal care provided by family and friends, or simply doing without any additional care. Moon (1988: 330–331) estimates the cost burden of privately financed formal and informal care due to premature hospital discharge at $400 million in 1985.

Determination and Assignment of Premiums. HI is not financed by premiums but by compulsory tax contributions paid during working years.

Until 1991, tax treatment under HI was identical to treatment under the OASDI program. An HI tax is assessed on a worker's earnings up to a maximum taxable amount (equal to $51,300), with an equal tax amount matched by employers (except for self-employed who pay the combined employee and employer portions). Beginning in 1991, the HI payroll tax will have a different maximum taxable level from OASDI. The maximum level increased to $125,000 in 1991. In 1991, the HI tax rate for both employee and employer was 1.45 percent. Beginning in 1984, the self-employed person was required to pay both the employer and employee portion of the HI tax, equaling 2.9 percent in 1991. All HI contributions are credited to the HI Trust Fund, which by law may be used only to defray the insurance benefit and administrative costs of the HI program. Premiums are paid only by ineligible persons 65 or older who voluntarily enroll into the program. In 1991, the monthly HI premium was $177.

The HI financing mechanism has workers contributing toward their hospital insurance during their working years, when they are best able to afford insurance contributions. That is, in principle, workers are spreading the cost of hospital insurance over their 40 years plus working lifetimes, so that only modest worker contributions (in the form of deductibles and coinsurance) would be required after retirement. Although this financing mechanism does provide the worker with the opportunity to spread costs over a long period of time, it cannot be justified on either individual equity or social adequacy grounds. A flat-rate tax on capped earnings implies that workers with unequal earnings profiles pay unequal prices for an equal benefit package upon retirement. In essence, the "price" for HI coverage is equal to the present value of the worker's HI tax contributions. Because these different prices are not related to risk exposure, they cannot be justified on individual equity grounds. Social adequacy principles would require that a greater tax burden be assessed on those with a greater ability to pay. But a ceiling on payroll tax contributions (even a ceiling higher than that used in OASDI) limits the extent to which this principle is employed.

Supplementary Medical Insurance

Insurance Pool. All persons in the HI insurance pool are eligible to enroll voluntarily in the Supplementary Medical Insurance (SMI) program. Participation in SMI is optional, but nearly universal because of the large general fund subsidy. Roughly 98 percent of those with HI insurance also enroll in SMI. Enrollment is conditional on payment of monthly premiums. Persons can enroll in SMI without penalty within a seven-month period surrounding their sixty-fifth birthday. For those who delay enrollment after the seven-month period, their premium rate is increased by 10 percent for each full year of delay. To guard against adverse selection, persons electing to delay enrollment in SMI past the seven-month period must wait to enroll during a general enrollment period. A general enrollment period is held annually from January 1 to March 31. Coverage is effective the following July 1.

A frequent criticism of the SMI financing scheme is that the plan's premium costs are overly burdensome for the near-poor aged. The combined annual cost of participating in the SMI program in 1991 was $459, equaling the sum of the $100 annual deductible and the $359 annual premium. In 1988, for the near poor living alone (mean income of $7,092), the SMI deductible and premium charges (exclusive of coinsurance) took approximately 5.3 percent of their disposable income. The financial burden of the SMI program for the poor was eliminated effective January 1, 1989, with the mandatory Medicaid buy-in provision. States, through their Medicaid programs, are mandated to pay the premiums, deductibles, and coinsurance for eligible persons who can demonstrate financial need. Medicaid "buy-in"— agreements are jointly financed by state and federal governments through a federal matching fund arrangement.

Insurable Event. Physician and ancillary medical care services are far from ideal insurable events. Although the aggregate use rate may be predictable, the rate of use for any individual is neither low nor random, and the associated costs are unlikely to have catastrophic financial consequences on a nonpoor person experiencing the loss. Use of outpatient services is particularly sensitive to the help-seeking choices made by insureds. Large reductions in the price of these services may also lead to excessive use. To avoid moral hazard behavior, deductibles and coinsurance are imposed on services covered by Medicare. Also, Medicare guarantees payment for only services that are reasonable and necessary for the diagnosis or treatment of illness or injury.

Benefit Coverage. SMI covers certain physician services in hospital, skilled nursing facility, office, and home settings; outpatient mental health services; ambulatory surgical services; optometrists' services; outpatient physical and occupation therapy; outpatient rehabilitation facility services; outpatient hospital services; limited dental services; home health services; and such other medical services as diagnostic tests, ambulance services, some prescription drugs, and medical supplies. SMI does not cover routine physical examinations, eye or hearing examinations, most immunizations, cosmetic surgery, routine foot care, preventive or routine dental care, eyeglasses, most prescription medications, or custodial care.

Services covered in Part B are subject to deductible and coinsurance provisions. For each year, beneficiaries are required to pay the first $100 of the costs of services covered by SMI and 20 percent of each approved Medicare (or "allowable") charge for covered services thereafter. Cost-sharing arrangements are different for mental health services (Lave and Goldman 1990). Costs related to the treatment of Alzheimer's disease and physician services associated with the "prescribing, monitoring, and changing of prescriptions" are subject to a 20 percent coinsurance payment. All other covered mental health services provided by physicians, psychologists, and social workers are subject to a 50 percent coinsurance payment.

Medicare pays 80 percent of "reasonable costs" for covered services. Medicare beneficiaries are required to pay more than the 20 percent coinsurance amount if their physician does not accept the Medicare-approved charge as payment in full. If the beneficiary's physician does not accept the Medicare allowable charge as full payment for services rendered, then the beneficiary must pay 20 percent of the allowable charge plus the "balance bill," that is, the difference between the physician's charge and the allowable charge. Physician charges are estimated to exceed Medicare-approved charges by approximately 25 percent (Moon 1988: 323).

Medicare supplemental insurance purchased in the private sector, more commonly known as "medigap" insurance, is typically purchased by the elderly to offset the financial burden of coinsurance, deductibles, and services not covered by Medicare. Medigap insurance has been purchased by an ever-growing number of elderly persons since the introduction of Medicare. In 1967, an estimated 46.7 percent of Medicare beneficiaries had supplemental private insurance (Mueller 1972: 10). Currently, more than 70 percent of Medicare beneficiaries have medigap coverage despite load charges (i.e., administrative costs) of 40 to 50 percent (Lave 1988: 12). The purchase of medigap policies has been found to be related to age, income, education, and health status (Long and Settle 1982; Phelps and Reisinger 1988: 134–36; Rice and McCall 1985). For example, elders with annual incomes of $25,000 are twice as likely as elders with annual incomes of $5,000 to purchase medigap insurance (Gordon 1986)., This is not too surprising since annual premiums for medigap policies in 1984 averaged $300 to $400 per elder (Blumenthal 1988b: 28). Overall, in 1984, approximately 30 percent of Medicare beneficiaries with incomes less than $8,999 were without Medicaid or medigap coverage, contrasted with 10 percent of those whose incomes exceeded $24,999 (Blumenthal 1988b: 29).

In recent years, employers have also provided tax-subsidized medigap coverage for retired employees. TEFRA of 1982 required employers to offer insurance benefits to working Medicare beneficiaries age 65 to 69 comparable to those offered younger workers. In addition, TEFRA made Medicare the secondary payer for workers with dual Medicare and employer insurance. That is, beginning in 1983, employer-sponsored health insurance plans were the primary payers for beneficiaries over age 65 who continued to work. Making Medicare the second payer for older workers shifted Medicare covered costs to employers. This is yet another example of an instrument used by Congress to control Medicare costs by shifting them to another payer. In 1983, approximately 31 percent of (worker and retired) Medicare beneficiaries had employer-sponsored insurance, although coverage has been found to vary with age, sex, race, and income (Farley Short and Monheit 1988: 308–314). Employer-sponsored supplemental plans have been found to be more generous than individual plans marketed by insurance companies at comparable prices (Cafferata 1984).

Additional insurance coverage provided by medigap policies tends to undermine Medicare's efforts to offset moral hazard. Elderly with no supplemental insurance have been found to consume less health care and pay fewer out-of-pocket expenses than their counterparts with supplemental insurance (Garfinkel and Corder 1985: Kasper 1986). For example, on average, a Medicare beneficiary with supplemental insurance incurs $1,818 in health care expenses per year, compared to $1,087 for a Medicare beneficiary without additional medigap insurance, a difference of $731. Part of this difference reflects increased Medicare costs. Per capita Medicare expenses were $988 and $729, respectively, for a Medicare beneficiary with and without medigap insurance. Despite their supplementary insurance, those with medigap policies also had higher out-of-pocket costs; Medicare beneficiaries with medigap coverage paid $363 out of pocket compared to $318 by the Medicare beneficiary without additional coverage (Garfinkel and Corder 1985). Supplemental insurance protection thus increased the per capita total health care cost by 67 percent, costs incurred by Medicare by 35 percent, and the out-of-pocket costs incurred by the individual by 14 percent.

In recent years, Medicare reimbursement for doctors had been sky-rocketing at double-digit rates. Medicare expenditures on physician services per enrollee grew at a compound annual rate of 16 percent per year between 1975 and 1990 (U.S. GAO 1991: 4). Total Medicare spending for physician services is expected to exceed $33 billion in 1991. SMI is the fastest-growing segment of the Medicare program. At present, Medicare uses historical patterns of "customary, prevailing, and reasonable" screens to determine Medicare physician payments. "Allowable charges" under Medicare are the lesser of (1) physician's submitted charge, or "the billed amount"; (2) the physician's "customary charge," defined as the physician's median charge for a specific service in the previous year; or (3) the "prevailing charge" equaling the seventy-fifth percentile of charges for all physicians for that service in a given geographical area. This method of reimbursement has been criticized for perpetuating fee and volume inflation and payment differences among physician specialties and across geographic areas (Blumenthal and Hsiao 1988; Yett et al. 1985).

Congress attempted to control physician prices in several ways in recent years. The Deficit Reduction Act of 1984 mandated a freeze on the "customary, prevailing, and reasonable" payments to physicians at the 1984 levels beginning July 1, 1984, and ending in May 1986 for participating physicians, and in January 1987 for nonparticipating physicians (Physician Payment Review Commission 1987). In addition to freezing physician reimbursement, the freeze legislation provided incentives for physicians to accept the Medicare-approved rate as the full payment for services provided. Recall that physicians may, on a claim-by-claim basis, choose to accept the Medicare allowable charge as full payment for services rendered, or they may bill Medicare patients for the entire amount, including that in excess of the Medicare allowable charge. The freeze legislation modified the definition of "participating physician." Under the new definition, participating physicians were required to sign a Medicare participation agreement in which they agree to accept assignment on all services for all Medicare patients (as distinguished from the earlier claim-by-claim basis). In exchange for agreeing to accept assignment, participating physicians were ensured future fee updating at the end of the freeze. More specifically, the fee freeze was lifted earlier for participating physicians, and Health Care Financing Administration (HCFA) permitted smaller rates of increase in charges for nonparticipating physicians than for participating physicians after the freeze. Indeed, these incentives precipitated a substantial increase in participating physicians; the assignment rate increased from 51 percent in 1983 to 67 percent in 1985 (Holohan and Zuckerman 1989: 68–69) and increased to 77 percent in 1988 (Helbing et al. 1991: 115).

A new physician payment system was introduced with the passing of the Omnibus Budget Reconciliation Act (OBRA) of 1989. The new system assigns physician fees according to a resource-based relative value scale. The new payment system evaluates the relative value of different health services on the basis of the resources the doctor provides to those services (Hsiao et al. 1988; Ginsburg, 1989; Ginsburg et al. 1990). Resources measured in the new fee system include the physician's time, mental effort, technical skills and stress involved in performing a health service, the costs of maintaining a practice (inclusive of office rent, salaries, equipment, and supplies), and medical malpractice costs. The new payment scheme will be phased in over five years beginning in January 1992. This fee system is expected to reallocate Medicare payments among physicians by service, specialty (e.g., decrease Medicare payments to surgeons but increase payments to internists), and geographic area, but not control the rapid growth in physician costs. Target expenditure limits were also included in this legislation to control the level of physician spending over time.

As mentioned above, Medicare provided a series of financial incentives in the Deficit Reduction Act of 1984 to encourage physicians to accept Medicare patients on assignment. OBRA of 1989 introduced yet another effort to limit physicians who do not accept assignment; this time charge limits were imposed. Congress stipulated the following absolute charge limits for nonparticipating physicians: the upper bound allowable charge on physician fees cannot exceed 125 percent, 120 percent, and 115 percent of the Medicare approved rates in 1991, 1992, and 1993, respectively.

Determination and Assignment of Premiums. SMI is not paid for during the worker's working lifetime. Beginning at age 65 (for disabled person, at time of entitlement to HI), a person may voluntarily participate in the SMI program by paying an annually adjusted monthly premium. Uniform monthly premiums are set annually so as to generate income to cover 25 percent of SMI costs. The remainder is subsidized by the federal government out of general revenues. States are required to pay the premiums (as well as deductibles and coinsurance) for persons eligible for Medicare whose incomes are less than 100 percent of the federal poverty level and assets are less than twice the supplement security income level, beginning January 1, 1991. OBRA of 1990 requires states to pay the SMI premiums for persons with incomes of 110 percent or less of poverty in 1993 and 1994 and 120 percent or less of poverty beginning in 1995.

Until 1974, the federal funds match rate was 1:1, with the annual premiums ranging from $36.00 in 1966 to $80.40 in 1974. Because of escalating health care costs and the concern that the financial burden of SMI premiums on the aged was excessive, the federal government assumed a larger fraction of the premium beginning in 1975—increasing the subsidy in excess of 50 percent. Since 1985, the monthly SMI premium has been calculated to equal 25 percent of the estimated SMI costs for Medicare enrollees age 65 and older. In 1991, the SMI enrollee paid a monthly premium of $29.90, and the federal government paid $95.30 for elders and $82.10 for disabled persons. Premiums are scheduled to increase to $31.80, $36.60, $41.10, and $46.10 in years 1992, 1993, 1994, and 1995, respectively. SMI benefits are paid from the SMI trust, a separate trust fund to which all premiums paid by the SMI enrollees and matching general funds are credited.

The uniform SMI general revenue subsidy is frequently criticized because it subsidizes the high-income elderly who have the ability to pay a larger portion of their full health care costs. Target group inefficiency is a common criticism of social insurance programs that do not, by design, impose means testing to determine benefit eligibility.

STYLISTIC MODEL OF MEDICARE INSURANCE

Because program inequities are defined in terms of benefits relative to costs (or in the case of Medicare, in terms of contributions or premiums), it is important to define clearly the value of the benefits to which the individual is entitled and the associated costs paid by the individual to gain access to these benefits. Who gains (loses) from participating in the program can then be determined by comparing the benefits received relative to the costs paid. In this section, the benefit and contribution streams for the HI and SMI programs are developed. Empirical estimates are provided in the following section.

The distributional impact of the Medicare program is isolated by using a "life cycle" insurance-transfer framework. This approach was first used to evaluate the distribution impact of the Medicare program by Vogel (1988). In using this framework, we are determining the lifetime value of Medicare benefits to an individual at retirement and then comparing it to the accumulated value of the contributions paid by the individual over the course of a lifetime. An attractive feature of this framework is that it permits the decoupling of the strictly insurance portion of the Medicare program (i.e., the benefit portion the elder actually paid for) from the redistributive or transfer portion (i.e., the benefit portion the elder did not pay for with his or her contributions or premiums).

Hospital Insurance

To evaluate the horizontal and vertical equity and the distributional impact of the Medicare program, the tax (premium) and benefit structure of program components must be clearly specified and then compared. This section builds on earlier work by Vogel (1988). Recall that the HI part of the program involves two flows of money: (1) the HI tax flow begins in 1966 (or, when covered employment begins if after 1966) and terminates when the individual reaches age 65 and is based on wage earnings up to a taxable maximum and (2) the service benefit flow, defined as an ex ante promise of defined service benefits covering hospital, nursing home, hospice, and home health care, begins at age 65 and ceases upon death. Because eligibility for Medicare benefits begins at age 65, aged cohorts are defined to include all persons who share the same birth year and who paid HI taxes some time over their lives.

First, consider the service benefit flow. The ex ante value of the HI service benefits, $HTE_{yj, MED}$, received in any year by experience group j within an aged cohort, MED, can be represented by

$$HTE_{yj, MED} = \sum_{i=1}^{n_j} \sum_{g=1}^{x} P_{gij} \, Q_{gij} + A_j \tag{6.2}$$

where

n_j	=	number of Medicare enrollees age 65 in each experience group j consuming services in year y
x	=	number of covered health care services
P_{gij}	=	price of the gth covered health care service
Q_{gij}	=	quantity of the gth covered service consumed by individual i in experience group j
A_j	=	administrative overhead cost for group j

The value of $HTE_{yj, MED}$ will depend on the frequency, types, cost, and duration of medical services used during the year by members of the experience group. Although Medicare does not experience rate, there may be naturally occurring experience groups within the Medicare pool; that is, aggregates of similarly aged persons with systematically different expenditure patterns and personal characteristics. These aggregates may be identified by their gender, race, marital status, health status, and/or income level.

Recall, however, that Medicare insurance covers service benefit costs for life in exchange for the payment of HI contributions. To capture the perpetual benefit structure of Medicare, a longitudinal perspective is required. The annuity-like benefit stream for the entire aged cohort, MED, can be rewritten as

$$LHTE_{MED} = \sum_{j=1}^{m} \sum_{y=MED}^{E_j} S_{yj} HTE_{yj, MED} \, (1 + r_y)^{MED-y} \tag{6.3}$$

where

$LHTE_{MED}$ = present actuarial value of lifetime HI benefits for an aged cohort reaching age 65 in *MED* year

m = number of experience groups

E_j = expected life span of the *j*th group

S_{yj} = survivor probability in year *y* for experience group *j*

r_y = discount rate in year *y*

Projecting the ex ante value of health insurance benefits becomes more difficult when a longitudinal perspective is used. The reason is that the value of $LHTE_{MED}$ depends on illness, longevity, medical care use, and cost patterns over time. Changes in mortality, technology, and quality of care, as well as consumer preferences for medical care services, will have an uncertain, yet significant, effect on the growth path of the benefit stream over time. Technology changes, in particular, will affect the composition and breadth of the services within the benefit package in each successive time period.

In addition, the value for E_j, or the length of the coverage period, is uncertain. Estimating the actuarial value of $LHTE_{MED}$ requires an assumption about the length of life for an aged cohort. Using a life certain approach assumes that all members of a cohort die at a specific age, say 14 years after reaching age 65. The present actuarial value of HI benefits for an elderly cohort using the life certain approach is expressed in equation 6.3 with E equaling a fixed age, say 79 and S_{jy} equaling 1. Alternatively, a life uncertain, probabilistic approach assumes that members die off at an increasing rate with age (implying the S_{jy} is less than 1 and diminishing monotonically with age). These rates can also be adjusted to reflect mortality differentials by gender, race, marital status, and income. The cumulative sum of HTE_y over the lifetime of the cohort calculated under each approach will differ if the growth in or length of health care costs after age 79 are not fully accounted for in the growth in the health care expenditures prior to age 79 in the life certain equation.

The present ex ante actuarial value of lifetime Medicare HI insurance for individual *i* within the *j*th experience group is represented by

$$B_{ij, MED} = LHTE_{j, MED}/n_j \qquad (6.4)$$

Next looking at the HI tax flow, each beneficiary in an aged cohort, *MED*, pays an HI tax on wage earnings. The present value of the HI tax stream at age 65, $C_{i, MED}$, paid by a representative worker, i, over his or her working life can be computed by[5]

$$C_{i, MED} = \sum_{y = F}^{MED} t_y E_{iy} (1 + r_y)^{MED-y} \text{ for } E_{iy} \leq M_y \tag{6.5}$$

where

MED	=	year individual i reaches age 65
F	=	first year HI tax was paid by individual i
t_y	=	HI tax rate in year y
E_{iy}	=	taxable wage earnings in year y for individual
r_y	=	interest rate in year y
M_y	=	maximum taxable wage earnings base in year y

The present value of HI tax payments will vary among individuals within the same aged cohort. The value of $C_{i, MED}$ varies with the level of taxable earnings, tax rate, self-employment status (until 1984 self-employed persons paid $1/2$ of t_y), and number of years of covered employment since 1966.

HI tax payments, expressed in present value terms, for an aged cohort, *MED*, can be expressed as

$$TC_{MED} = \sum_{i = 1}^{n} C_{i, MED} + \sum_{p = n + 1}^{T} C_{p, MED} \tag{6.6}$$

where T equals the total number of individuals who paid HI taxes over time and who were born in the same year ($MED -65$), and n equals the number of cohort members who survived to age 65. Not all contributing workers survive to age 65, but their HI taxes must be included in an analysis of the distributional equity of the system. To exclude the HI taxes of the "fallen comrades" would result in an overestimation of the net transfer of resources across the generations (Hurd and Shoven 1983: 9). The value of TC_{MED} is sensitive to the phase-in date of the program, as well as to other legislated changes in the HI tax rate, taxable maximum earnings level, definition of covered employment, and mortality experience of the cohort. For example, individuals in the first HI aged cohort

(1966) did not pay HI taxes in previous years; therefore, TC_{1966} equals zero for the 1966 cohort. As the system matures, the value of TC will increase because of the longer HI payment period for each advancing cohort and the increasing HI tax rate and base.

In summary, individual workers pay $C_{i,\,MED}$ and an elderly cohort pays TC_{MED} to secure perpetual drawing rights to hospital, nursing home, hospice, and home health care agency service benefits covered by Medicare.

Supplementary Insurance

The structure of the SMI program differs from that of the HI program. In modeling this program, several key features must be accounted for, including (1) the program is term health insurance that is rolled over annually, (2) premiums are subsidized from general revenues, and (3) elders pay federal taxes and, hence, contribute to general revenues used to subsidize SMI. Unlike HI insurance, SMI insurance is comparable to term health insurance for which disenrollment occurs when SMI premium payments lapse. Since most elders maintain their SMI coverage over their lifetimes, it is modeled using a longitudinal perspective.

Turning first to the benefit stream, the annual (lifetime) present value of the SMI benefit package for an experience group (aged cohort) is calculated using equation 6.7 (6.8) and is summarized below with new variable acronyms to identify the SMI program.

$$STE_{yj,\,MED} = \sum_{i=1}^{n_j} \sum_{g=1}^{x} P_{gij}\,Q_{gij} + A_j \tag{6.7}$$

$$LSTE_{MED} = \sum_{j=1}^{m} \sum_{y=MED}^{E_j} S_{yj}\,STE_{yj,\,MED}\,(1+r_y)^{MED-y} \tag{6.8}$$

where $STE_{yj,\,MED}$ equals the expected total SMI expenditures in year y for an experience group j in aged cohort MED, and $LSTE_{MED}$ equals the present actuarial value of lifetime SMI benefits for all experience groups composing an aged cohort reaching age 65 in MED year.

The present actuarial value of lifetime Medicare SMI insurance for individual i within the jth experience group in the MED cohort is

$$SB_{ij,\,MED} = LSTE_{j,\,MED}/n_j \tag{6.9}$$

Turning next to the payment side of the program, SMI enrollees pay premiums for SMI service benefits upon reaching age 65. According to the legislation, SMI premiums are set to defray a fixed percentage (currently 25 percent) of expected program costs. The different financing of SMI insurance requires several additional equations.

The present discounted value of SMI premium payments for an experience group in an aged cohort (MED) at age 65, $P_{j, MED}$ and for an entire aged cohort, TP_{MED} can be computed by

$$P_{j, MED} = \sum_{y = MED}^{E_j} S_{yj} \ (F_y \ STE_{yj, MED}) \ (1 + r_y)^{MED-y} \tag{6.10}$$

and

$$TP_{MED} = \sum_{j=1}^{m} \sum_{y = MED}^{E_j} S_{yj} \ (F_y \ STE_{yj, MED}) \ (1 + r_y)^{MED-y} \tag{6.11}$$

where

E_j	=	expected life span for the jth group
S_{yj}	=	survivor probability for year y for the jth group
F_y	=	the fixed percentage of premiums paid by elders
$STE_{jy, MED}$	=	the expected total SMI expenditures in year y for experience group j in MED cohort
r_y	=	interest rate in year y

Although SMI premiums are based on a community-rating experience principle, whereby all enrollees are assessed the same premium independent of age, earnings, health, or other identifiable health-risk and use-related factors, the actuarial value of the SMI benefits to an individual depends on his expected SMI expenditures.

The SMI program also redistributes income directly across age cohorts since general revenue funds are used to subsidize SMI premium payments. The size of the intergenerational subsidy is not, however, the simple sum of all general revenue SMI subsidies in a given year, because many elderly still pay federal taxes after age 65. Taxes paid by the elderly are reflected in general revenue funds, which are then used to pay SMI premiums. In practice, it is very difficult to disentangle the taxes paid by the elderly from those paid by the nonelderly and even more difficult to track how tax monies were used after they have been paid to the government. A simple approximation of the present discounted value of the elderly portion of SMI premiums paid from general revenues paid by an aged cohort, GRE_{MED}, is

$$GRE_{MED} = \sum_{y=MED}^{E} GR_{y,MED} \ (GFE_{y,MED}) \ (1+r_y)^{MED-y} \tag{6.12}$$

where GR_y equals the total SMI premium financed from general revenues in year y (or, $(1-F_y) STE_y$); and GFE equals the proportion of general revenue funds paid by the MED elderly cohort in year y. GRE_{MED} represents the present value of general revenue SMI premiums financed from taxes paid by all persons comprising the elderly cohort. To allocate the present value of general revenue SMI premiums to specific individuals within the cohort, information is needed on each elder's post-age 64 expected lifetime total federal tax liabilities expressed as a proportion of all expected tax liabilities of the elderly, or TL_i.

For each Medicare beneficiary, the present discounted value of the SMI direct and indirect premiums paid by a representative individual at age 65 in experience group j, SP_{ij}, for any year can be computed by

$$SP_{ij,MED} = P_{j,MED}/n_j + GRE_{MED} \ TL_{i,MED} \tag{6.13}$$

And the present value of SMI direct and indirect premiums paid by the aged cohort equals

$$LTP_{MED} = TP_{MED} + GRE_{MED} \tag{6.14}$$

Redistributional Equity

In the previous section, the life cycle model of the HI and SMI programs was developed. The redistributional impact of the HI and SMI programs can be determined by examining the relationship between lifetime insurance payments and benefits, expressed in present value terms. Formal conditions for intracohort and intercohort redistribution and companion definitions of horizontal and vertical equity are presented below for the HI and SMI programs. Definitions of equal treatment of equals (horizontal equity) and unequal treatment of unequals (vertical equity) within and across aged cohorts depend on whether one is subscribing to principles of individual equity or social adequacy.

Intracohort Redistribution. To examine the extent to which individuals within an aged cohort are expected to receive more or less than their "fair" share from the Medicare programs requires (1) a comparison of the ex ante present actuarial value of lifetime HI (SMI) insurance to present value of the HI (SMI) payment streams and (2) a specification of a standard of equity. If for a Medicare beneficiary either condition holds, for HI

$$
B_{ij,\,MED} \begin{array}{c} > \\ < \end{array} C_{i,\,MED} + 1/n \left(\sum_{p=n+1}^{T} C_{p,\,MED} \right) \tag{6.15}
$$

or, for SMI

$$
SB_{ij,\,MED} \begin{array}{c} > \\ < \end{array} SP_{ij,\,MED} \tag{6.16}
$$

then the enrollee is expected, on average, to receive Medicare benefits that are greater than (less than) the compounded value of insurance payments. Equations 6.15 and 6.16 are program-specific conditions for intracohort redistribution.

The redistributive share, HRS_{ij} for HI and $SRS_{ij,\,MED}$ for SMI, for individual i in the jth experience group is, therefore, defined for each program as

$$
HRS_{ij,\,MED} = B_{ij,\,MED} - \left[C_{i,\,MED} + 1/n \left(\sum_{p=n+1}^{T} C_{p,\,MED} \right) \right] \tag{6.17}
$$

for HI and

$$
SRS_{ij,\,MED} = SB_{ij,\,MED} - SP_{ij,\,MED} \tag{6.18}
$$

for SMI.

Whether individuals receive their "fair" redistributive share depends on the definition of "fairness." Within an individual equity context, standards of actuarial fairness are imposed. Individuals purchasing health insurance would pay a price equal to an actuarially fair premium plus load. Thus, an equitable assignment of premiums requires that each insured be assigned a premium that closely approximates his or her risk exposure level, or average expected medical expenditures. Therefore, an actuarially fair health insurance program would satisfy the following conditions:

$$B_{ij, MED} \ = \ LHTE_j/n_j \tag{6.19}$$

for HI, and

$$SB_{ij, MED} \ = \ LSTE_j/n_j \tag{6.20}$$

for SMI.

Equals are, therefore, defined in terms of their average expected medical expenditures, or the ex ante present actuarial value of medical expenditures for a lifetime health insurance policy. Actuarial equals (unequals) are defined as those with equal (unequal) Bs or SBs. It is wholly consistent with individual equity principles to charge different premiums to individuals for the same package of service benefits providing the premium differentials reflect differences in expected average medical expenditures. To charge equal premiums to persons with different expected risk levels would result in overcharging low-risk persons and undercharging high-risk persons. In so doing, the health insurance plan would, by design, redistribute income ex ante.

Defining equals and unequals within the context of a social program founded on social adequacy principles requires a different standard of fairness. Indeed, the Medicare program may be viewed as an attempt to extend a basic human right—a minimum standard of medical care access and financial protection—to needy elders in the pursuit of social justice. The central issue, therefore, is whether the program redistributes resources to reflect the absolute or relative neediness of members composing an aged cohort. "Social" fairness depends on whether those with equal (unequal) need receive equal (unequal) redistributive shares from the social insurance program.

Many standards of need could be used to proxy social fairness; for illustrative purposes, two will be discussed: adjusted income and combinations of income and medical need.[6] A traditional standard used to define need is adjusted (family, household, or per capita) income, Need, in this case, is negatively associated with adjusted income. Using this standard of need, elders within a cohort would be rank ordered by adjusted income and those with equal (unequal) adjusted incomes would receive equal (unequal) redistributive shares from the program. The value of the redistributive share for each income class would depend on the subsidy weight assigned to each income class and the size of its insurance premium. The size of the subsidy weight, a_c, for income class c would depend on the threshold income standard, Y^*, and the income classes level of income, Y_c, or, more formally,

$$a_c = \frac{Y^* - Y_c}{Y^*} \quad \text{for } Y < Y^* \tag{6.21}$$

As written, income groups with incomes exceeding Y^* are not considered to be "needy" and, therefore, would not receive a public subsidy. This condition, however, may not be socially acceptable or socially fair if comparably well-off nonaged persons receive public subsidies. Because employer contributions to health insurance are not treated as taxable income, nonaged individuals do receive a premium subsidy. Conditions for parity across the nonaged and aged cohorts would require that elders with Y above Y^* receive a tax subsidy equal to that of their nonaged equivalent income group (adjusted, of course, for differences in administrative costs of public versus private group plans and other price advantages associated with a large public payor of services).

The intended (i.e., that which is designed to occur) redistributive share for a representative individual i in income class c for the HI program is

$$IHRSI_c = a_c \, B_i, \tag{6.22}$$

and, for SMI is

$$ISRSI_c = a_c \, SB_i, \tag{6.23}$$

where B_i (SB_i) is the actuarially fair HI (SMI) insurance premium for each member of an aged cohort. According to equations 6.22 and 6.23, health insurance premiums are assigned on a sliding income scale to reflect differential need of public subsidization by cohort members. The size of intended public subsidy would then be compared to the actual public subsidy (estimates from equations 6.17 and 6.18) received from the program.

Intended redistributive shares will be fairly distributed within the aged cohort by using explicit subsidy weights for the assignment of premiums provided members of each income class have equal health care needs, medical care use patterns, and life expectancies—factors affecting insurance premiums. If expected medical care expenditures systematically vary within an income class but premiums are standardized, unintended redistribution for individual i in experience group j and income class c will occur and equal

$$UHRSI_{ijc} = a_c\ (B_{ijc} - B_i) \quad \text{for } a_c > 0; \text{ and}$$
$$(B_{ijc} - B_i) \quad \text{for } a_c = 0 \tag{6.24}$$

for the HI program, and

$$USRSI_{ijc} = a_c\ (SB_{ijc} - SB_i) \quad \text{for } a_c > 0; \text{ and}$$
$$(SB_{ijc} - SB_i) \quad \text{for } a_c = 0 \tag{6.25}$$

for the SMI program, where B_{ijc} (SB_{ijc}) equals the experience-adjusted, actuarially fair HI (SMI) premium for individuals in j experience group and c income class. That is, ex ante unintended redistribution of resources would occur, transferring resources from low-risk to high-risk elders.

An alternative standard of need is an income-medical need measure that accounts for differential medical and financial need. Here, need is defined more comprehensively and recognizes that individuals with equal incomes may differ in their medical need. One possible measure of income-medical need is the individual's experience-adjusted premium expressed as a proportion of his or her adjusted income, or B_{ij}/Y_c. The experience-adjusted premium captures differential medical need and use, and adjusted income captures financial ability. Using this measure, income-medical need equals would be defined as

$$\frac{B_{1j}}{Y_1} = \frac{B_{2j}}{Y_1}, \tag{6.26}$$

for those individuals in the same experience group, B_j, and income class, Y_1, or

$$\frac{B_{i1}}{Y_1} = \frac{B_{i2}}{Y_2}, \tag{6.27}$$

such that individuals in more costly experience groups (e.g., $B_{i1} > B_{i2}$) have offsetting difference in income (e.g., $Y_1 > Y_2$).

Again, the intended redistributive share for each income-medical need group q would depend on the size of the subsidy weight, im_q, assigned to each group and the value of the experience-adjusted insurance premium.

The subsidy weight, im_q, for each group q would depend on the threshold income-need standard, B^*/Y^*, and the income-need measure for the group q, B_{ij}/Y_c, or, more formally,

$$im_q = \frac{B_{ij}/Y_c - B^*/Y^*}{B^*/Y^*} \tag{6.28}$$

The intended redistributive share for group q is

$$IHRSIM_q = im_q\, B_{ijq} \tag{6.29}$$

for the HI program, and

$$ISRSIM_q = im_q\, SB_{ijq} \tag{6.30}$$

where B_{ijq} (SB_{ijq}) is the experience-adjusted, actuarially fair HI (SMI) insurance premium for group q. According to equations 6.29 and 6.30, experience-adjusted health insurance premiums are assigned on a sliding income-medical need scale to reflect differential need of medical and financial subsidies by the government. The intended redistributive shares will be distributed within the aged cohort such that those with equal medical and financial needs receive equal redistributive shares. Again, an additional subsidy weight would be needed to equalize treatment of aged and nonaged persons with income-medical needs exceeding the target threshold level.

Intercohort Redistribution. Aged cohorts, in aggregate, may have ex ante expected benefits from the Medicare program that are greater than, less than, or equal to the present value of their contributions. When contributions are less than expected health care costs, then funds are redistributed from current tax payers. The intercohort redistribution condition for the HI program is

$$LHTE_{MED} \; \overset{>}{<} \; TC_{MED} \tag{6.31}$$

and, for the SMI program is

$$LSTE_{MED} \; \overset{>}{<} \; LTP_{MED} \tag{6.32}$$

The intended redistributive share for the cohort *MED* is

$$CHRS_{MED} = LHTE_{MED} - TC_{MED} \tag{6.33}$$

for HI, and

$$CSRS_{MED} = LSTE_{MED} - LTP_{MED} \tag{6.34}$$

for SMI.

Corollary conditions for actuarial and social fairness developed for intracohort redistribution can be established for intercohort redistribution. An actuarially fair insurance program would require that each member of the cohort pay actuarially fair premiums so that on average there would be no redistribution across age cohorts. Each age cohort would internally fund its expected medical expenditures over its life cycle. Cohort equals (unequals) are those with equal (unequal) lifetime expected ex ante medical expenditures.

Social fairness across the cohorts also requires the specification of a need standard so that cohorts of equal need are treated equally and cohorts of unequal need are treated unequally. Preservation of horizontal and vertical equity across the cohort equivalents (defined in terms of real income or real income–need) would be accomplished by applying constant weights to the actuarially based premiums for each cohort. Although this equity rule will preserve the relative distribution of the redistributive shares across the cohorts, the absolute size of the intercohort transfer will not be equal across the cohorts. The absolute size of the transfer will depend on the number of members and the size of the actuarially fair premium of each need group.

EMPIRICAL EVIDENCE

Little research has been done on the distributional impact of the Medicare program. Wilensky (1982) examined the distributional impact of 1977 government expenditures on three leading government programs on health: tax expenditure subsidies, Medicare, and Medicaid. Per capita government expenditures (exclusive of premiums and prior contributions) on Medicare declined with income when all Medicare beneficiaries were included in the analysis, but the relationship between per capita expenditures and income became U-shaped when only beneficiaries receiving benefits in 1977 were analyzed separately. Total expenditures on Medicare were roughly proportional with income. With the exception of the study by Vogel (1988), no research has focused on the distributional impact of Medicare within an intertemporal framework. Vogel uses an annuity certain–transfer approach to examine the distributional impact of the Medicare program (HI and SMI) from 1966 to 1985. A microsimulation model is used to compute the annual present value of the ex ante stream of HI (SMI) benefits and accumulated HI taxes at age 65 (annual present value of SMI premiums at age 65) for each elderly cohort from 1966 to 1985. A welfare component, or redistributive share for HI (SMI) is then calculated for each aged cohort by subtracting the present value of HI (SMI) benefits from the accumulated tax contributions (present value of premiums). Dividing the welfare component by the present value of HI (SMI) benefits renders the welfare ratio. Vogel's intercohort subsidy results for HI and SMI appear in Tables 6.3 and 6.4, respectively.

Column 1 of Table 6.3 shows the estimated present value of HI benefits by year. To calculate column 1, Vogel used equation 6.3 and assumed (1) all persons at age 65 live a uniform and fixed life span, (2) each elderly cohort includes the "new" elderly reaching age 65 in that year only, (3) all new beneficiaries became eligible for Medicare on January of each year, and (4) no additional tax contributions are paid after age 65. Expenditure data from 1966 to 1982 and projected expenditures from 1983 to 2003 were obtained from the Office of the Actuary, HCFA. The annual present value of HI benefits for the 1966 elderly cohort (the phase-in year that added 18.9 million enrollees to the program) was $42.4 billion. The present value of HI benefits, expressed in absolute dollars, increased for each successive cohort after 1968 because both life expectancy and the intensity of medical services increased over time. For those retiring in 1985, it reached $54.5 billion.

Column 2 presents the computed HI contributions for each retirement cohort. HI contributions were compounded using an equation comparable to equation 6.5 and were aggregated over workers, and it is assumed that (1) payroll taxes are paid annually at the end of each year; (2) employer's taxes are shifted fully to the employee[7]; and (3) a 1.45 HI tax rate applied for years after 1986. The tax base equaled the weighted median earnings for male and female full-time workers for each year. Because the 1966 elderly group paid no taxes, its contribution to HI equals zero, reflecting a pure windfall gain to the initial group of enrollees. Accumulated contributions have been increasing with each successive cohort.

Column 3 displays the welfare component, the present value of HI benefit amount that the elderly cohort did not pay for through prior HI taxes. The initial group of elderly (1966 cohort) received a pure transfer with the phase-in of the program. This result is consistent with earlier reported start-up findings for the OASI program (Burkhauser and Warlick 1981; Freiden et al., 1976; Hurd and Shoven 1985; Leimer and Petri 1981; Wolff 1987). In general, the first generations participating in a pay-as-you-go benefit program will always reap large windfalls because they have few

Table 6.3
Welfare Component of the HI Program under Medicare, 1966–85 (dollar values in thousands)

Year	Annual present value of stream of HI benefits (1)	Accumulated tax contributions at interest (2)	Welfare component (3)	Welfare ratio (4)
1966	42,361,531	0	42,361,531	1.00
1967	5,036,582	21,391	5,015,191	1.00
1968	5,665,582	57,676	5,607,582	0.99
1969	6,572,258	104,776	6,467,482	0.98
1970	8,159,647	162,036	7,997,611	0.98
1971	9,282,552	225,766	9,056,785	0.98
1972	10,604,079	296,708	10,307,370	0.97
1973	12,664,028	389,413	12,274,616	0.97
1974	14,600,940	540,531	14,060,409	0.96
1975	18,309,443	749,372	17,560,061	0.96
1976	19,827,798	899,258	18,928,539	0.95
1977	22,815,506	1,103,997	21,711,509	0.95
1978	25,852,952	1,348,860	24,504,092	0.95
1979	29,280,959	1,659,111	27,621,848	0.94
1980	32,481,695	2,076,074	30,405,621	0.94
1981	35,322,948	2,548,087	32,774,862	0.93
1982	38,849,013	3,229,316	35,619,696	0.92
1983	43,436,652	3,982,853	39,453,800	0.91
1984	49,940,744	4,732,427	45,208,318	0.91
1985	54,534,974	5,572,012	48,962,962	0.90

Total value of HI benefits compounded forward to 1985: $962,818,235

Total value of HI taxes compounded forward to 1985:   45,469,018

Total welfare: $917,349,217

Global welfare ratio: 0.95

Source: Ronald J. Vogel, "An Analysis of the Welfare Component and Intergenerational Transfers Under the Medicare Program," in Mark V. Pauly and William L. Kissick, eds., *Lessons from the First Twenty Years of Medicare* (Philadelphia: University of Pennsylvania Press, 1988), Table 4.2, p. 82. Reprinted with permission of the University of Pennsylvania Press.

or zero years of taxation and a relatively long expected benefit collection period. The diminution of the windfall gains over time are most evident by looking at column 4, showing the welfare ratio (column 3 divided by column 1). As the system matures, the intercohort subsidy decreases from 100 percent in 1966 to 90 percent in 1985. This finding could be interpreted as being consistent with social adequacy principles since over this time

Table 6.4
Welfare Component of the SMI Program under Medicare, 1966–85
(dollar values in thousands)

Year	Annual present value of stream of SMI benefits (1)	Annual present value of SMI premiums (2)	Welfare component (3)	Welfare ratio (4)
1966	14,360,035	7,968,009	6,391,936	0.45
1967	1,726,660	828,903	897,756	0.52
1968	1,945,049	905,989	1,039,060	0.53
1969	2,339,342	1,106,848	1,322,494	0.57
1970	3,017,318	1,204,581	1,812,737	0.60
1971	3,510,761	1,309,010	2,201,751	0.63
1972	4,127,706	1,456,571	2,671,135	0.65
1973	5,055,507	1,690,203	3,365,304	0.67
1974	6,009,405	1,902,218	4,107,187	0.68
1975	7,930,557	2,316,297	5,614,260	0.71
1976	8,858,747	2,464,377	6,394,369	0.72
1977	10,443,955	2,779,940	7,654,014	0.73
1978	12,143,343	3,103,562	9,039,782	0.74
1979	14,043,292	3,468,666	10,574,626	0.75
1980	16,104,505	3,828,988	12,275,517	0.76
1981	18,079,710	4,154,832	13,924,878	0.77
1982	20,495,903	4,560,873	15,935,030	0.78
1983	24,503,805	5,115,776	19,388,030	0.79
1984	28,883,129	5,907,443	22,975,686	0.80
1985	32,474,239	6,412,910	26,061,329	0.80

Total value of SMI benefits compounded forward to 1985: $433,580,878

Total value of SMI premiums compounded forward to 1985: 131,690,199

Total welfare: $301,890,679

Global welfare ratio: 0.70

Source: Ronald J. Vogel, "An Analysis of the Welfare Component and Intergenerational Transfers Under the Medicare Program," in Mark V. Pauly and William L. Kissick, eds., *Lessons from the First Twenty Years of Medicare* (Philadelphia: University of Pennsylvania Press, 1988), Table 4.3, p. 83. Reprinted with permission of the University of Pennsylvania Press.

period, the economic status of elders showed marked improvement. However, a more careful analysis of cohort "need" would be necessary to determine the rate at which the need for public subsidization was diminishing for the members of each advancing aged cohort. Vogel estimates that over the program's 20-year history, a $917 billion intercohort subsidy has been received by Medicare enrollees, representing a 95 cent subsidy, on average, for every dollar of HI outlay from 1966 to 1985.

Table 6.4 shows comparable calculations for the SMI program. Note that the SMI welfare ratio appearing in column 4 has increased from 0.45 in 1966 to 0.80 in 1985. This result should not be surprising given the program's growing reliance on general revenues since 1974. This estimated welfare component, however, cannot be interpreted as a pure intercohort subsidy. Vogel does not try to disentangle the elderly population's contribution to general revenues; consequently, some of the intercohort transfers represent tax payments made by the elderly, which are used to finance some of their SMI premium payments.

Two other cautionary notes about Vogel's intercohort estimates should be mentioned. First, Vogel's estimates do not include the contributions made by workers who die before age 65 (i.e., "fallen comrade" contributions). These workers paid in tax dollars but do not draw benefits; hence, their funds could be used to subsidize surviving members of the aged cohort. The estimates of compounded HI contributions are biased downward by the exclusion of HI contributions made by fallen comrades. Second, Vogel uses an annuity-certain framework (which assumes all members of a cohort live a fixed number of years) to calculate the ex ante present actuarial value of a stream of health care benefits. This actuarial assumption is likely to bias downward the estimates of the ex ante actuarial value of HI (SMI) benefits in light of the highly inflationary costs for medical care and the longer life expectancies of advancing cohorts. More realistic estimates would be generated from the life annuity framework, which would incorporate differentiated expected life contingencies for the members of the cohort and their medical care costs in those later years.

Vogel presents a crude measure of intracohort redistribution for HI. To shed some light on relative gains for members of the same aged cohort, Vogel estimates a benefit-tax ratio for a representative male worker who reaches age 65 on January 1, 1980. The worker's estimated ex ante actuarial value of HI benefits in 1980 was $11,200. Tax contributions were compounded from January 1, 1966, to January 1, 1980, assuming the worker's previous earnings were 100, 75, 50, and 25 percent of the maximum taxable wage base in each year. The worker's ratio of the present value of benefits to HI taxes at the four different earnings levels of 100, 75, 50, and 25 percent were 2.9, 3.9, 5.8, and 11.60, respectively. As expected under these assumptions, there is unambiguous pro-poor intracohort redistribution based on the earnings levels of beneficiaries.

Vogel's estimation of intracohort redistribution reflects that the HI program assesses different insurance prices for the same benefit package to elders who are presumed to be risk equals. The different HI prices are related to income, not risk exposure. Indeed, if all members of the HI insurance pool had the same expected health expenditures after age 64, higher earners would pay a larger share of their expected medical care expenditures than lower income earners. This result is actuarially unfair, but potentially socially fair if differences in return closely correlate with society's accepted definition of differences in financial need.

There are several reasons to question the completeness of Vogel's estimation of intracohort redistribution. First, the present actuarial value of HI benefits depends on the mortality experience and medical expenditure patterns of members comprising the aged cohort. Mortality studies show that specific socioeconomic characteristics, such as age, gender, race, marital status, income, and education (Antonovsky 1972; Gove 1973; Hu and Goldman 1990; Iams and McCoy 1991; Kitagawa and Hauser 1973; Verbrugge 1989), as well as health status (Iams and McCoy 1991), influence survivor probabilities. Examining the death profile of a sample of newly retired workers over an eight-year period, Iams and McCoy (1991) found a significantly higher probability of death for beneficiaries who were male, unmarried, older, poor, more health impaired, and less educated, ceteris paribus. In a "lifetime" health insurance program, persons with lower survivor probabilities (or shorter life expectancies) subsidize persons with relatively higher survivor probabilities (or longer life expectancies). Charging higher prices for an identical "lifetime" insurance package is consistent with principles of actuarial fairness if prices vary with a significant predictor of survivorship.

The lifetime value of health insurance benefits will also depend on the medical care utilization patterns of members of the aged cohort. Many studies have shown differences in medical service use according to gender, race, ethnicity, and income. In particular, lower income persons have repeatedly been found to use more medical care than higher income persons (Aday and Andersen 1981; Butler et al. 1985; David et al. 1981; Freeman et al. 1987). The negative correlation between medical care use and income, however, may be confounded by the association between health and income. Health and income are positively associated; those in poor health are likely to be poor because their health limits their earnings potential and/or prior treatment costs have resulted in large debts. Gottschalk and Wolfe (1991: 11–14) found that the nonpoor elderly had higher, not lower, average health care expenditures than the poor elderly after controlling for race, ethnicity, education, health insurance coverage, and health status. For example, elders with health limitations were found to have $1,400 more in health expenditures, and those with incomes twice the poverty line had roughly $600 more in health expenditures, ceteris paribus.

In addition to the above-mentioned factors that affect the expected medical expenditures of an elder, derivative HI benefits for the spouses and survivors of workers lead to differential treatment of HI beneficiaries on the benefit side of the equation. Some HI beneficiaries essentially receive two HI insurance policies—one for the worker and one for the dependent spouse—for their contributions. In effect, one worker is given drawing rights for two people but pays for the rights of only one. Provision of 2-for-1 drawing rights would have a neutral effect within an aged cohort provided all workers claimed these extra drawing rights. However, this is not the case. Both workers in dual-earner households pay for some fraction of these benefits. These extra drawing rights fall disproportionately on single-earner households. Most empirical evidence suggests that there is an inverse relationship between family income and a wife's labor force participation (Boskin 1973; Cain 1966; Garfinkel and Masters 1977). Choosing to be a homemaker appears to be a more viable option for high-income wives. A retirement sample of 781 single-earner couples retiring between 1962 and 1972 drawn from the 1973 Current Population Survey-Administrative Match File shows that 14 percent of single-earner couples were low-income as compared to roughly 43 percent with middle or high incomes (Wolff 1985: 51).

Tables 6.5a and 6.5b show a series of adjustments to Vogel's intracohort estimates that take into account differential survivorship by gender, income, and health status; differential medical expenditures by income and health status; and the 2-for-1 drawing rights of the HI program. Under assumptions of constant risk exposure (columns 1 and 2) used by Vogel, a representative male with maximum taxable contributions for fourteen years (1966–1979) received a redistributive share equal to $7,338 (row 3), or a public subsidy of 65 cents on each dollar of the present actuarial value of expected HI benefits (row 4). In comparison, the male with a 25 percent contribution rate received approximately a 91 percent public subsidy on HI benefits, equaling $10,235. Clearly, both individuals gain more than their money's worth from the HI program; however, the largest relative gain went to the male with the lower taxable contributions. On its face, the HI program would appear to be horizontally and vertically inequitable, in actuarial terms, since presumed risk equals are charged different prices for the same benefit package, but socially fair since lower-contributing individuals are receiving a larger subsidy weight on their "premiums."

To examine the program feature of "free" HI benefits for dependent spouses and the effect of the wife's work status on benefit incidence,

Table 6.5a
Intracohort Redistribution of HI Program: Male Worker and Female Spouse

	CONSTANT RISK EXPOSURE		ADJUSTED RISK EXPOSURE[b]	
Contribution Level	100% maximum tax base	25% maximum tax base	100% maximum tax base	25% maximum tax base
MALE WORKER				
(1) 1980 present actuarial value of HI benefits	$11,200[a]	11,200[a]	16,128	10,640
(2) 1980 present value of tax contributions	$ 3,862[a]	965[a]	3,862	965
(3) Absolute difference (1)-(2)	$ 7,338	10,235	12,266	9,675
(4) Percentage difference (3)/(1)x100	65.5%	91.4	76.1	90.9
(5) Benefit to tax ratio (1)/(2)	2.9	11.6	4.2	11.0
FEMALE SPOUSE				
(6) 1980 present actuarial value of HI benefits	$11,200[a]	11,200[a]	17,696	11,928
(7) 1980 present value of tax contributions	0	965[a]	0	965.43
(8) Absolute difference (6)-(7)	$11,200	10,235	17,696	10,963
(9) Percentage difference (8)/(1)x100	100%	91.4	100	91.9
(10) Benefit to tax ratio (6)/(7)	----	11.6	----	12.4

a Reported values from present actuarial value of HI benefits and tax contributions are estimates reported by Vogel (1988).

b Iams and McCoy (1991) report logit coefficients on likelihood of death by health status, sociodemographic and income factors for persons aged 65 and older; Gottschalk and Wolfe (1991) report estimates on the effect of health and income on the average medical expenditures for elders. These estimates were used to adjust Vogel's estimates.

Sources: Ronald J. Vogel, "An Analysis of the Welfare Component and Intergenerational Transfers under the Medicare Program," in Mark V. Pauly and William L. Kissick, eds., *Lessons from the First Twenty Years of Medicine* (Philadelphia: University of Pennsylvania Press, 1988), p. 87; Howard M. Iams and John L. McCoy, "Predictors of Mortality among Newly Retired Workers," *Social Security Bulletin* 54, no. 3 (1991), p. 7; and Peter Gottschalk and Barbara L. Wolfe, "How Equal Is the Utilization of Medical Care in the United States?" Paper presented at the Association for Public Policy and Management meetings, San Francisco, November 1990, Table 5.

Table 6.5b
Intracohort Redistribution of HI Program: Household Unit

	CONSTANT RISK EXPOSURE		ADJUSTED RISK EXPOSURE[b]	
Contribution Level	100% maximum tax base	25% maximum tax base	100% maximum tax base	25% maximum tax base
HOUSEHOLD UNIT				
(11) 1980 present actuarial value of HI benefits	$22,400[a]	22,400[a]	33,824	22,568
(12) 1980 present value of tax contributions	$ 3,862[a]	1,931[a]	3,862	1,931
(13) Absolute difference (11)-(12)	$18,539	20,469	29,963	20,637
(14) Percentage difference (13)/(1)x100	82.8%	91.4	88.6	91.4
(15) Benefit to tax ratio (11)/(12)	5.8	11.6	8.8	11.7

[a] Reported values from present actuarial value of HI benefits and tax contributions are estimates reported by Vogel (1988).

[b] Iams and McCoy (1991) report logit coefficients on likelihood of death by health status, sociodemographic and income factors for persons aged 65 and older; Gottschalk and Wolfe (1991) report estimates on the effect of health and income on the average medical expenditures for elders. These estimates were used to adjust Vogel's estimates.

Sources: Ronald J. Vogel, "An Analysis of the Welfare Component and Intergenerational Transfers under the Medicare Program," in Mark V. Pauly and William L. Kissick, eds., *Lessons from the First Twenty Years of Medicine* (Philadelphia: University of Pennsylvania Press, 1988), p. 87; Howard M. Iams and John L. McCoy, "Predictors of Mortality among Newly Retired Workers," *Social Security Bulletin* 54, no. 3 (1991), p. 7; and Peter Gottschalk and Barbara L. Wolfe, "How Equal Is the Utilization of Medical Care in the United States?" Paper presented at the Association for Public Policy and Management meetings, San Francisco, November 1990, Table 5.

spousal benefits and household benefits are examined separately. Because roughly 90 percent of single-earner families in 1973 have high or middle income, we assume that the spouse of the high-contributing male receives dependent HI benefits, as compared to the worker HI benefits for the working spouse of the lower-income male. When combining the benefits and contributions of the couple (Table 6.5b), the relative public subsidy decreases sharply between the lower- and higher-income groups, from a 26 percentage point (row 4) difference calculated by Vogel to a 9 percentage point difference (row 14). Since the 2-for-1 drawing rights fall disproportionately on the higher-contributing households, social adequacy is obfuscated. Still, the lower-contributing household receives $1,930 more HI benefits, in present value terms, from the program than the higher-contributing household given their risk status.

In the next set of columns (labeled Adjusted Risk Exposure), adjustments are made in the present actuarial value of the HI benefits to reflect effects of gender, health status, and income on survivorship and the effects of income and health status on medical expenditures. Rows 11 and 12 in Table 6.5b indicate that the household benefit and contribution levels are higher for the higher contributing household vis-à-vis the lower-contributing household. With these adjustments, unequal households are treated roughly equally by the program; that is, the contribution-level differential within the cohort diminishes toward zero when risk exposure differences for identifiable subgroups are included in the analysis (rows 14 and 15). It is also interesting to note that the higher-contributing household can expect on average to receive approximately $9,300 more in HI benefits relative to the lower-contributing household (row 13). Each household is required to pay roughly 10 percent of the expected present actuarial value of HI benefits. These results suggest that by assessing higher-contribution rates on higher earners, the HI program is maintaining subsidy parity between the lower- and higher-contributing households.

Vogel does not construct estimates of intracohort redistribution for SMI. He argues (1988: 83) that "because SMI monthly premiums, beginning at age sixty-five, are not a function of income, there is no direct SMI intragenerational transfer, or redistribution, of income." In fact, the SMI program would be distributionally neutral within an aged cohort if SMI premiums were independent of income and the actuarial price for SMI was treated as constant. However, not all SMI beneficiaries receive an equal subsidy from the program since SMI beneficiaries with incomes at or below poverty receive a 100 percent public subsidy through the Medicaid buy-in arrangement and the remaining beneficiaries receive a 75 percent public subsidy financed through general revenues. Hence, some direct redistribution occurs through the program.

Two additional sources of indirect redistribution arise from the way the program is designed. First, federal taxes paid by elders are partially reflected in the general revenues used to finance the SMI subsidy. Since federal taxes are an increasing function of income, higher-income elders, on average, pay larger indirect premiums (as reflected in equation 6.13). Second, as shown above, average medical care expenditure differences across income groups will affect the actuarial value of SMI insurance.

Higher average expenditures for higher-income persons may arise because of the effect of medigap insurance on the price of outpatient and physician services facing them in the market and/or because higher-income elders have preferences for a greater quantity or quality of medical care services. In the presence of these expenditure differences across income groups, an income-conditioned premium is necessary to prevent redistribution of resources in favor of the wealthy through this program. To a limited degree, the extra indirect premium paid by higher-income persons offsets their greater risk exposure (that is, greater use of medical services). Whether the additional indirect premiums are sufficiently large to pay for the higher Medicare costs is an empirical issue requiring further research.

REFORM RECOMMENDATIONS AND CONCLUSIONS

The "original intent" of Medicare was to target scarce public resources to assist a financially and medically needy group. Because all persons 65 and older were presumed to be equally needy of collective protection, the program was designed to treat all elders alike, affording them equal access and coverage to social insurance. Medicare's financing mechanism, however, reflects a perception that workers have an unequal ability to pay for future HI benefits but that retirees have an equal ability to pay for present SMI benefits. Indeed, undergirding Medicare's social adequacy design is a form of discrimination in favor of the aged, or what Binstock (1985: 429–430) refers to as "compassionate ageism." *Ageism* refers to "the attribution of the same characteristics, status, and deserts to an artificially homogenized group labelled 'the aged' " (Binstock 1985: 422). In the case of Medicare, elders as a group are envisaged as medically frail and economically vulnerable—a group warranting collective compassion.

Social fairness among members of a cohort and across aged cohorts was to be preserved by treating all equals equally and unequals unequally. There was no need to be concerned about fairness between the rich and poor within an aged cohort since all members were equally needy upon retirement. However, because earlier cohorts were in greater relative need, fairness between aged cohorts required that the redistributive share be set high for phase-in cohorts and then allowed to diminish to a socially acceptable level of redistribution as the economic status of advancing cohorts improved.

As shown in the empirical section, the intercohort redistribution has been diminishing over time for the HI program, but increasing for the SMI program. This seems at odds with principles of social equity on which the program was founded. The evidence is more ambiguous regarding intracohort redistribution. Medicare does have pro-poor (e.g., assessing HI taxes as a function of taxable earnings and Medicaid buy-in arrangements) and pro-nonpoor (e.g., capping taxable earnings, payment of benefits to nonworking spouses, assigning equal public subsidies for SMI to unequals) features built into both the HI and SMI programs. Moreover, the extent of redistribution depends on factors incidental to the program but coincidental with characteristics of Medicare beneficiaries (e.g., differences in longevity and medical utilization patterns). The confluence of intentional and incidental factors makes the direction and extent of redistribution uncertain.

Reform Proposal

In recent years, the Medicare program has been the focus of public attention and controversy. Many basic challenging questions have been raised: Can we afford Medicare? Can program costs be controlled? Are benefit services adequate and appropriate? Do elders need or want the program? Is the program fair to elders and nonelders alike? Issues of fairness have received the least attention, but bear heavily on the long-term political and economic feasibility of the program. Historical and future changes in the demographic, economic, and medical status of the elderly challenge the principles of equity undergirding the current Medicare program.

The contemporary facts are clear: The number and proportion of elders are increasing, and the age composition is changing. Elders are living longer, healthier lives. Age 65 and older are neither necessary nor sufficient conditions of need for public subsidy. Elders widely differ in their medical and economic needs. Medical and economic needs change over the aged life cycle. If the system is to meet the current and future needs of older Americans, equitably and reliably, reform that focuses on fairness between the poor and nonpoor within an aged cohort is in order. Moreover, reform proposals need to be sensitive to issues of fairness across generations. Intergenerational tensions are building. Antagonistic and invidious questions are repeatedly being raised. Are elders getting or taking too much collective protection? Is the burden of supporting elders too high on workers? Are the needs of children and other vulnerable populations being compromised in the process? The nation appears to be on the cusp of change between compassionate and antagonistic ageism.

Any future reform of Medicare should begin with a restatement of its objectives. Of foremost importance in designing or redesigning a social risk-bearing program is a formal and clear statement of the program's protective and redistributive objectives. Since once the program is enacted, public expectations and claims of individual entitlement evolve. Leonard and Zeckhauser (1983: 156) speak to this point:

When the state becomes involved in the provision of economic security, an evolutionary process is set in motion. The end result of this process is a pattern of dependency and redistribution. The original purpose of protecting individuals confronting a common risk through a form of insurance gets lost. Once the dependency situation has been created, matters may deteriorate further. The transfer process may create entitlements, and those entitlements may evolve into rights.

To moderate the "nonmarket" failures associated with public programs, policymakers need to be forthright in explaining the intended objective of the program.

In our reform proposal, we draw on the four objectives for an insurance system proposed by Gottschalk et al. (1989: 352–355). They include the following: (1) risks should be spread across individuals within an insurance pool, (2) risks should be spread over an individual's life cycle, (3) resources should be distributed according to criteria of health and economic need, and (4) the system should encourage a socially efficient use of medical care services. We add one additional objective: (5) financial burden should be fairly assigned within and across the generations. Our reform embraces principles of social adequacy and individual equity, but they are disentangled to reflect and preserve redistributive intent. Conditions for horizontal and vertical equity are defined within each set of principles.

We propose a two-tier, age-stratified comprehensive health insurance plan for elders 65 and older that is financed by a combination of income-conditioned premiums and payroll tax contributions.

Equity Principle 1: Groups of similarly aged individuals with unequal "average" needs are treated unequally by a social insurance program. Our reform proposal stratifies elders into two age groups: Tier 1, age 65 to 74, and Tier 2, age 75 and older. Because these two groups of elders are not equal in average ability to pay or average medical need, they should not be pooled into the same program under the implicit assumption that they are equals. Our stratification scheme is intended to capture systematic, age-related differences in both measures of need.

Equity Principle 2: Individuals should pay according to their medical and financial ability. Elders in the first tier have widely varying abilities to pay for insurance benefits and diverse medical needs during this phase of their life cycle. We use income as a proxy measure for medical and financial need. To satisfy the second equity principle, income-conditioned premiums are used to finance the costs associated with the healthier elders in Tier 1. Those with equal (unequal) need are treated equally (unequally) regarding the payment for insurance protection. All Tier 2 costs are financed by payroll taxes.

By using this financing scheme for the older group of elders, the social insurance program allows individuals to spread risks over their life cycle (one of five objectives of an insurance system) and accounts for the systematically higher medical needs and lower financial ability of this age group, on average, during the final phase of the life cycle. In keeping with the ability to pay principle, individuals with higher earnings during their working years contribute more toward the health care costs associated with their declining health in the concluding phase of their life cycle.

Equity Principle 3: Those in greater need should be given greater collective assistance. In both Tiers 1 and 2, public subsidies are targeted for those in greater medical and financial need. Our income-conditioned premium schedule assigns larger subsidy weights to those young elders with lower incomes during their retirement years. For Tier 2, public subsidies are negatively related to income since prior tax contributions are a function of taxable earnings. Those who are relatively less able to save during their working years for health care risks associated with the last phase of their life will receive greater collective assistance when they reach age 75. Public subsidies in each tier are designed to target those in greater need—when need reflects being poor when old and being poor when young.

In the next section, we develop our equity-based reform of Medicare in greater detail.

Insurance Pool. All persons age 65 and older would be covered by the program, forming one large insurance pool for risk spreading.[8] Although we do not think that age per se is a marker for medical and economic need, we do think that persons in this age group are subject to unacceptable "uninsurance" risks at retirement because employers may terminate retirees' group policies or because reasonably priced, comprehensive individual policies are unavailable. Creating an insurance pool inclusive of well over 30 million people results in nontrivial administrative cost savings, as well as price negotiation power, which would also confer savings to the program.

Insurable Event. Acute and chronic medical care costs associated with impaired physical and mental health are covered.

Benefit Coverage. HI and SMI would be merged and combined with new long-term care benefits into a comprehensive health insurance (CHI) program. Costs for each program component for the year 2000 expressed in 1985 prices appear in Table 6.6. These cost projections are based on the Harvard Medicare Project (Blumenthal et al. 1988: 193–197).

Table 6.6
Equity-Based Reform Population, Cost, and Revenue Projections (in 1985 dollars)

Projected Population[a] (in thousands)	Total	AGE GROUP 65-74	75+
	34,882	18,243	16,639

Projected Program Costs[b] (in billion dollars)			
Hospital Care (HI)	$ 70.0	$ 28.0	$ 42.0
Physician Care (SMI)	21.0	8.4	12.6
Reduced Co-payment	9.1	3.6	5.5
Long-Term Care with Residential Co-payment	47.8	8.6	39.2
TOTAL	$147.9	$ 48.6	$ 99.3

Projected Program Revenues (in billion dollars)			
Income-Conditioned Premiums			
1 > 250% poverty, no subsidy	$ 33.5	$ 33.5	N.A.
2 > 250% poverty, 5% subsidy	32.3	32.3	N.A.
3 > 250% poverty, 10% subsidy	31.1	31.1	N.A.
4 > 250% poverty, 15% subsidy	29.9	29.9	N.A.
General Revenue Subsidy of SMI 75% of Projected Year 2000 costs	15.7	15.7	N.A.
HI Trust Fund Total Income Alternative II, Year 2000[c]	$ 97.4	N.A.	$ 97.4
Total 1	$146.6	$ 49.2	$97.4
2	145.4	48.0	97.4
3	144.2	46.8	97.4
4	143.0	45.6	97.4

a Data from U.S. Bureau of the Census, *Current Population Report* 1989, Series P-25, no. 1018, p. 62.

b Adapted from David Blumenthal, Mark Schlesinger, and Pamela Brown Drumheller, *Renewing the Promise, Medicare and Its Reform* (Oxford: Oxford University Press, 1988), pp. 193–195.

c Data from Social Security Administration, Office of the Actuary 1991.

All existing services covered by Medicare would be maintained. All cost sharing (i.e., deductibles and coinsurance), however, would be removed from HI and SMI. This raises legitimate concerns regarding moral hazard. However, we do not expect to see a dramatic change in program use or cost with the removal of existing cost-sharing arrangements given that poor elders do not face cost-sharing barriers under Medicaid buy-in arrangements, and 70 percent of elders purchase additional supplemental insurance to offset Medicare cost sharing provisions. Long et al. (1982) found that Medicare beneficiaries who do not face copayments use approximately 30 to 50 percent more services than their counterparts facing copayments. Since eliminating existing cost sharing will affect only the 30 percent of elders without supplemental policies, we expect that our reform will increase physician and hospital costs by approximately 10 percent. The Harvard Medicare Project proposed to eliminate 66 to 75 percent of cost-sharing liability at a projected "4-to-5 percent increase in physician utilization and a 6-to-8 percent increase in hospital costs" (Blumenthal et al. 1988: 195).

Programmatic safeguards against moral hazard behavior and physician-induced demand are likely to be well established by the year 2000. Recent legislation has expanded the authority of Peer Review Organizations to nursing homes, home health agencies, hospital outpatient departments, and physicians' offices (Russell 1989: 18–19, 65). PROs have already begun their oversight of health maintenance organizations and outpatient surgery sites. Physician practice guidelines are also likely to be in place and used in the utilization review process. Physician expenditure targets would be used to guard against physician-induced demand incentives. Target expenditure levels and research for practice guidelines were included in the physician payment reform of the 101st Congress.

The long-term care services and expanded mental health services would be identical to those proposed by the Harvard Medicare Project (Blumenthal et al. 1988: 179–181). All Medicare beneficiaries would be insured for the full medical costs associated with extended nursing home care, inclusive of limited, rehabilitative stays. Beneficiaries, however, would be assessed a residential copayment for lodging expenses equal to "80 percent of their Social Security benefits" (Blumenthal et al. 1988: 179). In addition, there would be a liberal expansion of outpatient long-term care services and mental health services.

Determination and Assignment of Premiums. We propose stratifying the beneficiaries into two age groups: young-old (65 to 74) and old-old (75 and older). Comprehensive health insurance for the young-old group would be financed by income-conditioned premiums paid during the young-old portion of the aged life cycle.[9] The subsidy weight varies with the ratio of income to the official poverty level.[10] Comparable insurance for the old-old would be financed by existing payroll taxes applied to earnings during working years. Old-old elders would not pay any medical costs except for those costs associated with prescription medications after age 74, and they would pay the residential copayment upon admission into a nursing home. This financing scheme satisfies three of our objectives: (1) risks are spread over an individual's life cycle by tying specific program costs to periods of the life cycle when the individual has the greatest ability to pay for needed medical care services in the future; (2) public resources are distributed on the basis of health and financial ability as reflected in the age–income-conditioned premiums paid for the young-old program and the payroll tax premiums paid for the old-old program; and (3) fairness within and between cohorts is preserved by consistently applying a constant premium scheme within a current cohort and across advancing aged cohorts.

As already noted, age per se is an imperfect predictor of medical and/or financial need. However, research shows that relative medical and financial need and use systematically change over the aged life cycle. Age-gradient differences in medical care utilization and income status were discussed earlier; persons age 65 to 74 have significantly lower utilization of hospitals, physicians, and nursing homes and lower rates of poverty than their 75-year-old and older counterparts. Also, average health care expenditures differ between the two age groups; persons age 65 to 74 have average health care expenditures equaling $1,435 as compared to $2,143 for persons age 75 and older (Gornick et al. 1985; 22, 44). By dividing elders in two age groups, we are formally recognizing the heterogeneity of their medical needs and financial ability and stylizing programs that better meet their respective sets of need. Because the health and economic status of elders is expected to improve (within limits) and retirement age limits are being moved up over time, the age bend points (65 and 75) should be adjusted to reflect contemporary conditions. Such an adjustment is necessary to preserve intergenerational equity.

Binstock (1985: 425) has taken issue with "policy options that would simply substitute age 75 (and other old ages) for a variety of younger ages now used as crude markers in public policies to approximate those within the older population who may need collective assistance." We agree that this is a form of "buck passing," which perpetuates ageism. Our reform, however, does not assume that this group needs or deserves collective assistance. The old-old program is not a welfare program, although some people within the program will be receiving welfare transfers from the public sector. The health care costs of persons age 75 and older would be financed by a flat-rate CHI (equal to the HI rate) tax applied to the legislated earnings taxable maximum. These CHI tax revenues are really a form of medical care savings held in the form of a social contract across the generations. It is only at age 75 that elders can start to draw on their medical care–saving reserve. Clearly, the present value of the CHI tax revenues (or the value of the medical care savings reserve) will be positively related to an elder's earnings level during his or her work history. Those who were less able to save due to low earnings will receive an intended public subsidy through the old-old program. Still, redistributive uncertainty exists for this part of the program; tax contributions for this coverage will reflect ability to pay, but high income elders are still likely to live longer and have preferences for higher quality and levels of medical care, leading to above average health care expenditures. The recent raising of the taxable maximum ceiling to $125,000, however, is likely to moderate the reversal of the redistributive intent.[11]

The young-old portion of the program would be financed by income-conditioned premiums. Research shows a strong negative association between health status and medical expenditures and use, and a positive correlation between health status and income. Given these associations, we argue that income, as distinguished from age, is a more precise marker of both medical and financial need. Public opinion evidence also shows that lower-income aged persons consistently and continually report problems with receiving medical care and affording medical care, and concerns about future medical care services. Similar problems and concerns are not reported by higher-income aged persons. For example, in a 1984 Gallup survey, roughly 35 percent of persons with incomes below 150 percent of the poverty level reported "lack of sufficient income during the previous year for medical care" as compared to less than 12 percent of elders with incomes 150 to 350 percent of poverty (Palmer et al. 1988: 21). Similarly, more than 20 percent of low-income elderly respondents reported that medical benefits were a serious problem. Less than 7 percent of elders with incomes exceeding $12,000 reported medical benefits to be a serious problem for them (unpublished results from a 1982 ABC News/Washington Post Survey). Low-income elders also worry more about future medical care costs; more than 70 percent of respondents in low-income aged households reported to be very concerned about future medical costs as compared to 25 percent of high-income elders (unpublished results from the 1987 Markle Foundation Survey).

Our premium schedule reflects evidence of differential need and principles of social adequacy: those with greater medical and financial need for collective assistance pay a smaller portion of actuarially fair premiums.

Table 6.7
Proposed Premium Schedule and Projected Tier 1 Program Revenues from Premiums

Ratio of Income to poverty level	Tier 1 premium schedule	Annual out of pocket reform expenditures		Percent of elderly population[c]	Total CHI revenues under reform (in millions)
		Premium[a]	Percent of income[b]		
0-124%	0	$ 0	0%	15.3%	$ 0
125-149%	25%	667	10.4 - 8.4	6.9	839
150-174%	40%	1,066	13.9 - 11.9	6.2	1,206
175-199%	60%	1,600	17.8 - 15.6	12.2	3,532
200-249%	80%	2,133	20.8 - 16.6	10.7	4,164
> 250%	100%	2,666	20.7	48.7	23,734
					$33,475

[a] Our reform does not include prescription medication coverage, except that currently covered by Medicare. Projected out-of-pocket prescription medication costs for elders in the year 2000 (expressed in 1985 dollars) ranges between $252 and $407. Mean annual expenditure projections for prescription medicines are calculated from the National Medical Expenditure Survey and Prescription Drug Expenditure Verification Survey. Data from Marc L. Berk, Claudia L. Schur, and Penny Mohr, "Using Survey Data to Estimate Prescription Drug Costs," *Health Affairs* 9, no. 3 (1990), pp. 146–156.

[b] Based on the poverty income guideline for an individual 65 and older in 1985.

[c] Data from U.S. Bureau of the Census, *Current Population Reports* 1990, Consumer Income, Series P-60, No. 171, Table 5, p. 25; and U.S. Congress House, Committee on Ways and Means, *The Green Book* (1991), Table 9, Appendix H, p. 1106.

The premium scheme is shown in Table 6.7. In a recent AARP survey, "58 percent of Americans favor basing Medicare premiums on beneficiaries' incomes," with 26 percent opposing such a plan (Schlesinger and Kronebush 1991: 22). Currently, Medicare beneficiaries spend 18 percent of their annual income on medical care and health insurance. Schlesinger and Drumheller (1988: 37) estimate per capita health care expenditures for noninstitutionalized poor and near-poor elders at $1,272 (expressed in 1984 dollars and inclusive of prescription medication expenditures). On average, elders with incomes below 125 percent of the 1984 poverty line "spend over a fourth of their annual income on health care and health insurance" (Schlesinger and Drumheller 1988: 37). In our plan, the actuarially fair premium in the year 2000 (expressed in 1985 dollars) is equal to $2,666. Persons with incomes below 200 percent of the poverty line will pay a CHI premium equaling slightly less than 18 percent of their income.[12] The poor and near poor (incomes less that 125 percent of the poverty line) would not be assessed a premium charge for the CHI insurance; however, they would be required to pay for their prescription medications. The CHI premium burden is capped at 21 percent of personal income, which occurs at the two bend points, 200 and 250 percent of the poverty index level. Premium burden for the poor, near poor, and low income in our plan are lower than the portion of their income spent on medical care in 1984. On average, premium rates for elders with modest to moderate income are likely to be higher than their current proportion of income spent on medical care and health insurance. However, they are afforded greater insurance coverage while they are age 65 to 74 at a lower time and inconvenience cost, and at age 75 they will be covered by acute and long-term care insurance and their out-of-pocket medical care costs will diminish sharply after age 75.

The financial feasibility of this two-tier reform proposal is shown in Table 6.6. The old-old CHI program is estimated to cost $99.3 billion (in 1985 dollars).[13] The projected total income for the HI Trust Fund in year 2000, expressed in 1985 dollars, is $97.4 billion, resulting in a $2 billion shortfall. We would propose that the earning ceiling on the HI payroll tax base be eliminated to make up for the Tier 2 revenue shortfall. Such a change would be consistent with our equity reform based on treating unequals unequally and equals equally. The young-old program has a projected surplus equal to $0.6 billion, assuming that no public subsidy is extended to persons with income above 250 percent of poverty. As noted earlier, however, because there is now a substantial health insurance tax subsidy for working aged employees of all incomes, intergenerational fairness may dictate providing some public subsidy to higher-income households while household members are between the ages of 65 and 74. If subsidy weights equal to 85, 90, and 95 percent were assigned to this income group, the program balance would be –$3.0 billion, –$1.8 billion, or –$0.6 billion, respectively. Because the aged are receiving more comprehensive insurance (no cost sharing plus long-term care) from a more efficient insurer (lower administrative costs and better price negotiation ability), a subsidy weight of between 90 and 95 percent for higher-income aged persons would satisfy reasonable standards for intergenerational equity.[14]

CONCLUSION

On average, the Medicare program redistributes resources to all persons age 65 and older, independent of their health or economic status. Rich and poor alike receive more than their money's worth from the program. The 1985 cohort of 65-year-olds paid roughly 10 (20) cents on every dollar of present actuarial value of HI (SMI) benefits. Intracohort redistributive shares are allocated by good fortune (e.g., living a long life, not needing both adult members of a family to work in the labor force, entering the program in its start-up years), misfortune (e.g., having poor health, being poor), and idiosyncratic preferences (e.g., a propensity for higher levels and quality of medical care). Relative gains are driven as much by luck and whim as by program design—to assist the needy. Such a program cannot be defended on principles of equity. Nor can we afford such a program; the price, in terms of unmet needs elsewhere, is too high.

As we begin to examine and plan for the economic, social, and demographic realities of the future, we need to take great care to distribute our scarce resources carefully, purposefully, and fairly. Our collective sense of fairness needs to be well honed, and then consistently applied and regularly consulted as we make choices about the treatment of equals and unequals in the future. Our Medicare reform proposal attempts to eliminate the redistributive capriciousness within the current Medicare program. We make explicit the redistributive intent of the program while recognizing the unique needs of elders in general and older elders in particular.

We design a program offering comprehensive benefits, but elders who are financially able are expected to pay their fair share. Higher-income elders, however, are afforded equivalent preferential premium treatment as that given to nonaged persons in the labor force. This kind of fairness requires each to pay according to his or her medical and financial ability. This kind of fairness promotes intergenerational accord. This kind of fairness we can afford. Binstock (1985: 447) warns "if we allow our thinking to be confined by our current policies and the principles they have come to reflect, we may very well find ourselves engaged in policy debates on age-group conflicts that are far worse than those we have experienced to date, trading off the value of one human life against another." The choice is clearly ours.

NOTES

1. Although adverse selection and moral hazard could have impeded or prevented the development of private health insurance for elders prior to the introduction of Medicare, private insurers had sufficient risk management techniques for managing both types of market impediments. The growth of this market, however, may have been slowed and/or hindered by high marketing

costs associated with the nongroup nature of these policies and the high administrative costs of monitoring the insurance pool.

2. Universal coverage also had roots of political incrementalism. Efforts in the 1950s to enact a national health insurance program in the United States had been resoundingly defeated. A tactical decision was made to refocus efforts on providing universal coverage for elders as a "first step" toward the enactment of compulsory national health insurance for all (Marmor 1970: 14–16; Annis 1963: 104–6; Blumenthal 1988a: 4–10).

3. Radner (1990) explored the relative economic standing of aged and nonaged under alternative definitions of economic well-being. He found improvements in the economic status of the aged relative to the nonaged when income and wealth (as opposed to just income) were included in the definition of economic well-being. However, the specific proportion of wealth (measured as financial assets only) included in the measure of resources available for current consumption did not have a significant impact on the relative standing of aged and nonaged groups.

4. Skilled nursing homes must be Medicare-certified and have staff and equipment to provide 24-hour skilled nursing and rehabilitative care under the supervision of physicians.

5. For illustrative purposes, we assume no additional contributions are made by the Medicare beneficiary after age 65.

6. Medicaid currently uses similar eligibility screens by way of a means test and the medically needy program.

7. The initial impact of the HI payroll tax rate is shared equally by employees and employers. However, it is generally assumed that the final burden of the tax is borne by labor (i.e., there is 100 percent backward shifting of the tax). The shifting assumption is controversial (Aaron 1982; Brittain 1972; Feldstein 1972; Hammermesh 1979; Vroman 1974), but conventional in most studies of individual equity of the OASI program (Burkhauser and Warlick 1981; Freiden et al. 1976; Hurd and Shoven 1983; Wolff 1987).

8. The minimum age for CHI eligibility would be tied to social security retirement age.

9. Income-conditioned premiums have also been proposed by Davis and Rowland (1989) and Blumenthal et al. (1986).

10. We used the official poverty rate to scale our subsidy weights. Alternative definitions of income and poverty should be explored to better approximate financial need. Ruggles (1990) comprehensively explores the problems with an alternative definition of poverty thresholds. She recommends a major overhaul of the official poverty measure. The new measure would be calibrated for standard of living changes, geographic differences, and family structure and need differences, in addition to incorporating assets into the measure of poverty.

11. In keeping with horizontal and vertical equity principles, we recommend the elimination of the taxable maximum ceiling on earnings.

12. Our reform does not include additional prescription medication coverage. Survey evidence (adjusted for underreporting of prescribed medicine expendi-

tures) from 1987 shows that the average Medicare beneficiary between the age 65 and 74 spent $393 per year on prescribed medicines (Berk et al. 1990: 153). Adjusting for the aging of the population, we project a mean annual expenditure for prescribed medicines of $374 (expressed in 1985 dollars) for elders age 65 to 74.

13. Administrative costs under our reform would be minimized by directly subtracting monthly income-conditioned premium payments from social security retirement benefits. The household's adjusted gross income (obtained from IRS records) from the previous year will be used to determine the subsidy weight for the forthcoming year.

14. Alternatively, the value of health insurance fringe benefits could be subject to income and payroll taxation (Munnell 1985).

7

Social Security and Individual Equity: A Summing Up

The Old Age, Survivors, and Disability Insurance program (OASDI) insures American workers and their families against earnings loss associated with retirement and long-term disability. Benefits are contingent on prior earnings, but a progressive benefit formula tilts benefits in favor of workers with lower average earnings. Additional benefits, noncontributory in nature, are payable to eligible dependents and survivors. This feature contributes to social adequacy but draws criticism for favoring single-earner couples at the expense of two-earner couples and single persons.

How one evaluates social security depends on the perspective from which one approaches issues of social policy. Robert J. Lampman (1984: 103–105) offers a convenient framework for evaluating competing perspectives. He refers to what he terms the four "mentalities" from which various perspectives emanate: the insurance mentality, which emphasizes offset of losses; the income tax mentality, which emphasizes horizontal and vertical equity; the minimum provision mentality, which emphasizes targeting of benefits to those who need them most; and the efficient social investment mentality, which focuses on transfers as a means of increasing national income. Each can serve as a basis for justifying or criticizing program features.

Of particular relevance for evaluating OASDI are the insurance and income tax mentalities. The insurance mentality emphasizes offset of losses and identifies justice with maintaining rank. This emphasis is embodied in the earnings-replacement feature of OASDI. The income tax mentality places high value on equal treatment of appropriately defined equals and on a narrowing of vertical inequality, both of which are features of the earnings-based, worker-only benefit structure. But this approach also countenances adjustments to the equality measure (average indexed monthly earnings, or AIME, in the case of OASDI) if justified by differences in individual circumstances. One may defend dependent's allowances and survivor's benefits on grounds of social adequacy in a manner analogous to the ability-to-pay defense of personal exemptions and medical deductions under an income tax. To extend the analogy, loss of noncontributory benefits because of dual entitlement might be likened to the difficulties of applying a graduated rate structure to single- and two-earner households. Horizontal and vertical equity play a key role in the design of both the OASDI benefit structure and the individual income tax, but ambiguities in the choice of an appropriate benefit or tax base and benefit or rate formula always seem to generate controversy.

The OASDI system as it has evolved remains true to the vision of Hohaus (1938), combining actuarial features of individual equity with an overriding goal of social adequacy. In broad terms, the Hohaus plan represents an amalgam of at least three of the mentalities identified by Lampman: insurance (earnings replacement), income tax (benefits linked to an earnings base), and targeting to those in need (progressive benefit formula and noncontributory family benefits). In mixing the three approaches, the system draws criticism from persons wedded to only one.

OTHER VISIONS OF SOCIAL SECURITY

Hohaus's vision of social security is reflected in the current OASDI system, but other visions have been put forth as being more equitable and, because they would strengthen the connection between contributions and benefits, as a means of improving market efficiency. These goals would be achieved by changing the system to conform more closely to actuarial standards.

An Actuarial Standard of Individual Equity

Under an actuarial standard, each worker would receive upon retirement a lifetime annuity, equal in present value to the compounded value of lifetime contributions. A retirement annuity insures retired workers against uncertainty of lifespan after retirement. An actuarial system can easily be extended to provide old age benefits to a surviving spouse, either by means of a joint-and-survivor annuity or by equal sharing of contributions made by spouses during marriage. Granting of survivor's benefits to dependent children could be accommodated within an actuarial system, but this would require additional contributions from affected households, a major departure from current practice.

Private insurers attempt to segregate the insured into homogeneous risk groups. Failure to separate poor from good risks will result in initial premiums that are too low for the former and too high for the latter. The good risks will seek to avoid the overcharge by taking their business to a competitor or, if that is not possible, by considering self-insurance. Insurers are therefore forced by adverse selection to establish separate risk categories and to charge appropriate premiums within each. The ability to establish homogeneous categories is limited by the availability and cost of information about each applicant, but categorization by age, gender, certain life-style factors such as smoking or drinking, and medical status are common practices in the issuance of life and annuity contracts.

When proponents of social security reform call for a standard of equity based on actuarial fairness, it is not always clear how far in this direction they want to go. OASI currently includes an actuarial adjustment for early or delayed retirement. This feature, although applied imperfectly, is not controversial and is recognized as necessary to prevent exploitation of the system by those who retire early. Available mortality data would allow segregation of risk groups according to gender, race, and socioeconomic status, but such efforts would be perceived by many as unfair or unjust and, perhaps, as unconstitutional. Because of the compulsory and nearly universal nature of the program, social security can collectivize these features within the beneficiary population without experiencing adverse selection. This allows substantial scope for creating a system that, even without homogeneous risk categories, would move us much closer to an annuity standard.[1]

One example is the two-tier proposal of Michael J. Boskin (1986: 139–171). Boskin argues (171) that his proposal would eliminate "enormous inequities" and inefficiencies in the present system. He would eliminate inequities by providing each worker with only those benefits that can be purchased with prior contributions. Boskin contends that such a system would eliminate serious sources of labor market distortion. The present system's weak and uncertain link between contributions and benefits causes workers to regard marginal contributions more as a tax than as an actuarially fair purchase of insurance, resulting in greater distortion in the labor market. Boskins's plan resembles an earlier proposal by Munnell (1977: 140–43), which would replace the progressive benefit formula with a proportional benefit formula that makes benefit awards a constant percentage of the benefit base.

A means-tested welfare program, such as Supplemental Security Income (SSI), adds the second tier to the Boskin and Munnell proposals. It would provide a safety net for workers whose social security annuity benefits are insufficient to meet standards of social adequacy. SSI already serves this purpose for about 5 percent of OASDI beneficiaries, but many more would qualify and come under the welfare system if actuarial benefits replaced the current redistributive arrangement. Precisely how many would depend on the level at which proportional benefits are set. For example, if average benefits remain at current levels, OASDI would pay higher benefits to workers with high earnings, lower benefits to workers with low earnings. It seems likely that average OASDI benefits would be reduced with a corresponding increase in welfare payments to those with low earnings.[2]

The Boskin and Munnell plans conform to the annuity-welfare model of Thompson (1983: 1437), combining the insurance mentality and the "minimum provision" mentality with its emphasis on targeting benefits only to those in need. Whereas the annuity component would be financed by payroll tax contributions to the individual account of each worker, the welfare component would be financed out of general revenues. In addition to the income test, potential recipients of SSI supplements presumably would be subjected to the rather rigid asset tests that currently restrict access to benefits.

Limits to Reform

If we are to retain a social insurance system that bases cash benefits on prior contributions of insured workers, it will almost certainly take the form of an earnings-based, partially redistributive model like the current system or evolve into an annuity-based model with a greater role for SSI. The need for a second-tier welfare safety net would recede over time if real earnings should continue to grow and if the intercohort adjustments built into the current formulas are retained because average benefits would then rise over time.

Other options seem less acceptable. Radical reforms such as Ferrara (1980) would phase out social security over time, but this option lacks political appeal. Even generations that expect low returns on contributions are likely to prefer some benefits to none.[3] Potential problems in the private pension system also increase the attractiveness of a tax-financed system, as do concerns about the ability of a private system to provide inflation protection after retirement. In the 1930s, Congress and the New Deal rejected a demogrant for the elderly (the Townsend plan) while assigning a secondary role to welfare programs for the aged and disabled. That decision is not likely to be reversed.

Nevertheless, pressures to reform the system are not likely to disappear. As Lampman has made clear, people evaluate the system from differing and sometimes conflicting perspectives, complicating efforts to reach a consensus. Abrupt changes, especially those affecting current retirement cohorts, are especially difficult to implement. The benefit tax, introduced in 1983, seems to be an exception, but Congress will not soon forget the reaction of the notch cohorts or the ill-fated attempt to finance Medicare catastrophic coverage with a tax on the affluent elderly. Delayed transitions, such as the phased advancement of the normal retirement age legislated in 1983, seem to be more acceptable even when they significantly redistribute wealth among cohorts. A similar phase-in period is likely if a consensus forms to rein in noncontributory benefits to dependents or to adopt earnings sharing.

COMBATTING MORAL HAZARD: THE DISABILITY DILEMMA

The OASI benefit formula has been extended to the Disability Insurance (DI) program with appropriate allowances for the shortened labor force tenure of many disabled beneficiaries. The work-disincentive or moral hazard problem associated with DI is more serious than that associated with OASI, which the minimum retirement age and early-retirement benefit reduction help to keep under control. Most of the controversy surrounding DI results from the apparently impossible task of determining in an equitable and consistent manner who is and who is not disabled. Changing standards of disability reflect the ongoing political struggle between fiscal constraint and compassion as well as the unpredictable and erratic role of federal courts. This fluidity again may be traced to differing perspectives on who among the population of impaired workers should receive public support or whether benefits, once awarded, establish a right to continued entitlement.

When DI was introduced in 1956, much attention was placed on rehabilitation, even though initially only workers age 50 and over were eligible for benefits. Rehabilitation efforts reflect the social investment mentality of Lampman, an approach marked by only limited success in spite of regulations requiring beneficiaries to cooperate or lose benefits.

MEDICARE AND INDIVIDUAL EQUITY

Medicare participants differ both in their need for medical care and in their ability to finance it. The program was introduced in recognition of the greater burden that medical costs impose on the elderly, and for the same reason, coverage was soon extended to workers receiving DI benefits (after two years). Medicare consists of two parts, Hospital Insurance (HI), financed by a payroll tax on insured workers, and Supplementary Medical Insurance (SMI), which covers physicians fees and related expenses. SMI is financed by monthly premiums paid by the insured, supplemented by a large federal subsidy.

As shown in Chapter 6, intercohort redistribution has diminished over time for HI, which provided a total windfall to initial enrollees who had paid no HI payroll tax while working. Because the payroll tax varies directly with taxable earnings, HI is redistributive within cohorts, and 1990 legislation raising the HI cap on taxable earnings to $125,000 in 1991 and indexing it thereafter makes it more so. At the same time that intercohort redistribution decreased under HI, it increased under SMI as Congress raised the general fund subsidy. The SMI premium is nonredistributive in principle, but Medicaid pays the premium of those who are poor, making the program redistributive in overall net impact.

Redistribution within cohorts depends on medical utilization patterns and longevity as well as on financing, making the overall direction of redistribution uncertain. The splitting of the system into HI and SMI with separate sources of finance for each fails to conform to any apparent equity principle.

A reform proposal presented in Chapter 6 illustrates how Medicare financing and benefits might be restructured to reflect and preserve redistributive intent. The elderly would be divided into younger and older cohorts. For younger cohorts, age 65 to 74, benefits would be financed jointly by income-conditioned premiums based on ability to pay coupled with continuing federal subsidies. All costs of older cohorts, age 75 and over, would be financed by a payroll tax on insured workers. Financial support and redistribution could be enhanced by removing the cap on taxable earnings for Medicare purposes. Thus, workers would establish a right to medical benefits during their advanced years when potential need is greater by paying an earnings-related, redistributive tax while they are working.

THE IMPENDING TRUST FUND SURPLUS

Social security trust funds never approached full funding and operated on close to a pay-as-you-go basis from the 1950s to the 1980s. Until the early 1970s, ad hoc tax and benefit increases allowed the system to grow, and retirement cohorts received large transfers from younger working generations. With passage of the 1977 Social Security Amendments, wage indexing of initial benefit allowances replaced the hastily adopted and poorly designed indexing scheme of 1972. A procedure for linking benefit awards to changes in real wages was put into place, beginning with the cohort that reached age 62 in 1979. The 1977 amendments also established future payroll tax rates and wage indexed the annual taxable maximum for individual workers. When the unexpectedly poor performance of the economy threatened short-term solvency of the trust funds, further tax increases and benefit reductions were approved in 1983. This legislation rescued the funds from short-term insolvency and brought them into near long-term balance over the next 75 years. To achieve these results, however, Congress adopted tax and benefit formulas that will generate historically unprecedented annual surpluses until about 2020. Fund accumulation will peak about 2030, only to disappear by 2050.

If the system is viewed in isolation, the buildup places on members of the baby-boom cohorts some of the burden of financing their own retirement. As a result, the cohorts that follow will pay less in taxes than would be required if currently legislated benefits were to be financed on a pay-as-you-go basis.[4] Whether this method of allocating burdens across generations is the result of a conscious decision with respect to intergenerational burden sharing or merely an accidental product of a long-term fund balancing scheme is not clear. Robert J. Myers, an adviser to the National Commission on Social Security Reform that recommended most of the changes incorporated into the 1983 Social Security Amendments, has testified that the temporary fund buildup is merely a coincidence. At the time, attention of commission members was focused on means of protecting the fund from insolvencies like those that threatened it in 1977 and 1983, not on longer-term issues.[5]

Macroeconomic Implications

Debate over the impending surplus and the subsequent sell-off seems to focus more on its effect on saving, investment, and deficit spending than on equity. An extended discussion of the macroeconomic implications of the surplus would carry us beyond the scope of this work, but the issue merits brief consideration because of its implications for the survival of the benefit structure so painstakingly created by the 1977 and 1983 amendments. Some economists express concern that Congress will dissipate the surplus by eliminating notches, bailing out Medicare, or simply raising benefits. Others expect a payroll tax cut, which would redistribute wealth toward the baby-boom cohorts and away from their successors.[6] It would also eliminate a potential source of aggregate savings. A frequently expressed fear is that the surplus, if allowed to accumulate, will be used to finance even larger deficits in the federal general fund. The suspicion that much of the surplus will be offset by larger general fund deficits gains credence in light of recent fiscal behavior (Buchanan 1990: 53–56).

In an attempt to highlight the economic and intergenerational consequences of the trust fund surplus, John Hambor (1987) analyzes the effects of two contrasting fiscal scenarios on saving, investment, and burden sharing. Each may be described as extreme, but they serve to highlight the implications of alternative fiscal responses. To limit the analysis to issues of growth and burden sharing, Hambor assumes that monetary policy maintains full employment.

Scenario One: Validation. The general fund remains in annual balance. As the trust fund builds up, it absorbs an increasing share of federal debt. As fund size peaks, full implementation of the policy may require investment in private sector financial instruments. The government, operating through the fund, becomes a large net saver, contributing to lower interest rates, a larger capital stock, and increased per capita earnings. As the baby-boom generation phases into retirement, a portion of its retirement cost is financed by a sell-off of fund assets. Given continuing balance in the general fund, the sell-off turns the government into a net dissaver. Interest rates rise. The capital stock declines, returning at the end of the sell-off to the level that would have prevailed in the absence of a trust fund buildup.

Scenario Two: Offset. The general fund deficit equals the trust fund surplus. This policy allows for a general fund deficit during the period of trust fund buildup but requires offsetting general fund surpluses during the sell-off. The interest rate, saving, investment, and aggregate output are not affected by the trust fund. Benefits of deficits accrue to current workers, whose retirement costs will be borne by future workers. During the sell-off, bonds are retired out of general fund surpluses as the shift from income tax to payroll financing during the buildup is reversed during the sell-off. As Hambor points out, the same aggregate effects could be achieved by cutting payroll taxes during the first phase and then increasing them during the second. This option would eliminate the buildup and the sell-off. Its only effect would be to redistribute tax burdens within the two generations.

Other Scenarios. Other combinations are possible. For example, if surpluses are validated during the buildup and offset during the sell-off, a permanent partially funded system could be created and a larger capital stock would be maintained. Economists such as Martin Feldstein (1977) favor this approach as a means of overcoming a perceived capital shortage in the U.S. economy.

A more frightening but perhaps more likely scenario combines offset during the buildup phase with validation during the sell-off. The economy enters the sell-off phase with no increase in capital stock, and the postbaby-boom generation would be called upon to honor benefit obligations in the face of a decline (at least in relative terms) in the capital stock and in aggregate output.

The model underlying these analyses is very simple. For example, it does not consider the possibility that increased public saving during the validation buildup may be offset, at least in part, by reduced private saving. Nor does it allow for the effects of international capital flows, which enabled investment to exceed domestic savings during the 1980s. Hambor is aware of these limitations. His intent is to highlight the fact that the way we handle the fund buildup has important implications both for the economy and for equity between and within generations.

The Brookings Simulations

Economists at the Brookings Institution constructed a simulation model for the purpose of projecting macroeconomic and trust fund performance through the year 2060 (Aaron, et al. 1989). The model, consisting of more than 100 equations, projects the effects of alternative trust fund and budgetary options on future values of key macroeconomic variables, including capital stock, national product, consumption, and wage rates. Budgetary assumptions are similar to those of Hambor.

The Brookings baseline projection assumes annual total federal deficits (general fund plus OASDHI trust funds) equal to 1.5 percent of GNP throughout the simulation period. Qualitatively, the baseline projection approximates Hambor's offset scenario, requiring general fund deficits during most of the trust fund buildup and general fund surpluses during the sell-off. General fund deficits prevent use of the trust fund to augment private savings and investment. The baseline is compared to an alternative simulation that assumes an annual general fund deficit equal to 1.5 percent of GNP. During the trust fund buildup, social security surpluses in excess of the modest general fund deficit contribute to increased national savings and capital formation, approximating Hambor's validation scenario. In both simulations, it is assumed that social security tax rates are increased as necessary to maintain close fund balance over a 75-year horizon. Benefit levels are established in accordance with the 1983 benefit formula. Because of timely tax increases, the trust funds become a continuing source of savings, thus avoiding the disinvestment that would occur if Hambor's validation policy were to continue throughout the sell-off phase.

Assuming that additional savings translate fully into domestic investment, the comparison simulation projects a capital stock exceeding that of the baseline projection throughout the first six decades of the twenty-first century. Capital stock exceeds the baseline level by a maximum of 23.7 percent in 2020, showing the effect of validation during three decades of fund surpluses. In spite of the drain on the fund occasioned by retirement of the baby-boom generation, the policy of increasing payroll taxes to maintain long-term balance results in a stock of capital 12.4 percent higher than under the baseline projection in 2060.

A larger capital stock increases labor productivity and earnings, which eventually increases social security benefits. Nevertheless, the simulation indicates that because of increased output, the social security pension program would impose no additional burden on future generations of workers. Increased consumption by the affected generations more than offsets the required increases in OASDI taxes. Prospects for the HI fund are less sanguine, but maintenance of long-term close balance by raising tax rates would, if channeled into domestic investment, offset much of the anticipated burden of financing this program.[7]

The authors of the Brookings study warn that long-term OASDHI benefit obligations can be accommodated without reducing the lifetime consumption of future generations only if we maintain fiscal discipline. This requires a willingness to restrain general fund deficits and to increase payroll tax revenues to keep the funds in close long-term balance. If, instead, the funds are used to finance current consumption, social security will impose substantial burdens on future generations. The future will be even more bleak if the recent sluggish growth in productivity persists into the next century (Aaron et al. 1989: 96–98).

A FINAL SUMMING UP

Our primary goal has been to discern and evaluate the principles of individual equity inherent in the OASDHI system. Since individual equity is only one of the factors to be considered in the design of a system of social insurance, it is not surprising that some components of the system fail to conform to any discernible equity standard. We have attempted to identify instances when this is so and to discover how they came about.

OASDI is a defined-benefit program. Except for the relatively minor fund stabilizer provision of 1983, the law does not prescribe how tax and benefit rules are to be amended to ensure fund balance. The program remains an open system with responsibility for correcting imbalances placed in the hands of future Congresses and presidents. This creates inevitable uncertainty for future generations. In particular, it leaves unanswered questions about how burdens will be shared among generations. Because the system is now mature, returns to future generations will be much lower than returns to their predecessors who enjoyed windfalls in both the retirement and Medicare programs. Intergenerational issues can be settled only in conjunction with other policies directed as deficit reduction, saving, and capital formation.

The special problems of Medicare must likewise be dealt with as part of an overall program for improving our ailing system of health care. Potential changes might include extension of Medicare coverage to children or a merging of the program into a system of national health insurance. If policymakers opt for the latter, the question of finance becomes important. If national health insurance is to be financed by payroll taxes, it raises questions of how much additional expenditure can be supported by this single tax base.

Finally, OASDHI represents only a part of our national safety net. How should it mesh with means-tested welfare? Should we cut the social adequacy role of OASDHI, including at least some of its noncontributory benefits, and place greater reliance on the welfare system? Issues such as these will require a reexamination of our attitudes toward benefit entitlement, means testing, and federal tax structure.

NOTES

1. Trowbridge (1989) provides a nontechnical introduction to actuarial principles of private and social insurance. A somewhat more advanced treatment appears in Barr (1987: 108–124).

2. Burkhauser and Smeeding (1981) discuss the relationship between social security and welfare, emphasizing that, because SSI benefits are essentially reduced dollar for dollar for persons also receiving OASDI benefits, the poor experience little net gain from social security.

3. Meyer (1987: 138–140) presents a simple arithmetic illustration of the effects of a phase-out. Browning (1973) provides a more extensive treatment. Stein (1987) offers a critique of Ferrara's plan.

4. Kotlikoff (1990) proposes generational accounts, denominated in present value terms, as a means of emphasizing the impact of fund financing and fiscal policy on different generations.

5. Testimony before the Subcommittee on Social Security, Ways and Means Committee, (U.S. Congress 1988: 36).

6. A volume edited by Carolyn L. Weaver (1990) provides economic and political analyses of the impending surplus by a number of economists and budget specialists. A variety of views are represented.

7. To the extent that increased savings are invested abroad, gains in domestic earnings and production will not occur. Income from foreign earnings and reverse capital flows from disinvestment will ease the burden of financing future benefits, and because earnings are lower, benefit obligations will be reduced (Aaron et al. 1989: 82–87).

References

Aaron, Henry J. 1977. "Demographic Effects on the Equity of Social Security Benefits," in Martin S. Feldstein, ed., *The Economics of Public Services*, pp. 151–173. New York: Macmillan.

_____ . 1982. *Economic Effects of Social Security*. Washington, DC: Brookings Institution.

Aaron, Henry J., Barry P. Bosworth, and Gary Burtless. 1989. *Can America Afford to Grow Old?* Washington, DC: Brookings Institution.

Acton, Jan P. 1976. "Demand for Health Care among the Urban Poor with Special Emphasis on the Role of Time," in R. Rosett, ed., *The Roles of Health Insurance in the Health Services Sector*, pp. 165–214. New York: National Bureau of Economic Research.

Aday, Lu Ann, and Ronald Andersen. 1981. "Equity of Access to Medical Care: A Conceptual and Empirical Overview," *Medical Care* 19 (12), pp. 4–27.

Annis, Edward R. 1963. "Government Health Care: First the Aged, Then Everyone," *Current History*, August, pp. 104–109.

Antonovsky, Aaron. 1972. "Social Class, Life Expectancy and Overall Mortality," in E. Gartly Jaco, ed., *Patients, Physicians and Illness*, pp 1–27. New York: Free Press.

Atkins, G. Lawrence. 1985. "The Economic Status of the Oldest Old," *Milbank Memorial Fund Quarterly* 63 (2), pp. 395–419.

Ball, Robert M. 1988. "The Original Understanding on Social Security: Implications for Later Developments," in Theodore R. Marmor and Jerry L. Mashaw, eds., *Social Security: Beyond the Rhetoric of Crisis*, pp. 17–39. Princeton, NJ: Princeton University Press.

Barr, Nicholas. 1987. *The Economics of the Welfare State*. London: Weidenfeld and Nicolson.

Berk, Marc L., Claudia L. Schur, and Penny Mohr. 1990. "Using Survey Data to Estimate Prescription Drug Costs," *Health Affairs* 9 (3), pp. 146–156.

Berkowitz, Monroe, and M. Anne Hill. 1986. "Disability and the Labor Market: An Overview," in Monroe Berkowitz and M. Anne Hall, eds., *Disability and the Labor Market*, pp. 1–28. Ithaca, NY: ILR Press.

Binstock, Robert H. 1985. "The Oldest Old: A Fresh Perspective or Compassionate Ageism Revisited?" *Milbank Memorial Fund Quarterly* 63 (2), pp. 420–451.

Blumenthal, David. 1988a. "Medicare: The Beginnings," in David Blumenthal, Mark Schlesinger, and Pamela Brown Drumheller, eds., *Renewing the Promise, Medicare and Its Reform*, pp. 3–19. Oxford: Oxford University Press.

_____. 1988b. "Medicare: The Record to Date," in David Blumenthal, Mark Schlesinger, and Pamela Brown Drumheller, eds., *Renewing the Promise, Medicare and Its Reform*, pp. 20–30. Oxford: Oxford University Press.

Blumenthal, David, and William Hsiao. 1988. "Payment of Physicians under Medicare," in David Blumenthal, Mark Schlesinger, and Pamela Brown Drumheller, eds., *Renewing the Promise, Medicare and Its Reform*, pp. 66–80. Oxford: Oxford University Press.

Blumenthal, David, Mark Schlesinger, and Pamela Brown Drumheller. 1986. "The Future of Medicare," *New England Journal of Medicine* 314 (11), pp. 722–728.

_____, eds. 1988. *Renewing the Promise, Medicare and Its Reform*. Oxford: Oxford University Press.

Boskin, Michael. 1973. "The Economics of Labor Supply," in Glen Cain and Harold Watts, eds., *Income Maintenance and Labor Supply*, pp. 163–80. New York: Academic Press.

_____. 1986. *Too Many Promises: The Uncertain Future of Social Security*. Homewood, IL: Dow-Jones Irwin.

_____, Lawrence J. Kotlikoff, Douglas J. Puffert, and John B. Shoven. 1987. "Social Security: A Financial Appraisal across and within Generations," *National Tax Journal* 40 (1), pp. 19–34.

Bound, John. 1989. "The Health and Earnings of Rejected Disability Insurance Applicants," *American Economic Review* 79 (3), pp. 482–503.

Brittain, John A. 1972. *The Payroll Tax for Social Security*. Washington, DC: The Brookings Institution.

Browning, Edgar K. 1973. "Social Insurance and Intergenerational Transfers," *Journal of Law and Economics*, 16, pp. 215–237.

Buchanan, James M. 1990. "The Budgetary Politics of Social Security," in Carolyn L. Weaver, ed., *Social Security's Looming Surpluses*. Washington, DC: AEI Press.

Burkhauser, Richard V., and Timothy M. Smeeding. 1981. "The Net Impact of the Social Security System on the Poor," *Public Policy* 29, pp. 159–178.

Burkhauser, Richard V., and Jennifer L. Warlick. 1981. "Disentangling the Annuity from the Redistributive Aspects of Social Security in the United States," *The Review of Income and Wealth* 27 (4), pp. 401–421.

Butler, John A., William Winter, Judith Singer, and Martha Wenger. 1985. "Medical Care Use and Expenditure among Children and Youth in the United States: Analysis of a National Probability Sample," *Pediatrics* 76 (4), pp. 495–507.

Cafferata, G. 1984. "Private Health Insurance Coverage of the Medicare Population," Data Preview 18. National Center for Health Services Research, National Health Care Expenditures Study. Rockville, MD: U.S. Department of Health and Human Services, Publication No. (PHS) 84-3362.

Cain, Glen. 1966. *Married Women in the Labor Force: An Economic Analysis.* Chicago: University of Chicago Press.

Campbell, Rita Ricardo. 1977. *Social Security: Promise and Reality.* Stanford, CA: Hoover Institution.

Chassin, Mark R., Robert H. Brook, R. E. Park, Joan Kessey, Arlene Fink, Jacqueline Kosecoff, Katherine Kahn, Nancy Merrick, and David H. Solomon. 1986. "Variations in the Use of Medical and Surgical Services by the Medicare Population," *New England Journal of Medicine* 314 (5), pp. 285–290.

Cohen, Wilbur J. 1963. "Medical Care for the Aged," *Current History*, pp. 98–103.

Corning, Peter A. 1969. *The Evolution of Medicare . . . from Idea to Law.* U.S. Department of Health, Education and Welfare, Research Report No. 29.

Davis, Karen, Marsha Gold, and Diane Makuc. 1981. "Access to Health Care for the Poor: Does the Gap Remain? *Annual Review of Public Health* 2, pp. 159–182.

Davis, Karen, and Diane Rowland. 1984. "Medicare Financing Reform: A New Medicare Premium," *Milbank Memorial Fund Quarterly/Health and Society* 62 (2), pp. 300–316.

Davis, Karen, and Cathy Schoen. 1978. *Health and the War on Poverty: A Ten-Year Appraisal.* Washington, DC: The Brookings Institution.

Derthick, Martha. 1979. *Policy Making for Social Security.* Washington, DC: The Brookings Institution.

_____. 1990. *Agency under Stress.* Washington, DC: The Brookings Institution.

Encyclopedia Britannica. 1970. "Insurance." Chicago: Encyclopedia Britannica.

Farley Short, Pamela, and Alan C. Monheit. 1988. "Employees and Medicare as Partners in Financing Health Care for the Elderly," in Mark V. Pauly and William L. Kissick, eds., *Lessons from the First Twenty Years of Medicare*, pp. 301–20. Philadelphia: University of Pennsylvania Press.

Feder, Judith. 1977. *Medicare: The Politics of Federal Hospital Insurance.* Lexington, MA: D. C. Heath.

Feldstein, Martin S. 1972. "The Incidence of the Social Security Payroll Tax Comment," *American Economic Review* 62, pp. 735–738.

———. 1977. "Facing the Social Security Crisis." *Public Interest* 47, pp. 88–100.

Ferrara, Peter J. 1980. *Social Security: The Inherent Contradiction*. San Francisco: Cato Institute.

Freeman, Howard E., Robert J. Blendon, Linda H. Aiken, Seymour Sudman, Connie F. Mullinix, and Christopher R. Covey. 1987. "Americans Report on Their Access to Health Care," *Health Affairs* 6 (1), pp. 6–18.

Freiden, Alan, Dean Leimer, and Ronald Hoffman. 1976. "Internal Rates of Return to Retired Worker-Only Beneficiaries under Social Security, 1967–70," in *Studies in Income Distribution No. 5*. Washington, DC: U.S. Department of Health, Education, and Welfare, Social Security Administration.

Garfinkel, Irwin, and Stanley H. Masters. 1977. *Estimating the Labor Supply Effects of Income Maintenance Alternatives*. New York: Academic Press.

Garfinkel, S. A., and L. S. Corder. 1985. "Supplemental Health Insurance Coverage among Aged Medicare Beneficiaries." Washington, DC: U.S. Government Printing Office, NMCUES Descriptive Report No. 5, DHHS Publication No. 85-20205, Office of Research and Demonstrations, HCFA.

Ginsburg, Paul B. 1989. "Physician Payment Policy in the 101st Congress," *Health Affairs* 8 (1), pp. 5–20.

Ginsburg, Paul, B., Lauren B. LeRoy, and Glenn T. Hammons. 1990. "Medicare Physician Payment Reform," *Health Affairs* 9 (1), pp. 178–188.

Gordon, N. M. 1986. Testimony before the Subcommittee on Health and the Environment, Committee on Energy and Commerce. U.S. Congress, House of Representatives, March 26.

Gornick, Marian, Jay N. Greenberg, Paul W. Eggers, and A. Dobson. 1985. "Twenty Years of Medicare and Medicaid: Covered Populations, Use of Benefits, and Program Expenditures," *Health Care Financing Review*. 1985. Annual Supplement. Washington, DC: U.S. Government Printing Office, HCFA Pub. No. 03217, Office of Research and Demonstrations, Health Care Financing Administration, pp. 13–59.

Gottschalk, Peter, and Barbara L. Wolfe. 1991. "How Equal Is the Utilization of Medical Care in the United States?" Paper presented at the Association for Public Policy and Management annual meetings, San Francisco, November 1990.

———, and Robert Haveman. 1989. "Health Care Financing in the US, UK, and Netherlands: Distributional Consequences," in *Changes in Revenue Structures*. Detroit: Wayne State University Press, pp. 351–373.

Gove, Walter R. 1973. "Sex, Marital Status, and Mortality," *American Journal of Sociology* 79, pp. 45–67.

Guterman, Stuart, and Allen Dobson. 1986. "Impact of the Medicare Prospective Payment System for Hospitals," *Health Care Financing Review* 7 (3), pp. 97–114.

Hambor, John C. 1987. "Economic Policy, Intergovernmental Equity, and the Social Security Trust Fund Buildup," *Social Security Bulletin* 50 (10), pp. 13–18.

Hammermesh, Daniel S. 1979. "New Estimates of the Incidence of the Payroll Tax," *Southern Economic Journal* 45, pp. 1208–1217.

Harris, Richard. 1969. *A Sacred Trust*. Baltimore: Penguin Books.

Haveman, Robert, and Barbara Wolfe. 1987. "The Disabled from 1962 to 1984: Trends in Number, Composition, and Well-Being." Madison: University of Wisconsin-Madison, Institute for Research on Poverty, SR #44.

Health Insurance Association of America. 1990. *Source Book of Health Insurance Data*. Washington, DC: HIAA.

Helbing, Charles, Viola B. Latta, and Roger E. Keene. 1991. "Medicare Expenditures for Physicians and Supplies Services, 1970–1988," *Health Care Financing Review* 12 (3) pp. 109–115.

Hohaus, Reinhard A. 1938. "Equity, Adequacy, and Related Factors in Old Age Security," *Record*, American Institute of Actuaries, 27, pp. 76–120.

Holden, Karen C. 1982. "The Housewife and Social Security Reform: A Feminist Perspective," in Richard V. Burkhauser and Karen C. Holden, eds., *A Challenge to Social Security*, pp. 41–65. New York: Academic Press.

Holohan, John, and Stephen Zuckerman. 1989. "Medicare Mandatory Assignment: An Unnecessary Risk," *Health Affairs* 8 (1), pp 65–79.

Hsiao, William C., Peter Braun, Daniel Dunn, and Edmund Becker. 1988. "Resource-Based Relative Values," *Journal of the American Medical Association* 260 (16), pp. 2347–2353.

Hu, Yuanreng, and Noreen Goldman. 1990. "Mortality Differentials by Marital Status: An International Comparison," *Demography* 27 (2), pp. 233–250.

Hurd, Michael D. 1989. "The Economic Status of the Elderly," *Science*, May, pp. 659–664.

_____, and John B. Shoven. 1983. "The Distributional Impact of Social Security." Working paper no. 1155. National Bureau of Economic Research, Inc. Working paper series.

_____. 1985. "The Distributional Impact of Social Security," in David A. Wise, ed., *Pensions, Labor, and Individual Choice*, pp. 193–215. Chicago: University of Chicago Press.

Iams, Howard M., and John L. McCoy. 1991. "Predictors of Mortality among Newly Retired Workers," *Social Security Bulletin* 54 (3), pp. 2–10.

Kaplan, Robert S. 1977. *Indexing Social Security*. Washington, DC: American Enterprise Institute.

Kasper, Judith D. 1985. "Perspectives on Health Care from the National Medical Care Utilization and Expenditure Survey, 1980." Draft Report. Baltimore, MD: Office of Research and Demonstrations, Health Care Financing Administration.

————. 1986. "Health Status and Utilization Differences by Medicaid Coverage and Income," *Health Care Financing Review* 7 (4), pp. 1–17.

————. 1988. *Aging Alone, Profiles and Projections*. Baltimore, MD: The Commonwealth Fund Commission on Elderly People Living Alone.

Keeller, Emmett B., Willard G. Manning, and Kenneth B. Wells. 1988a. "The Demand for Episodes of Mental Health Services," *Journal of Health Economics* 7, pp. 369–392.

————. 1988b. "The Demand for Episodes of Treatment in the Health Insurance Experiment," *Journal of Health Economics* 7, 337–367.

Kennedy, Edward M. 1972. *Critical Condition*. New York: Simon and Schuster.

Kitagawa, Evelyn, and Philip Hauser. 1973. *Differential Mortality in the United States: A Study of Socioeconomic Epidemiology*. Cambridge: Harvard University Press.

Koitz, David. 1984. "Social Security: Reexamining Eligibility for Disability Benefits." Congressional Research Service, Library of Congress.

Kollmann, Geoffrey, and David Koitz. 1988. "Social Security: Illustrations of Current Benefit Levels for Persons Born from 1895–1935," Congressional Research Service, Library of Congress, March 28.

Kotlikoff, Laurence J. 1990. "The Social Security 'Surpluses'—New Clothes for the Emperor?" in Carolyn L. Weaver, ed., *Social Security's Looming Surpluses*, pp. 17–27. Washington, DC: AEI Press.

Lampman, Robert J. 1984. *Social Welfare Spending: Accounting for Changes from 1950 to 1978*. Orlando, FL: Academic Press.

Lando, Mordechai E., Malcolm P. Coate, and Ruth Kraus. 1979. "Disability Benefit Applications and the Economy," *Social Security Bulletin* 42 (10), pp. 3–10.

Lando, Mordechai E., Alicia V. Farley, and Mary A. Brown. 1982. "Recent Trends in the Social Security Disability Insurance Program," *Social Security Bulletin* 45 (8), pp. 3–14.

Latta, Viola B., and Roger E. Keene. 1990. "Use and Cost of Short-Stay Hospital Inpatient Services under Medicare, 1988," *Health Care Financing Review* 12 (1), pp. 91–98.

Lave, Judith R. 1988. "The Structure of the Medicare Benefit Package: Evolution and Options for Change," in Mark V. Pauly and William L. Kissick, eds. *Lessons from the First Twenty Years of Medicare*, pp. 2–24. Philadelphia: University of Pennsylvania Press.

Lave, Judith, and Howard Goldman. 1990. "Medicare Financing of Mental Health Care," *Health Affairs* 9 (3), pp 6–19.

Leimer, Dean R. 1978. "An Empirical Analysis of Alternative Social Security Benefit Structures," in *Studies of Income Distribution*, Washington, DC: U.S. Social Security Administration, Office of Research and Statistics, No. 9.

_____ , and Peter A. Petri. 1981. "Cohort-Specific Effects of Social Security Policy," *National Tax Journal* 34 (1), pp. 9–28.

Leimer, Dean R., Ronald Hoffman, and Alan Freiden. 1978. "A Framework for Analyzing the Equity of the Social Security Benefit Structure," in *Studies in Income Distribution* Washington, DC: U.S. Social Security Administration, Office of Research and Statistics, No. 6.

Leonard, Herman B., and Richard J. Zeckhauser. 1983. "Public Insurance Provision and Non-Market Failures," *The Geneva Papers on Risk and Insurance* 8 (27), pp. 147–157.

Leonard, Jonathan S. 1986. "Labor Supply Incentives and Disincentives for Disabled Person," in Monroe Berkowitz and M. Anne Hill, eds., *Disability and the Labor Market*, pp. 64–94. Ithaca, NY: ILR Press.

Long, Steve H., and Russell F. Settle. 1984. "Medicare and the Disadvantaged Elderly: Objectives and Outcomes," *Milbank Memorial Fund: Health and Society*, 62, pp. 609–656.

Long, Steve H. , and Charles R. Link. 1982. "Who Bears the Burden of Medicare Cost Sharing?" *Inquiry* 19 (3), pp. 222–234.

McBride, Timothy D. 1986. "Old-Age and Survivors Insurance in the Demographic Crunch." University of Wisconsin-Madison.

Manning, Willard G., Joseph P. Newhouse, Naihua Duan, Emmett B. Keeler, Arlene Leibowitz, and M. Susan Marquis. 1987. "Health Insurance and the Demand for Medical Care: Evidence from the Randomized Experiment," *American Journal of Economics* 77 (3), pp. 251–277.

Marmor, Theodore, R. 1970. *The Politics of Medicare.* Chicago: Aldine.

Mashaw, Jerry L. 1983. *Bureaucratic Justice.* New Haven: Yale University Press.

_____ . 1988. "Disability Insurance in an Age of Retrenchment: The Politics of Implementing Rights," in Theodore R. Marmor and Jerry L. Mashaw, eds., *Social Security: Beyond the Rhetoric of Crisis.* Princeton, NJ: Princeton University Press.

Meyer, Charles W. 1987. "The Economic and Political Implications of a Phase-Out: A Summing Up," in Charles W. Meyer, ed., *Social Security: A Critique of Radical Reform Proposals*, pp. 127–148. Lexington, MA: D. C. Heath and Company.

Moon, Marilyn. 1988. "Increases in Beneficiary Burdens: Direct and Indirect Effects," in Mark V. Pauly and William L. Kissick, eds., *Lessons from the First Twenty Years of Medicare*, pp. 321–340. Philadelphia: University of Pennsylvania Press.

Mueller, Margorie S. 1972. "Private Health Insurance in 1970," *Social Security Bulletin* 35, pp. 3–19.

Munnell, Alicia. 1977. *The Future of Social Security.* Washington, DC: The Brookings Institution.

_____ . 1985. "Paying for the Medicare Program," *New England Economic Review*, January/February, pp. 46–66.

Myers, Robert J. 1985. *Social Security*. 3rd ed. Homewood, IL: Richard D. Irwin.

Nagi, Saad Z. 1969. *Disability and Rehabilitation*. Columbus, OH: Ohio State University Press.

National Center for Health Statistics. 1991. *Health, United States, 1990*. Hyattsville, MD: Public Health Service.

National Commission on Social Security Reform. 1983. *Report*. Washington, DC: U.S. Government Printing Office.

Neugarten, Bernice L. 1974. "Age Groups in American Society and the Rise of the Young Old," *Annals of the American Academy of Political and Social Science* 415, pp. 187–198.

Newhouse, Joseph. 1978. "Insurance Benefits, Out-of-Pocket Payments, and the Demand for Medical Care: A Review of the Literature," *Health and Medical Care Services Review* (1), pp. 3–15.

_____. 1981. "The Demand for Medical Care Services: A Retrospect and Prospect," in J. van der Gaag and M. Perlman, eds., *Health, Economics, and Health Economics*, pp. 85–102. Amsterdam: North-Holland.

Okonkwo, Ubadingko, 1976. "Intragenerational Equity under Social Security." Washington, DC: International Monetary Fund.

Packard, Michael. 1990. "The Effects of Removing 70- and 71-year-olds from Coverage under the Social Security Earnings Test." Washington, DC: Social Security Administration, ORS Working Paper Series, No. 44.

Palmer, John L., Timothy Smeeding, and Christopher Jencks. 1988. "The Uses and Limits of Income Comparisons," in John L. Palmer, Timothy Smeeding, and Barbara Boyle Torrey, eds., *The Vulnerable*. Washington, DC: The Urban Institute Press.

Pattison, David, Benjamin Bridges, Jr., Michael V. Leonesio, and Bernard Wixon. 1990. "Simulating Aggregate and Distributional Effects of Various Plans for Modifying the Retirement Earnings Test." Washington, DC: Social Security Administration, ORS Working Paper Series, No. 46.

Pellechio, Anthony, and Gordon Goodfellow. 1983. "Individual Gains and Losses from Social Security before and after the 1983 Amendments," *Cato Journal* 3 (2), pp. 417–442.

Phelps, Charles E., and Joseph Newhouse. 1974. "Coinsurance, the Price of Time, and the Demand for Medical Services," *Review of Economics and Statistics*, 56, pp. 334–342.

Phelps, Charles E. , and Anne L. Reisinger. 1988. "Unresolved Risk Under Medicare," in Mark V. Pauly and William L. Kissick, eds, *Lessons from the First Twenty Years of Medicare*, pp. 117–150. Philadelphia: University of Pennsylvania Press.

Physician Payment Review Commission. 1987. "Medicare Physician Payment: An Agenda for Reform," March 1, 1987.

Rabin, David L. 1985. "Waxing of the Gray, Waning of the Green," in *America's Aging, Health in an Older Society*. Washington, DC: National Academy Press.

Radner, David B. 1987. "Money Incomes of the Aged and Nonaged Family Units, 1961–84," *Social Security Bulletin* 50 (8), pp. 9–28.

Radner, Daniel B. 1990. "Assessing the Economic Status of the Aged and Nonaged Using Alternative Income-Wealth Measures," *Social Security Bulletin* 53 (3), pp. 2–14.

Rice, Dorothy. 1986. "Living Longer in the U.S.: Social and Economic Implications," *Journal of Medical Practice Management* 1 (3), pp. 162–169.

_____ , and Mitch LaPlante. 1988. "Chronic Illness, Disability and Increased Longevity," in S. Sullivan and M. E. Lewin, eds., *The Economics and Ethics of Long Term Care and Disability*, pp. 9–55. Washington, DC: American Enterprise Institute for Public Policy.

Rice, Thomas, and Nelda McCall. 1985. "The Extent of Ownership and the Characteristics of Medicare Supplemental Policies," *Inquiry, The Journal of Health Care Organization, Provision, and Financing* 22 (2), pp. 188–200.

Rowland, Diane. 1989. "Measuring the Elderly's Need for Home Care," *Health Affairs* 8 (4), pp. 39–51.

Ruggles, Patricia. 1990. *Drawing the Line: Alternative Poverty Measures and Their Implications for Public Policy*. Washington, DC: The Urban Institute.

Russell, Louise. 1989. *Medicare's New Hospital Payment System: Is It Working?* Washington, DC: The Brookings Institution.

Schlesinger, Mark, and Karl Kronebush. 1991. "Intergenerational Relations, Tensions and Conflict: Attitudes and Perceptions about Social Justice and Age-Related Needs." Paper presented at the American Gerontological Association annual meetings, San Francisco, November 1991.

Schlesinger, Mark, and Pamela Brown Drumheller. 1988. "Beneficiary Cost Sharing in the Medicare Program," in David Blumenthal, Mark Schlesinger, and Pamela Brown Drumheller, eds., *Renewing the Promise, Medicare and Its Reform*, pp. 31–57. Oxford: Oxford University Press.

Schulz, James H. 1988. *The Economics of Aging*. 4th ed. Dover, MA: Auburn House.

Sherman, Sally R. 1985. "Reported Reasons Retired Workers Left Their Last Job: Findings From the New Beneficiary Survey," *Social Security Bulletin* 48 (3), pp. 22–30.

Shoup, Carl S. 1969. *Public Finance*. Chicago: Aldine.

Snee, John, and Mary Ross. 1978. "Social Security Amendments of 1977: Legislative History and Summary of Provisions," *Social Security Bulletin* 41 (3), pp. 3–20.

Social Security Administration. Office of the Actuary. *1991 Annual Report of the Board of Trustees of the Federal Hospital Insurance Trust Fund* and the *1991 Annual Report of the Board of Trustees of the Federal Supplementary Medical Insurance Trust Fund*. Office of the Actuary, Health Care Financing Administration.

Social Security Bulletin. 1991. 54 (5).

Social Security Bulletin. 1990. Annual Statistical Supplement.

"Social Security Technical Panel Report to the 1991 Advisory Council on Social Security." 1991. *Social Security Bulletin*, 53 (11), pp. 2–34.

Stein, Bruno. 1987. "Phasing Out Social Security: A Critique of Ferrara's Proposal," in Charles W. Meyer, ed., *Social Security: A Critique of Radical Reform Proposals*, pp. 35–48. Lexington, MA: Lexington Books.

Stone, Deborah A. 1984. *The Disabled State*. Philadelphia: Temple University Press.

Thompson, Lawrence H. 1983. "The Social Security Reform Debate," *Journal of Economic Literature* 21 (4), pp. 1425–1467.

Trowbridge, Charles L. 1989. *Fundamental Concepts of Actuarial Science*. Actuarial Education and Research Fund.

U.S. Bureau of the Census: Projections of the Population, by Age, Sex, and Race, for the United States: 1988 to 2080. 1989. *Current Population Report*, Series P-25, No. 1018, p. 62, U.S. Department of Commerce. Washington, DC: U.S. Government Printing Office.

U.S. Bureau of the Census: Age, Sex, Household Relationship, Race and Hispanic Origin, by Ratio of Income to Poverty Level in 1989. 1990. *Current Population Reports* Series P-60, No. 171, Table 5, p. 25. U.S. Department of Commerce. Washington, DC: U.S. Government Printing Office.

U.S. Congress. House, Committee on Ways and Means. 1985. *Report on Earnings Sharing Implementation Study*. WMCP: 99–4. 99th Congress, 1st Session.

————. 1988. *Social Security Trust Fund Reserves*, pp. 100–58. 100th Congress, 2nd session.

————. House, Committee on Ways and Means. 1991. *Green Book*. 102nd Congress, 1st session.

————. House, Select Committee on Aging. 1990. *Emptying the Elderly's Pocket Book—Growing Impact of Rising Health Care Costs*. 101st Congress, 2nd session.

————. Senate, Special Committee on Aging. 1984. "Special Tabulations of the March 1984 Current Population Survey."

U.S. Department of Health and Human Services. 1988. *Social Security Handbook*, 10th ed. Washington, DC: U.S. Government Printing Office.

U.S. Government Accounting Office. 1991. *Medicare: Further Changes Needed to Reduce Program and Beneficiary Costs*. Washington, DC: GAO/HRD-9167.

United States Statutes at Large. 1968. Vol. 81. Washington, DC: United States Government Printing Office.

Verbrugge, Lois. 1984. "Longer Life But Worsening Health? Trends in Health and Mortality of Middle-Aged and Older Persons," *Milbank Memorial Fund Quarterly* 62, pp. 475–519.

―――――. 1989. "The Twain Meet: Empirical Explanations of Sex Differences in Health and Mortality," *Journal of Health and Social Behavior* 30 (3), pp. 282–304.

Vogel, Ronald J. 1988. "An Analysis of the Welfare Component and Intergenerational Transfers under the Medicare Program," in Mark V. Pauly and William L. Kissick, eds., *Lessons from the First Twenty Years of Medicare*, pp. 73–116. Philadelphia: University of Pennsylvania Press.

Vroman, Wayne, 1974. "Employer Payroll Taxes and Money Wage Behavior," *Applied Economics* 6, pp. 189–204.

Weaver, Carolyn L. 1990. "Social Security Disability Policy in the 1980s and Beyond," in Monroe Berkowitz and M. Anne Hill, eds., *Disability and the Labor Market*. Ithaca, NY: ILR Press.

―――――., ed. 1990. *Social Security's Looming Surpluses*. Washington, DC: AEI Press.

Wennberg, John, Benjamin A. Barnes, and Michael Zubkoff. 1982. "Professional Uncertainty and the Problem of Supplier-Induced Demand," *Social Science and Medicine* 16 (7), pp. 811–824.

Wilensky, Gail. 1982. "Government and the Financing of Health Care," *American Journal of Economics* 72 (2), pp. 202–207.

Wolff, Nancy. 1985. "Women and the Equity of the Social Security Program," Paper presented at the 1985 Eastern Economic Association Meetings, Pittsburgh, PA, March 1985.

―――――. 1987. *Income Redistribution and the Social Security Program*. Ann Arbor: UMI Research Press.

Yett, David, William R. Ernest, and J. Hay. 1985. "Fee Screen Reimbursement and Physician Fee Inflation," *Journal of Human Resources* 20 (2), pp. 278–291.

Index

About the Authors

CHARLES W. MEYER is professor of economics at Iowa State University. He is also author of *Social Security: A Critique of Radical Reform Proposals* (1987).

NANCY WOLFF is assistant professor in the Department of Urban Studies and Community Health at Rutgers University. She was formerly an assistant professor in the Department of Preventive Medicine at the University of Wisconsin. She is the author of *Income Redistribution and the Social Security Program* (1987) and of several articles on the social security system.